THE BIG HAIRY
HAIRY
GREEN BOOK

ALL ABOUT ARTIFICIAL GRASS

MARK J O'LOUGHLIN

Published by Grassland Publishing, 2022

Typeset in Plantin MT Pro and Myriad Pro
Printed by Lettertec

Grassland, Military Road Industrial Park, Naas, County Kildare, Ireland.
mark@sanctuarysynthetics.ie

June '25

Hi Ciaran,

Very best Wishes

— Mark ó Foyle

'The grass is always greener on the other side'
'Is glas na cnoic i bhfad uainn'
~ Proverb

Dedication

*All my late mother Gemma ever wanted was for myself and my
six siblings to get on well in life. To do our best.
I'm dedicating this book to her memory.
I tried my best, Mother.*

*Oh, and to my loving wife, Anne, and our teenagers Orla and James,
without whom this book would have been completed
at least two or three years sooner.*

Foreword

'Nobody cares how much you know until they know how much you care'
~ Attributed to Theodore Roosevelt

My brother Eamon is a cop. One day at an event he introduced me to his boss's boss, the assistant garda commissioner. 'This is my brother Mark. He is Ireland's biggest importer of high-quality Dutch grass.' The commissioner looked at me askance so I quickly explained it was the synthetic kind. Still he remained nonplussed ...

'Eh, the artificial stuff, you know, fake grass for lawns.'

'Oh ... right so ... I have you now.'

Thanks, Eamon.

I'm going to do you a favour and cut right to the chase.

Many people are either downright hostile to, or at least somewhat sceptical of, artificial grass. I get that. If that's you, I urge you to drop this book immediately and slowly back away.

In my 20 years in the business I've never tried to convert the unwilling and have no intention of wasting my time or yours pushing artificial turf. Is a tightly mown, immaculately striped lawn your pride and joy? Are you perhaps a green-fingered horticulturist and among the 4–5 per cent who avidly grow their own food? Do you own sandals (or Crocs) and deliberately wear them even if not on holidays (perhaps with socks)? Are you unwilling to spend money on your outdoor space? Are you a renter? Too set in your ways to consider alternative solutions? Are you easily offended (there might be some mild swearing in some of the stories in this book)?

If your answer is yes to any of the above, then I'm probably *not* talking to you. Please, and I can't emphasize this enough, move on. We are all busy people.

Many citizens have neither the time nor inclination to garden. That's OK, it's not a sin. For some the very thought of tackling their garden arouses frustration, anger even.

If you would like more time and less work, read on. If you are a homeowner, have a 'garden' maybe with children or pets and ever wondered what the story is with artificial grass, then you've come to the right place. Well, really the only place. As fake grass is a relatively new and controversial phenomenon, despite its growing proliferation, there is virtually no literature on the topic, just superficial online stuff, often propaganda.

So you are stuck with me. I'm the one who cares.

The assertions and conclusions contained herein are my own. So too are any mistakes. Now let me set the scene for you in the introductory chapter.

Oh, and to my detractors, let me get my retaliation in first – *A dog only barks at moving cars.*

Contents

Keeping it real

'The love of gardening is a seed that once sown never dies'
~ Gertrude Jekyll

I had just been fired. Again.

My sister Jen heard that poor Mark was at yet another loose end and invited me out stateside. So in the spring of 1998 I found myself labouring for a plasterer in San Francisco. At almost 30, I was stretching out my young and reckless days for as long as possible.

My new boss had two young children, a busy wife and a completely overgrown garden. Turns out there was a connection. His business was good. All that was needed for months more work was the occasional earthquake tremor. They had a kid's birthday party coming up and because he either was too tired, hungover or just couldn't be bothered, I was asked to sort out their garden for an extra couple of hundred bucks over the weekend. To supplement my hard partying lifestyle I readily agreed. There was often way too much month left at the end of the money. Long story short, I tore into their jungle and after some blood, sweat and splinters, managed to restore it into a thorn- and bramble-free approximation of a garden. Chaos transformed into order.

Mom and indeed many of the party guests were suitably impressed. Still young(ish), fit and strong, I had enjoyed doing it. Five thousand miles from home I found my vocation and decided, overnight, to become a landscaper. I was hooked.

For many of us our gardens are a disaster zone and gardening is a real drag. Can we at least agree that most people dread the thought of garden work, especially having to mow the lawn? Again and again. Rather than being a pleasurable hobby it's a monotonous, never-ending chore.

Many homeowners are embarrassed to even show us their gardens. They find them intimidating. Those lucky enough to have one have been sold a dream. Barbecuing on sunny summer afternoons, laughing kids running after the barking dog – down, boy – chilling in the evening twilight, nursing a G&T under the gazebo.

Sadly for most, the reality can be quite different.

The large glass patio doors are destroyed with paw prints. Again. The once white kitchen floor tiles are all muddy and marked. Little and large footprints everywhere. "Wipe your feet!' Getting to the wheelie bins is an ordeal. The slippy deck is a death trap, especially when frosty. The green patch is strictly off limits from October to May. Maybe it'll recover during the summer … yeah, right. Basically it sucks.

Overwhelmed, even before the Covid-19 pandemic, seems to be the standard operating mode in modern society. Being quarantined at home has certainly given the public a better appreciation of their private outdoor spaces, or at least their potential.

Can artificial grass really be the ultimate garden life hack?

Some of the 'before' photos in this book might look familiar? Are you sick to the back teeth of your own ugly lawn? Tired of the constant muck, mowing and maintenance?

Don't despair. Take consolation from the fact that you are far from alone. Most people's gardens are, to be kind, not great. If you want a nice, hassle-free, pet and play friendly lawn and garden, this *could* be the book you need. Although fake lawns are anathema to many, you might have finally found the answer. Maybe you are a neat freak or are simply at your wits' end. I understand you'll need to know more. After all, investing lots of moolah in your garden can easily exceed the price of a much-needed family holiday. It behoves you to investigate it properly. Remember you usually only get one chance to get it right.

Critics be like: 'A plastic lawn, over my dead body!'

Once upon a time I had to contend with a doubting spouse.

We were not long married when I went off on a golfing trip to Florida.

'Guess what, honey,' I said on my return (that's a lie actually – I never call her honey. She'd thump me.)

'Guess what, Anne? I've got a new business idea and we'll be starting with our own lawn. Front and back.'

'Oh, will you now?' (That's code for: no bloody chance, mate!)

In the end she indulged me.

Now she too is a convert. Our kids have grown up knowing nothing else.

I often thought someone should write a book all about artificial grass.

This, at last, is that book.

Who knows, maybe it will help you avoid some of the cold sweats I suffered. It might also make your job of persuasion that little bit easier. Alternatively, it's weighty enough to use to threaten to hit any doubters over the head.

I'm aware that the effectiveness of some of my arguments can depend on the time of year you are reading this, along with your geographical location. Wintertime, certainly in our corner of the Atlantic, can make tending a lawn a bit of a nightmare as it's often far too wet. Come to think of it, it's often too wet in summer too, only the rain drops are that bit warmer. This in turn makes the grass grow much faster. It grows, well, like a weed.

Determined gardeners admittedly love tending to their lawns and I would never deprive them of their fetish, the therapeutic kick and that sense of satisfaction from getting a job done. Maybe they've been fighting with software all day and need something physical to do, preferably more tangible than with a mouse and computer screen. Others still think manual labour is a Spanish musician! The rest of us are just too damn busy. Or too lazy. For most people yard work is an unwelcome chore.

Either way that's why I'm in business.

An idea whose time has come

There are good reasons why the subject of this book is the fastest growing (no pun intended) sector of the home and garden industry despite many gardening snobs calling it a plague and an insult to nature. Critics are complaining that it's spreading across back gardens as ferociously as Japanese knotweed. There is real vitriol in their attacks. They find it offensive and see it as 'the last straw'.

It has long irked me that a majority remain flippantly dismissive of artificial grass. Now it's my turn to set the record straight. Having barely registered in the public's consciousness for years, it has suddenly become mainstream, with its popularity growing exponentially. Once upon a time fake grass was blatantly unconvincing and literally rough around the edges. It has come a long way. Lifestyle changes, product improvements, Covid-19 and affordability have helped. Besides the allure of low maintenance just what is behind the appeal of artificial grass? Inspired by fond memories of foreign sun holidays, there's a yearning for Mediterranean al fresco living. People want and expect more from their gardens. Far more than just a place to hang out the clothes and park the bike, gardens are now expected to transform into entertainment spaces.

My promise is this: I'll give you a comprehensive understanding of what looks increasingly like an unstoppable trend – the world of artificial grass. I could never keep a secret* and I want to help you make up your own mind. My hope is that this book will help free you from a major mundane chore and frankly give you back your garden and your weekends – to make your own sanctuary. Who knows, there's a danger you might then find time to do a bit of actual gardening. It's my mission to cut through the established thinking and myths, to give you a thorough understanding of the product, the industry, the installation process, the pitfalls and the results to expect.

I aim to impart knowledge and give insights from my discoveries following two decades of professional experience. If you are even remotely considering investing in *frass* (eh, fake grass!), then it's time to educate yourself, to become an expert without all the pain. You'll notice that, rather than getting bogged down in weeds, so to speak, I've relegated some of the more technical stuff to the Buyer's Guide and Technical Information at the end of this book, where some of us grass geeks can go for even more fun. As I pioneered the industry in Ireland, there was no such manual for me. In Chapter 3 I explain the difference between AstroTurf and artificial grass for domestic lawns, and explain why I won't touch the former.

A pariah ploughing his own furrow

In writing this synthetic grass bible I'm braving begrudgery and will not hide my light under a bushel. I think the best way to share my knowledge is by telling you the story of how I became the Fake Grass Man, warts and all. How did a big clueless labourer go from hand to mouth living, often not knowing where his next beer was coming from, to market niche domination? Business life was not all beer and skittles. We were far from an overnight success but I'll spare you the false modesty. Spoiler alert: I now run a successful multi million euro business called Sanctuary Synthetics with 20+ employees serving thousands of customers from our Grassland HQ.

This book examines two conflicting trends. The sudden proliferation of fake grass alongside a growing awareness of the environmental damage caused by plastic waste. Both issues are addressed at length including my personal struggle with reconciling this conflict (see Chapter 6). I intend to prove the folly of having a real lawn. I'm painfully aware this makes me something of a maverick and a black sheep of the gardening world but I can live with any ignominy my chosen career might bring.

* One of my few faults. Also I can't really sing.

Really it's two books mushed together and certainly no academic treatise. Ostensibly a practical guide, it also includes a candid chronicle of my own adventures. How the west was won so to speak. Stand by for irreverent anecdotes as well as unvarnished home truths. Hopefully you'll end up being better able to haggle and immune to being ripped off. I'll share what people wished they knew before getting started, what artificial grass should cost, how long it will last, how to work out the size of your lawn area, the benefits, the drawbacks. With both the cupcake and the recipe, it contains basically everything you ever wanted to know about artificial grass but were afraid to ask. I had considered that as my book title. Naw, too unoriginal.

It's been quite the journey. It only took about seven years procrastinating and several months actually writing the damn thing. Please indulge my occasional digressions. I've been very strict on insisting that we exclusively use photos of our *own* work.

Real lawns are not to be taken for granted. The first chapter has a bit of history (groan) about their evolution to help you see the big picture. I then proceed to happily desecrate them. Turns out there might be no good reason for keeping it real.

We love what we do and try to have fun doing it. Our reward for doing good work is the opportunity to do more. I'm here to help. After all I'm the **lawn ranger**, the expert pioneer in my field.

I'll leave you with this thought.

'Man without a smiling face should not open shop'
~ Ancient Chinese proverb

I sure hope you'll be rewarded with a smile or two reading this book.

PART 1
THE STORY
OF ARTIFICIAL GRASS

Chapter 1

The history of lawns and why they suck

Bíonn gach duine go lách go dtéann bó ina gharraí
Everybody is good-natured until a cow goes into their garden
~ Old Irish saying

An origin story
Ever before there were lawns there were gardens.

The Garden of Eden, enjoyed, however briefly, by Adam and Eve, was not necessarily even the very first garden. News flash for those who insist on interpreting the Bible literally (at least when it suits them) – this original story, much like many suspiciously similar ones in other world religions, is most probably allegorical. Many ancient religions feature mystical gardens in their writings which seem to fulfil both a spiritual and physical yearning.

Was plan A not something about creating paradise here on earth? I do know there was a flooding issue at one stage. Is this not what we are all subconsciously trying to do – to recreate our own Eden, albeit on a far smaller scale, at home?

From Babylon's hanging gardens to Islamic oases, from mythical Grecian Elysian Fields and medieval monastery cloisters to contemporary flower shows like Chelsea, gardens continue to evolve and intrigue, according to the needs and desires of each age of humanity.

They represent, ever since that unfortunate incident with a snake, mankind's dominion over nature. It's a microcosm of the natural world. Wikipedia says a garden is 'a planned space, usually outdoors, set aside for the display, cultivation, or enjoyment of plants and other forms of nature … Some gardens are for ornamental purposes only, while others also produce food.'[1] I would add that these days many are neither.

Humanity's instinct has always been to manipulate the landscape. Tim Ingram, writing in 'thinkinGardens', says a garden is part of the environment, a synthetic but hopefully functional ecosystem. While writer Michael Pollan

---

1 See Wikipedia, 'Garden', en.wikipedia.org/wiki/Garden.

suggests they 'might be a place where we can meet nature halfway'.[2] I like that. We generally don't tend to think too deeply about our gardens. Why do they even exist? They are just there.

That is not to say we don't worry and fret about them. Ditto the ubiquitous lawn. That thing that ties a garden together.

My star sign is Virgo and we are known to be logical and systematic, perfectionists at heart (we're also quite sceptical so I don't believe in any of that shite). Thus unfolds the following detail.

In my research I was amused to learn that the word 'lawn' came from the Celtic word *laune* (Middle Irish *lann* – land) which described a communal grass enclosure for grazing livestock. It's akin to the old French *launde*, meaning wooded district, or heath – that open space between woods.

On the island now known as Britain such demesnes were eventually owned by the medieval aristocracy who rented them out to their tenants to graze.

Not the tenants to graze per se, more for their livestock.

The main stage

According to author Dr DG Hessayon it was inside these aristocrat's mottes, baileys and castles where the English lawn truly began. There was usually an area of grass on which knights and their ladies could walk and sit, well away from the smells and vermin of indoor living.

While gardening may be largely a solo pursuit, gardens are very much a social space, lawns being the main stage. There were turf-topped seats and even rectangular 'greens' on which games such as bowls and pall-mall (a precursor to croquet) were played. It is interesting, he notes, that even from the very beginning there seems to have been a division between ornamental and sports turf, which we'll look into in more detail later.

Later this lawn area was extended to cover large open spaces for wealthy landowners around their castles or manor houses so that any potential attackers could be more easily spotted, depriving them of the cover of surrounding forests.

So basically the lawn was there to protect you from surprise attacks. Famously, one day in 1588, Sir Francis Drake, utter scoundrel that he was (look it up), delayed his attack on the Spanish Armada in order to complete his bowling game on a chamomile lawn. Because of some terrible weather and his clever tactics, the invading fleet fled and Elizabethan and later Tudor palaces continued to be adorned with classic Chamomile, so beloved of

2   Michael Pollan, *Second Nature: A Gardener's Education*, New York, Grove Press, 1991, p. 64.

17

poets, and grassy mounds, designed to display their owner's wealth.

Then in the 1600s the Jacobeans in turn were big fans of lawns, the eminent Francis Bacon exclaiming, 'Nothing is more pleasant to the eye than green grass kept finely shorn.' But it was the aristocracy of seventeenth and eighteenth century Europe who really got the whole cult of the lawn thing going.

French 'Sun King' Louis XIV included large squares of *tapis vert* (green carpet) in his magnificent Versailles gardens. This haute couture of landscaping quickly spread. An early form of conspicuous consumerism, it was a way of showing that landowners could afford to dedicate their grounds to aesthetic rather than primarily agricultural purposes. Back in England, as elsewhere, the cropped lawn became a status symbol, though early lawnmowers more often than not had four legs and were woolly.

In all fairness, compared to the time and resources spent on them today, lawns were considerably more sustainable back then. Scale helped. No harmful chemicals were ever deployed. There was no need. A mixture of meadow plants (including clover) grew – tasty nutritious food for their lawnmowers who then fertilised it with neat little dark round pellets of poo as they ambled around. If it was scythed, it would be gathered and saved as fodder.

All nature is a garden

Italian landscape artists' later glorification of idyllic pastoral scenes fed into the next romantic lawn mania. As a backlash to the splendid formality of continental gardens, English landscape designers like Capability Brown believed all nature is a garden. Entire country estates were converted to vast expanses of grass, copses of trees, lakes and the odd folly. Armies of labourers were employed to do some serious earth moving. If something undesirable, say a local village, was spoiling the view, well then, moved it would be.

As an aside, when invited to give a bit of a makeover in Castletown House, the Connolly estate just up the road from us in Celbridge, County Kildare, Mr Brown declined, declaring he was not yet done with England.

Ha-ha

Another clever innovation at the time was the ha-ha, from the French *hâ-hâ* or *saut de loup*. It's a recessed retaining wall that creates a vertical barrier, typically with a tufted incline sloping to meet masonry, which preserves an uninterrupted view of the landscape beyond.

This invisible ditch was used to prevent grazing livestock from straying too close to the big house. No more cow or sheep shite on one's shoes. The name might have stemmed from reactions to the sudden discovery of its existence (possibly having fallen into said ditch, unseen until the last second). Thus the gentry could have poo-free strolls around the big house, enjoying splendid views of the greater expanse, plus the occasional good laugh watching unsuspecting first-time visitors fall over said precipice.

Enslaved

Meanwhile, in the colonies, the concept of the grass lawn was being enthusiastically imported by the wealthy. Their white picket fences were safer than ha-has. The east coast of America had once been a pristine wilderness, but by the 1620s the livestock of its colonists had eaten all the available grass and more had to be seeded. In 1776, during the American Revolution, General George Washington even found time to write to his estate manager at home about his garden design plans. No doubt he was conscious of the symbolism of eschewing the agricultural value of his land in favour of sprawling lawns and gardens. Typical American homesteads merely had packed dirt or wildflower-strewn untamed areas outside. Think *Little House on the Prairie*. Mind you, I'd say the Olesons, especially Nellie, would have loved a nice lawn, regardless of the endless upkeep and expense for her long-suffering pa.

Another notable early American adopter was Thomas Jefferson at his Monticello plantation. Principal author of the Declaration of Independence, big fan of human rights, anti-slavery advocate and third US president, his expanses of shorn grass served no other purpose but to send a message about the ambitions of this newly founded and proud nation. I submit it's fair comment to record that he somewhat hypocritically deployed lots of his enslaved Black people to keep the lawn in tip top condition. Without modern equipment, this was gruelling endless work.

Olmsted's vision

After the American Civil War ended new suburbs sprang up everywhere. These often had large grassy areas inspired by the ubiquitous urban city parks. The spread of railway lines to and through these same suburbs had the unexpected side effect of providing a raised and moving platform for commuters who could now sit gazing out the windows (Long Island iced teas had yet to be invented) no doubt comparing the now visible yards of their neighbours with their own.

Later again in the 1800s one Frederick Law Olmsted, founding father of

American landscape architecture, also admired and envied the uninterrupted green swards of grand English estates. Back then designers thought on a big scale and in long time frames. Many schemes would take generations to mature to their full potential. Think how long it takes for trees to grow to full maturity. Mr Olmsted envisioned carpets of lawn throughout the new suburban developments that were springing up everywhere.

And so it came to pass.

'The lawn,' he declared, 'would be an expression of democracy.'

Drive down any American suburban street, no matter what city, and one can readily observe Olmsted's vision, one front lawn flowing into the next all the way down the block. This is the case regardless, or even in defiance of the geography, location or prevailing climate. Having started out as a status symbol such berms became an even more entrenched aesthetic.

The culture really shifted following the 1870 publication of Frank J Scott's highly influential bestseller *The Art of Beautifying Suburban Home Grounds of Small Extent* (by that rationale there's hope for this book's commercial success yet). It declared that having a perfect lawn was part of what makes a perfect citizen.[3] Perhaps my humble treatise can finally help reverse this belief.

Just one year later, one Mr Joseph Lessler filed a new patent for his easily connected garden hose sprinkler system. Thanks to Joe's sprinklers, most US lawns don't even use native grass. For example, the famous Kentucky blue grass originates from north-western Europe while Bermuda grass comes from Africa (rather than Bermuda). Like the Victorians back in Blighty where lawns were already being taken for granted, contemporary middle-class America was hooked.

Victorian convention

It's slightly different on our side of the Atlantic. The cool damp climate of this Northern European archipelago happens to suit the growing of grass very well. Ireland, aka the Emerald Isle, even got its nickname from it.

Here it's the back garden where the lush lawn reigns supreme. The formula being: lawn plus border = classic convention. It's easy enough to see why lawns became so popular. Castles and villas gave way to smaller, more modest homes and city gardens. This was the age of enlightenment and Victorian plant hunters. Filled as they were with exotic plants brought back from all around the globe,

---

3   David Botti, 'The Great American Lawn: How the Dream Was Manufactured' [video], *The New York Times*, 9 August 2019, Morning Briefing, www.nytimes.com/2019/08/09/video/lawn-grass-environment-history.html.

lawns set off the snazzy beds very nicely thank you. They covered the ground superbly and were installed relatively cheaply. Much like the dude's rug in *The Big Lebowski*,[4] the lawn really, like, tied the space together, man.

Great for play and relaxation, the tidy openness of the lawn became comfortably familiar. A patch of grass into which many poured their heart and soul. After all, an Englishman's home is his castle.

'Lawnageddon' – revolution and evolution

As for the question of maintenance, well, the Industrial Revolution took care of that. Before the advent of lawnmowers, lawns remained an expensive luxury. By 1832 an enterprising chap named Edwin Budding, observing the cutting machines in the busy textile factories (make a mental note of those machines – we'll be seeing more of them in the next chapter) was inspired to invent the manual cylinder mower thus facilitating keeping lawns neatly shorn. The first ones were pulled by a pony in soft leather boots to protect the grass. There were absolutely no sheep, very little skill and minimal brawn required.

The Americans soon came up with an even more efficient Archimedean mower. A steam-driven mower appeared in 1893, although I'm not sure it was particularly practical given its weight. Petrol models followed in the early 1900s and the famous Flymo appeared in the late 1960s.

Thus along with apple pie and that white picket fence, the neatly cut lawn was now finally an entrenched part of the American dream. Stay with me here, I'm getting to the point. Despite all this progress, according to historian Ted Steinberg in *American Green*, citizens spent 150 hours a year maintaining their lawns.

Order over squalor

In her seminal piece 'The Life and Death of the American Lawn' for *The Atlantic*, Megan Garber declares that 'lawns became aesthetic extensions of Manifest Destiny, symbols of American entitlement and triumph, of the soft and verdant rewards that result when man's ongoing battles against nature are finally won … [They] came, too, to represent a triumph of another kind: the order of suburbia over the squalor of the [inner] city.'[5]

So what started as defence and envy, morphed into vanity and then evolved

---

4   *The Big Lebowski*, Directors Joel Cohen and Ethan Cohen, Gramercy Pictures (I), 1998.
5   Megan Garber, 'The Life and Death of the American Lawn', *The Atlantic*, 28 August 2015, Culture, www.theatlantic.com/entertainment/archive/2015/08/the-american-lawn-a-eulogy/402745/.

into a cultural convention. A 1914 *New York Times* headline literally read 'Roosevelt cuts grass'.[6] Today it's so pervasive in society that we simply expect people to have and maintain a lawn and it's even enforced by law in many instances. They are a non-negotiable part of the package of home ownership. One is, of course, expected to keep a certain uniformity.

Mowing mania

During World War II US citizens were encouraged to continue lawn maintenance as a show of strength and unity. After the war their returning veterans were given cheap loans to buy even more new suburban houses. These would not, of course, be complete without a yard. The new interstate highway system also helped. Like Hitler's autobahns these roads were originally built to facilitate the efficient movement of troops and war materials. One side effect of this infrastructural investment was a further explosion of suburbia along with its inevitable gardens, which apparently take up over 20 per cent of urban areas. The *American Green* book called these rows of tidy lawns an expression of 1950s conformity. Have a listen to Pete Seeger's 1963 hit song 'Little Boxes'.

'Did you see the state of number 49's garden? It's a disgrace.' Social pressures and hubris drove dissatisfaction. The phrase 'keeping up with the Joneses' is particularly apt in this context (it was a syndicated US comic strip which ran from 1915 to 1940 – long enough to enter the popular lexicon).

Cultural historian Virginia Scott Jenkins observed in her book '*The Lawn: A History of an American Obsession*', when contemplating the lust for lawns, that 'a well-manicured patch of grass somehow is synonymous with status and good citizenship.'[7] She noted that in the early 1900s the Garden Club of America successfully fostered the lawn aesthetic by promoting community contests. Indeed, many local ordinances still dictate the required height of the grass.

There have been countless books written about lawns. This ain't one of them. I am here to declare that the lawn is dead. This book lays them to rest.

Lawns. Have. Had. Their. Day.

Here's today's news: maintaining a lawn is, in fact, a high maintenance, wasteful and labour intensive affectation.

A lawn is a chemically dependent monoculture whose genesis lies in the

---

6   'Roosevelt Cuts Grass: Disregards Politics for a Day and Pushes Lawn Mower', *The New York Times*, 18 July 1914, p. 1.
7   Lynn Van Matre, 'A Historian Digs into America's Lawn', *Chicago Tribune*, 16 May 1994, www.chicagotribune.com/news/ct-xpm-1994-05-16-9405160090-story.html.

expression of power and wealth *over* nature.

It is a multimillion dollar and multi million acre fetish.

A pandemic of utterly redundant pastures.

A middle-class affectation.

A cultural juggernaut.

And, dare I say it, a male obsession.

Oh, lawns and lawn care are big business alright, the pursuit of this weedless swathe being the holy grail of suburbia. This pursuit of nirvana is a mirage.

Let's face it, we've all been brainwashed into accepting a sacred cow – the lawn. We prostrate ourselves over its care. We genuflect in servility to, and in the pursuit of, its perfection. We are unwittingly enslaved by our lawns. What a sad state of affairs.

I don't wish to be sacrilegious but I hereby declare independence from the lawn. These neatly trimmed symbols of civic virtue of dubious morality have completely outlived their usefulness. They ought to be an endangered species.

Are you starting to see where I'm going with all this? With a whiff of croquet and afternoon tea about lawns, few suspected that the sacrosanct icon they'd become was a really bad idea.

Do not walk on the grass. Really? It's not just the college authorities in charge of the quads of Oxbridge that prohibit their actual use. The pressure to protect and maintain this manicured monstrosity, this al fresco green rug has led to an unhealthy, unthinking national obsession with its appearance. Countless hours are spent – I would say squandered – raking, spiking, scarifying, fertilising and feeding this monster. More fertiliser equals more growth equals even more mowing. And people have the temerity to tell me my synthetic solution is an abomination. Please. Besides, we typically don't replace lovely lawns, we remove mud patches.

You will recall the story of 'The Emperor's New Clothes', Hans Christian Andersen's famous tale. Well, think of me as the boy crying, 'The emperor has *no* clothes.' If I can undermine cultural bias and your faith, even just a little, I'll be happy.

The good news is that there is a realistic alternative. Park your guilt. You no longer need to suffer the tyranny of lawn care, forever trapped on the mowing treadmill. I'll help you escape from the hamster wheel of endless lawn maintenance, or worse, paying someone else to look after it. It was Pat Howell who said, 'Grass is the cheapest plant to install and the most expensive to maintain.'

Read on and discover a world where lawns are no longer needed for defensive purposes, where gardens are accessible, gardening is enjoyable and where it's a pleasure to step outside your back door.

In Chapter 6, we'll look at the biological and ecological footprint of lawns a lot more closely. Before we trace my own evolution as the Fake Grass Man, let's discover how artificial lawns came about in the first place – how they grew, so to speak. I would argue they were an evolutionary inevitability and bound to appear.

Let me leave you with this *Washington Post* headline from 2015, which I think neatly summarises my own conclusion:

'Lawns are a soul-crushing time-suck and most
of us would be better off without them'[8]

8   Christopher Ingraham, 'Lawns are a soul-crushing timesuck and most of us would be better off without them', *The Washington Post*, 4 August 2015, Economic Policy, www.washingtonpost. com/news/wonk/wp/2015/08/04/lawns-are-a-soul-crushing-timesuck-and-most-of-us-would-be-better-off-without-them/.

Chapter 2

The growth of artificial grass and why it's not so bad

'If you have a garden and a library, you have everything you need'
~ Marcus Tullius Cicero

On sunny days I love to jump onto the ride-on, pop in the ear buds and go into zen mode. In harmony with the machine, I mow neat lines, row upon row, smelling the freshly clipped grass, listening to music and leaving behind an orderly shorn lawn for my dad. Beautiful.

The job gives one a lingering sense of satisfaction. I've done something tangible, and there's visual proof. In an era when many spend all day pushing a cursor around a computer screen it can be an underappreciated task.

Trouble is, it needs to be done all over again within a week or so. Next time around it could well be raining. Or the big match will be live on TV. Now I'd hate to be responsible for depriving people (let's face it, mostly men) of this task if that's what they *want* to do. For many it's an obsession. An escape. I get that.

On the flip side, picture the traditional nuclear family. A frazzled mother, possibly holding down a full-time job, in a typical suburban family setting. Say a three-bed semi-detached, with a couple of young kids and that dog they got when they were practising for having actual kids. She's seen the idealised version of gardens in magazines, on Houzz and the TV makeover shows. She really wants that beautiful but low maintenance dream garden. But she's discovered that with the commute and demands of modern life they simply don't have time to maintain that lawn (except maybe during Covid-19 lockdowns), certainly not without sacrificing social media or wine time. Once work finishes on a Friday, picking up the kids from the childminder's is just the start of the weekend's not-for-profit taxi service. I won't depress the reader by listing their endless activities.

The brief grass-mowing window on Sunday morning passes as it's raining again / there's no petrol for the mower / it won't start / we really ought to go to church / whatever. Then the nagging starts, the match is on and Mum and Dad

25

want to chill out and read the paper. Meanwhile looking out the windows at the increasingly unkempt garden becomes more painful by the day. When the kids go outside to play — or get sent out away from under their parents' feet — they come back in mucky, the dog drags in dirt every single time, the lawn gets cut up and never seems to recover. So it gets put off limits. Then what's the point?

We all know that the grass is not always greener on the other side. But perhaps it can be. What if I was to tell you not to despair, that there might be an answer to your prayers. A silver bullet that delivers all the benefits with a fraction of the effort.

Really though. A *fake* lawn?

The definition of the word fake is 'to give a better appearance through artificial means'. It refers to something not genuine or presented fraudulently, i.e. counterfeit. So it's a word with largely negative connotations.

Nobody likes canned laughter, a fake smile or indeed fake news. Artificial sweeteners? No thanks. Soon there will be fake steaks (alternative to meat) available. As for fake boobs, my editor thinks it's best not to comment further. Is cosmetic surgery not booming all the same?

Consider what lurks in the corner of your living room for a few weeks each December? Do you buy a 'real' tree, specifically grown to be chopped down at a tender age to decorate our homes, or have you invested in a synthetic and therefore reusable one? What thought process informed that decision? So climb off your high horse about fake grass if there's a fake tree stuffed up in your attic.

Who remembers *The Brady Bunch*? Subliminally I've been aware of artificial lawns since the early 1970s. Can you picture that TV household's backyard? Ever notice anything strange about it? Well, between 1969 and 1974 the Bradys' blended family, plus Tiger the dog and housekeeper Alice — helpful factoids for table quizzes right there — enjoyed a nice novel synthetic lawn. Not to mention a catchy theme song. (Legendary golfer Tiger Woods was born only one year after that show ended. Just sayin'.)

That's half a century ago. So the whole phenomenon has hardly been an overnight success. The once novelty product has of course evolved immensely in the interim. Please don't let the fact that they now use it in the *Big Brother* house and on *Love Island* put you off.

A synthetic lawn is essentially a surface manufactured from artificial fibres made to mimic natural grass. Early adopters realised that their lawn was the most labour intensive, high maintenance and unsustainable part of their gardens and did something about it. For many it's an effective, affordable, guilt-free choice that blends well into any setting and which needs comparatively very little care. It can transform a sad looking patch into a functional play area. But be warned, at the end of a long hot summer it might not fool anyone. Why? Because yours will still be green and healthy looking in contrast to your neighbour's yellow, burned and dead grass. Zoom in on Google Earth, have a look around your neighbourhood and you'll see for yourself.

To use an unedifying analogy, traditional grass cutting is like constantly going to the barbers/hairdressers, whereas having a synthetic lawn is more like going to your wig maker. Once. Fake grass might have previously been considered the bad toupee of landscaping but no more. Hey, if you can't tell, you can't tell. I also know that a synthetic lawn is, much like the garden gnome, most definitely not for everyone. As a *Daily Mail* article caustically asserted, fake lawns 'are to horticulture what microwaves are to haute cuisine or what Twitter is to rational debate.'[9]

From potatoes to playgrounds

So what was the seed that first sprouted artificial grass?

In fact it all started with a persistent blight which, along with criminal laissez-faire indifference from Westminster, caused the Great Famine of 1845 to 1852.

This forced the Ford family from West Cork, along with over a million others, to flee to America. Some years later a second generation Ford, an enterprising chap named Henry, became very interested in machinery and how mechanisation could save back-breaking farm labour. His innovations changed the world and made him a fortune. Then he died.

Stay with me here.

Before his demise Henry and his son Edsel (remember that preposterous looking car?) established a major institution in 1936, the Ford Foundation. With an initial grant of $25,000 the Foundation's charter stipulated that its resources be used for 'scientific, educational and charitable purposes, all for the public welfare'.[10] Such a generous initial bequest made it among the largest philanthropic organisations in the world at that time. Don't forget the world was still in the grips of the Great Depression. Science and industry were together funded and tasked with the development of new concepts.

We're getting closer now.

In the 1950s there was a drive to improve the physical fitness of the youth

9   Robert Hardman, 'Yes it's Chernobyl for worms, but we love it', *Irish Daily Mail*, 23 July 2020, p. 37.
10 Ford Foundation, 'About Us: Our Origins', www.fordfoundation.org/about/about-ford/our-origins/.

of America's inner cities. I can't say for sure if this was connected to what the army had learned from the physical health of their World War II city recruits or if it was related to their ongoing Korean War needs. Maybe it was even out of concern for their general welfare.

This is where it really all began.

One particular Ford Foundation project arose from a perceived need to provide underprivileged inner city kids with a safer alternative to the hard asphalt that covered their playgrounds. Thus the Foundation's education facilities laboratory, in conjunction with the company Chemstrand, began work on the development and use of synthetic fibre outdoor carpeting designed especially for school playgrounds.

From 1962 to 1966 Chemstrand's research and development arm, called the 'creative group', continually tested samples for flammability, water drainage, resistance to foot traffic, traction and durability. In 1964 the first 'ChemGrass' installation was carried out at the Moses Brown school in Providence, Rhode Island. The concept soon migrated from the playground to both the sports ground and the garden.

Got there at last.

It's taken decades for the artificial grass development timeline to play out. In Sanctuary Synthetics we pioneered it in the primary school sector in Ireland in the early 2000s.

'Plastics, my boy'

Who remembers the 1967 classic film *The Graduate*?[11] Our hero, Benjamin Braddock, played by a young-looking Dustin Hoffman, had just finished college, hence the title, and gets some sage advice at a party.

'Ben, just one word. Plastics.'

(Instead he gets mixed up with a mother/daughter combo.)

Turns out it was pretty good advice at that time. Enough said.

By 1965 *Popular Mechanics* magazine was reporting that plastic grass was 'a work saving alternative to real lawns'. Boston-based Biltrite Rubber Co said their Neo-Turf could be spread over a patch of soil and 'you have a lawn without weeds, without gophers [thank God for that], that never needs mowing, watering or fertilization'.[12]

11 *The Graduate*, Director Mike Nichols, Embassy Pictures, 1967.

12 Richard Dunlop, 'Fresh Ideas for Easier Home Owning', *Popular Mechanics*, March 1965, p. 105.

Chevron advertised its 'leisure grass for the leisure class' promising that 'the grasslike surfacing of Poly-loom II' [and I thought our brand name was far out] really does look like real grass, only it never grows, so you never need to water, weed or mow it.'[13]

So there you have it. That's well over half a century ago, and it's come a long way since those days. In truth it was its adaptation to sporting uses that really drove the evolution.

Weekend leisure

When do people have leisure time and when do most sporting occasions take place? Yes, that's right – during the weekend. Guess who more or less invented the weekend? Right again, Mr Henry Ford. Almost 100 years ago, back in the 1920s, as his novel assembly lines were churning out lots of suddenly affordable Model Ts, Henry backed up his rhetoric and did something that was unprecedented: He gave his workers Saturdays off. The idea soon caught on and is something we now take for granted.

Houston, we've got a problem

Why on earth is it called 'AstroTurf'?

It all started with the great game of baseball. To cope with its growing popularity and to accommodate fans in maximum comfort a fancy new stadium opened in Houston, Texas in 1965. It was to be called the Harris County Domed Stadium. Instead, thanks to the nearby space programme, it became the Astrodome. Which is *not* the primary reason AstroTurf got its moniker. We'll get to that.

While the philanthropists and white coats up in New England were struggling to perfect their synthetic surfaces formula, the Astrodome developers had a series of problems of their own.

This new stadium had a roof. Such an innovation meant that fans would be nice and snug, cool and dry. The field itself boasted specially selected grass bred to thrive indoors. But as a natural grass it still needed both water and sunlight. A sprinkler system took care of the former and the architects had, of course, fully thought through the requirement for sufficient daylight. The Astrodome came complete with a transparent roof.

So far so good.

---

13 Virginia Jenkins, *The Lawn: A History of an American Obsession,* Washington DC, Smithsonian Institution Press, 1994.

Sadly it turned out the glinting of the sun above was accentuated by the transparent panels and blinded the outfield players looking up trying to field high balls. They and their fans were not best pleased as you can well imagine. Lots more home runs for whoever was batting.

Ha! No problem.

They simply painted the roof. Problem solved.

Only now the grass wouldn't grow properly.

The stadium owners were up in arms and the engineers were under pressure. Developer Judge Hofheinz consulted with Chemstrand employees James M Faria and Robert T Wright. These guys in turn called North Carolina State University, specifically the dean of the college of textiles, David Chaney. Dave was later declared by *Sports Illustrated* to be the man responsible for both the success of indoor Major League Baseball and for the appearance of millions of 'Welcome' doormats of the same material around the country. His research team, known as Research Triangle Park, duly created the first notable artificial sports turf. Made from nylon fibres it was initially named ChemGrass (a somewhat less than inspiring name, I think you'll agree) and came in any colour you wanted so long as it was green. OK, I just made that last bit up but it was probably true back then. It was the solution to the Astrodome's problems and installation promptly commenced there in 1966, within a year of its opening.

Because of insufficient light, the Dome's suited-up groundskeepers had to paint the dirt green. Then with not enough yardage of the new fake turf immediately available this continued, as surfacing the entire park was completed in stages. During this process these staff, in their kitschy spacesuit-type overalls (a marketing gimmick), were also deployed to sweep off debris from the fancy new 'grass' between innings. The viewing public were both intrigued and amused and soon started to call it moon grass.

By now President JF Kennedy's ambitious Apollo programme was gaining momentum and capturing the nation's attention. Slick marketeers, in tune with the zeitgeist at the dawn of the space age, canned 'moon grass' and came up with something better: 'astro turf'.

Manufacturer Chemstrand Co was later renamed Monsanto Textile Co and an official trademark was issued on 25 July 1967. We'll revisit their work in Chapter 6. Spoiler alert, it's not all good.

In 2016 AstroTurf filed for chapter 11 bankruptcy protection. It's still a trademark but more commonly used as a generic name. It's now a subsidiary of German-based Sport Group.

Maintaining real grass in an indoor stadium had proven both awkward and expensive. AstroTurf reduced ongoing maintenance costs drastically and was soon adopted in several other similar stadia throughout the US.

This was far from plain sailing of course and it took the solving of many teething problems and several generations to achieve something approaching acceptability. Next let's explore its evolution in more depth and how it has become virtually indistinguishable from the real thing.

Chapter 3

How artificial grass made the cut

Leisure grass for the leisure class

Remember George Eliot's novel *Silas Mariner* (1861), with Silas toiling away in his cottage on his loom, saving up his pennies?

Besides the invention of steam-driven pumps to clear water from coal mines and later for the locomotive transportation of the coal, another main driver of the Industrial Revolution was Mr James Hargreaves's 'spinning jenny'. Before his invention weaving was a cottage industry. His spinning jenny speeded up this process considerably and soon factories sprang up to supply the growing urbanised populace with linen and cotton clothing.[14]

From these humble beginnings developed today's large carpet-weaving/tufting machines for making artificial grass. The advent of artificial turf fortuitously coincided with the carpet manufacturing industry having spare capacity. Both carpets and fake grass (essentially an outdoor carpet) are made by the same machines with some relatively minor modifications. Thus several carpet manufacturers spun off (pun definitely intended) artificial grass divisions. These in turn are further divided into a sports grass arm and a smaller landscape/leisure grass arm. We'll examine the difference shortly. These guys then hook up with national distributors such as yours truly.

Picture a 4m wide tufting machine – it's basically a giant sewing machine. Think of your granny's Singer. Now imagine a long line of them working in tandem, typically up to 250 individual needles punching away, forming a loop, spewing out row upon row, metre after metre of carpet.

These needles insert filaments of fibre, fed via long narrow tubes from large spools of yarn, into a fabric backing. Knives then cut it to a set depth, anything between 8mm and 60mm, the machine trundles on another centimetre or so

---

14 The whole thing could have kicked off a lot sooner had it not been for a certain queen's reluctance. Way back in 1598 innovator William Lee applied to the English court for a patent for his invention, a knitting machine. Sadly, none was granted. According to *The Economist*, Elizabeth I said, 'Consider thou what the invention could do to my poor subjects. It would assuredly bring them to ruin by depriving them of employment.' (See www.economist.com/books-and-arts/2020/01/23/robots-may-well-take-your-job-eventually.) Thus, 'Good Queen Bess' may have forestalled the Industrial Revolution for many years. I wonder what she'd make of today's robotics.

Fake grass factory in the Netherlands

Fake grass back home

Rosanna Davidson (above left); not Rosanna Davidson (above right)

Warehouse and yard manager Tommy with Mark in Covid times

and the process is repeated. Usually they produce a linear metre a minute. After 20–25 metres the entire fabric is cut and another roll begins.

Afterwards, a flexible adhesive latex material is applied to bind the fibres to the backing. This backing material, similar to that of carpets, can be made from jute, plastic or polyester. A latex layer is typically coated twice at controlled temperatures. This is called curing. As it dries, hot pins then burn sequential holes into it to facilitate good permeability and drainage. It's then visually inspected for flaws and manually trimmed if necessary before being cooled, rolled up and sealed in wrapping and – hey presto – ready for storage and transport.

Plastic fantastic

So far so good but what about the main raw material used in the process? How is plastic made into a beautiful lawn with millions of individual strands or 'blades'? In Chapter 6 we'll have a look further back in the process but for now let's start with thermoplastic polymers – the millions of plastic pellets, whether virgin or recycled, used as the base raw material.

Nowadays these pellets are usually made of polypropylene with additives like UV stabilisers and dyes blended into a hopper melting them together. Mixed into a thick consistency, the liquid is then extruded through a petrified steel plate, a mould – think of a baker applying icing by squeezing that triangular-shaped piping bag with a small hole at the bottom – and then into a trough of water which acts to solidify the resulting threads. The shape of this mould's cross section naturally dictates the shape of the yarn produced. This shape, flat or V-shaped for example, is supposedly what gives the grass certain performance characteristics – a softer feel, better bouncebackability or whatever. See Buyers guide Chapter 14 for more on this. The quality of this resulting yarn is crucial to the performance of grass systems.

Once the yarn is cooled, pulleys and rollers separate and stretch these thin strands of material, initially like a loose rope, to make them just as thin as blades of real grass. Reheating can give them a twisted shape if desired. They are then wound onto spools set up manually or by robots, to feed into the tufting machines. Multiple spools, often in different combinations and yarn types, make up variations of grass.

The tech specs

These are easily glossed over but it's important to understand in order to judge and compare different grasses. After many years in the industry, this writer, even with a relatively trained eye, still can have difficulty separating the wheat from the chaff, so to speak. The market is currently getting swamped with often poor quality grasses made from cheap yarn that just won't perform or give the expected or promised longevity.

So don't be fooled.

Compare the specs. If it's cheaper, there's a reason. One prominent brand is entirely made in China, its customers blissfully oblivious to this unstated fact. Note: Some Chinese yarns and grasses *can* be decent quality too.

One of the oldest tricks in the book is to sell cheap grass on the basis of technical specifications that the vast majority of people, even many within the industry, simply don't understand. Thus an uninformed punter, trying to decipher the good from the possibly not so good, is left with no choice but to choose on price and appearance. So please do take the trouble to request and study respective spec sheets.

 TIP
When comparing, try to make sure the spec sheet correctly matches the actual sample you have. Take out your ruler. (See page 313–317 for more information)

Comparing apples with oranges

Fact: it's easy, if unscrupulous, to provide a high standard spec sheet along with a dodgy sample. Oh, and get physical samples – never rely on pictures.

The data describes the primary characteristics of grasses. And yes, different parameters and combos are often used purely for the sake of differentiation and marketing. News flash! A nice soft-feeling grass ain't necessarily the best choice as it ends up flattening too quickly once *in situ*. Basically the thinner the fibre, the weaker it is. Thin monofilament fibres are more easily split. As a rule, the thicker and wider the individual fibres are, the better, particularly when destined for heavy use or for sports applications.

The constant evolution of grass technology means some of this information may be invalidated by technological improvements such as the coming on stream of recyclable materials. Comparing can be as much fun as figuring out the relative charges of different mobile phone providers or health insurance plans. You would almost think they are trying to confuse you. Don't be intimidated. Be informed. Looking past the jargon, it's mostly common sense.

Pile height and gauge are among the most important criteria and can be verified using a simple ruler. If you can get your hands on a magnifying glass that would help.

Sports grass v Landscape grass

> *'What do you prefer, Rodney – AstroTurf or grass?'*
> *'Oh, I dunno. I never smoked AstroTurf.'*
> ~ Only Fools and Horses

To better understand the differences let's continue our study of the evolution of fake lawns.

This book is definitely *not* about sports grass aka AstroTurf. In the same way that well-known brand Hoover became synonymous with the generic vacuum cleaner, and to 'google' is to do an online search, the brand name AstroTurf has unsurprisingly been used for all sports grasses. It is also much less accurately (and somewhat annoyingly) used to describe artificial lawn turf.

As we've seen from the Astrodome challenges earlier, all was not all plain sailing.

Because of the challenges and prohibitive expense of maintaining natural grass indoors, AstroTurf, with its supposedly predictable ball ricocheting properties, was soon adopted in several other US baseball stadiums. However, it was to take several generations of product and the solving of many teething problems to get to the prominence synthetic sports grasses enjoy today. This in turn drove its spread in commercial, educational and residential applications. Far from the flaky green carpet seen under fruit and vegetable displays in the greengrocer's, it now has the look and feel of the real thing.

Unlike the actual grass, the market for both sports and domestic grass is growing rapidly.

Generations

Inevitably the appearance and quality of both AstroTurf and artificial lawns have improved dramatically over the last fifty years. Now it's possible to have a synthetic lawn that not only looks just like the real thing but outperforms it.

We've seen that the first generation of sports grasses were an array of short pile height versions. Unfortunately the ball would bounce all over the place and the nature of the surface caused joint injuries as well as nasty carpet burns, especially on knees and thighs. Players and fans became disillusioned.

In baseball early adopters even switched back to natural turf. Meanwhile in American football, the football stadium of the University of Pennsylvania, Franklin Field, home of the Philadelphia Eagles, converted to artificial turf in 1969. Crucially this allowed the hosting of many other sporting and musical events, despite frequent poor weather, without damaging or compromising the playing surface. The extra revenue generated took the pain out of the initial investment.

Synthetic sports grass did enjoy sustained success with both tennis and field hockey, in fact it significantly changed the latter. Unlike other sports, hockey did not demand a real grass feel. Indeed the short fibre structure allowed a considerable increase in the speed and appeal of the game. This led to changes in the shape of hockey sticks, and different playing techniques developed such as reverse stick trapping and hitting.

There were some unavoidable consequences. One drawback was that such pitches were only suitable for hockey, which was rather restrictive. Another was that due to the expense of installation, richer Western European teams suddenly enjoyed more success over Indian and Pakistani teams which had dominated the sport for years.

As synthetic sports grasses started to appear in Europe in the early 1970s the closely packed synthetic fibres began to be made from polypropylene rather than nylon. This was not only cheaper but also softer and more comfortable to play on. This change reduced injuries and friction burns.

Changing fashions

Another major factor in the advent of artificial grasses, for both sports and landscaping application, was as a result of the explosion in popularity of alternative indoor floor coverings such as laminated wood.

Linoleum, made from linseed oil, powdered cork and cotton, had been around for decades but cheaper, tougher PVC lino took off big time in the 1950s. Think back, why did granny have carpet in the bathroom? What was that all about?

All this in turn led to a downturn in carpet sales and the aforementioned unexpected spare capacity in many carpet-weaving factories. So, much like the head-scratching engineers following the painting of the Astrodome roof, carpet manufacturers now had to come up with a new plan. Hence their interest in, and the development of, new artificial grass lines using largely the same machinery and methodology as in their core business.

Later versions used more weather-resistant synthetics and, thanks to chemical treatment for resistance to ultraviolet sunrays, were now suitable for permanent outdoor use. Older types had been prone to bleaching and fading in the sun but, despite being a lingering and common misconception, this is no longer an issue in Sanctuary. We give a 10 year UV warranty.

With the 1970s in full swing artificial grasses followed the shag carpet trend and fibres became longer and less densely stitched. Sand began to be used to stabilise the roots. Dry sand was simply swept in and settled at the base. This also served to weigh it down, aiding the installation process. These were known as second generation grasses.

In due course scientific research and technological advances soon led to the introduction of third-generation (3G) pitches. It is generally acknowledged that these were a significant improvement. With ever longer fibres (55 mm+) and spaced further apart, the yarn of these grasses was made largely from polypropylene and was to prove kinder to athletes' skin than earlier versions.

Another key difference is that 3G grasses required rubber granule infill in addition to sand infill when laid. Boot studs could sink into the surface as per natural sod and there was less stress on the joints, so better for games like soccer. There are two material properties that affect injury rates: the coefficient of friction (resistance) and the coefficient of restitution (capacity for shock absorption). The lower the latter, the higher the injury and concussion rates. The higher the former, the more often lower extremity injuries occur. According to medics, early injuries included ACL (anterior cruciate ligament) tears, concussions and ankle sprains. In addition there were increased incidents of both turf burns and 'turf toe', a stiff big toe caused by arthritis.

FIFA, not surprisingly, flip-flopped on the acceptability of artificial grass. More on this later. Usually these rubber granules, regardless of manufacturer's specifications, were not made from virgin rubber, rather from ground-up old car tyres. Many readers will be familiar with the troublesome and ubiquitous 'little black balls' transported home in boots, socks and gear after playing on 3G and 4G pitches. Certainly parents will have cursed them while loading up the washing machine. UEFA and FIFA were soon on board however and certification of new pitches proceeded apace. Having appeared for the first time in the 2010 Soccer World Cup in South Africa a version is now being widely used for professional rugby too. As of 2017 according to the US's Synthetic Turf Council there are more than 12,000 synthetic turf sports fields in use throughout the US. The

UK has an estimated 4,000 artificial football pitches, with many more in the pipeline. Sports grass is not without its detractors. A cursory online search (try Google images) will show plenty of photos of nasty skin abrasions. A high price for diving over to score the winning try. We will examine this rubber infill and its potential health implications in Chapter 6.

In parallel with developments on the sports side, new applications and improvements for the leisure/domestic grass side of things also occurred. Although still the 'little brother' in terms of volume and revenue, sports grass makers began to see an increase in enquiries from the domestic market and they took steps to meet that demand. New companies (like us in Ireland) sprang up, specialising in serving that particular niche. Later we'll look at how fake lawns gradually gained acceptance, but suffice it to say that early adopters were quite pleased, despite some raised eyebrows.

The introduction of thatch

Thatch is a curled twisted fibre base layer in the carpet, often brown not green, introduced between the longer strands which has revolutionised the domestic synthetic grass industry. It made a huge difference to the look and feel of the grass. Besides giving it a more natural appearance it also increased its durability and did away with the need to add a layer of sand dressing on top post-installation. This development first came about due to efforts to give grasses a more burned, dry look for the hotter southern US and Mediterranean markets by mixing in brown fibres. More northerly markets liked it too as it looked like dead grass or moss and consequently appeared more natural.

Different paths

With increased specialisation, the two sister products, sports and landscape, continue to diverge, one to accommodate specific sports performance criteria and the other to maximise appearance and performance in the home.

So in summary, sports grasses (aka AstroTurf) and artificial lawn grasses, called leisure or landscape grasses, are clearly not the same. The former typically require sand and rubber infill and have far longer pile heights, and the latter nowadays need no such infill and tend to be shorter. Both however share common characteristics and go through a similar production process.

Not my circus, not my monkeys

From day one, my chosen niche was in landscape grasses. I continue to steer well clear of rubber infill AstroTurf. I will expand upon this later. As a student of marketing I understand the value of dominating your own niche. Sanctuary Synthetics became Ireland's first full service specialist in artificial grass for gardens. Sure, some big sports grass companies operate here but, for a long time merely dabbled in domestic lawns. Over the years however some sports-related challenges did occasionally crop up.

'Sanctuary settles Sallins stampede at soccer grounds'[15]

This is one of my favourite newspaper headlines involving our company. It appeared in a local newspaper, *Leinster Leader*, some years ago.

It tells of the sorry tale of the Sallins Celtic soccer team grounds getting destroyed by Sanctuary. More precisely, getting destroyed by my father's herd of rampaging bullocks who stampeded all over their newly mowed, rolled and marked pitch. At the time I was using the yard on the farm to store grass and equipment. It's quite close to the football grounds on the edge of the village. One of the lads, unused to boisterous livestock, had inadvertently neglected to tie the farm gate shut properly.

It is really not the kind of phone call one wants to receive on a wet Saturday afternoon while relaxing after a hard week's work.

'Eh, you might wanna come quick.' Having had their fun on the soccer pitch, the cattle continued to run amuck, making their way up Main Street heading God knows where. First I had to round up a posse to catch the strays and get them corralled back onto the farm. Then we turned to the now clearly unplayable pitch. Their first game of the season was scheduled for the following day.

Because of heavy rain there were hundreds of hoof marks deep in the wet grass. Not to mention copious amounts of cow dung. We sprang into action. Early on Sunday morning a crew of my lads, including the rather sheepish culprit, along with some disgruntled club officials and players, volunteered to spend several hours repairing and replacing the damaged areas with fresh natural sod. Many hands make light work and we managed to save the day. There had, however, been mutterings of legal action and it was a potential PR disaster locally.

So, taking the bull by the horns (sorry) I contacted a journalist from the local

15 Paul O'Meara, 'Sanctuary Settles Sallins Stampede at Soccer Grounds', *Leinster Leader*, 23
    May 2012, Local News, www.leinsterleader.ie/news/local-news/61607/Sanctuary-settles-Sallins-
    stampede-at-soccer.html.

paper, told him the whole story and arranged to be photographed making amends by handing over a €500 cheque for 'sponsorship' to the club's chairperson. In the subsequent article the official promptly and wholeheartedly praised his good neighbour Sanctuary Synthetics. Disaster averted.

Although, they did lose to Dunlavin later that afternoon (1–0).

Flatteringly our expertise has been called upon in the sports arena for more than just bullshit (again, sorry) reasons even though I draw the line at laying rubber infill AstroTurf.

I played a bit of rugby back in the day. I still coach at underage level and, as a Leinster and Ireland rugby fan, have endured terrific highs and lows over the years. In November 2016 my wife and I travelled to Chicago for a long weekend and witnessed not one but three momentous events.

First the Cubs won their first World Series in 109 years of trying.

Then, on Saturday afternoon in Soldier Field an Irish rugby team beat the famed All Blacks (New Zealand) 40 to 29 for the first time ever after more than a century of trying. It's a treasured memory I'll take to my deathbed.

The third event was even more unexpected and outlandish. As we left downtown Chicago, I saw long queues outside polling stations. Although he didn't actually win in *that* city, an Orange celebrity 'Apprentice' TV host was soon deemed elected to the presidency.

Back home Munster had long been rivals of my home province Leinster. They had won the European (Heineken) Cup twice before Leinster went on to claim four titles (so far). Their headquarters is in Thomond Park, a fantastic modern new stadium in Limerick city. When I got the call to ask if we could take a look at solving an ongoing pitch-side drainage problem they were having, I couldn't refuse. We successfully sorted them out and subsequently did work for Leinster Rugby too.

Anyway now that you have a handle on how the grass is made, it's high time to expand on how Sanctuary Synthetics came about.

Chapter 4

Finding Sanctuary

'When you come to a fork in the road, take it' [16]
~ Yogi Berra, legendary Yankee baseballer

As George W Bush said, 'When I was young and irresponsible, I was young and irresponsible.'[17] It took me quite a long time to get with the programme.

Any programme. It wasn't for the want of opportunities. I bounced around, oblivious to fake grass, hitting 30 before even starting to focus on anything like building a meaningful career or business. I sowed wild oats and had my fun. Equally I'd suffered through soul crushing torment. Who am I? Where am I going? Where's my next beer coming from?

I was born a year after the film *The Graduate* came out and right before *The Brady Bunch* TV series started. In 1968 flower power and the hippy movement were in full flow, the Vietnam war was hotting up and the Beatles were more famous than Jesus. Thanks to the suppression of civil rights and gerrymandering, the Troubles in Northern Ireland were about to kick off. Life expectancy was getting longer and miniskirts were at their shortest. Within months a man was to walk on the moon.

My first small steps were taken in Kill House on the edge of Kill village just inside the (actual) Pale[18] in rural County Kildare, aka the 'short grass' county. I grew up on a 215 acre farm bordering the dual carriageway, only 26 kilometres from the centre of Dublin city. The State had compulsorily purchased a chunk of what had been called our 'lawn' field from my grandfather, Joe Loughlin (who won a couple of All-Irelands in the 1920s) to make way for the N7, eventually a six-lane motorway. My other Granddad, Mark Deering, was also a Farmer as well as a TD and was capped for Ireland.

---

16 Yogi Berra, *When You Come to a Fork in the Road, Take It!: Inspiration and Wisdom from One of Baseball's Greatest Heroes*, 1st ed., New York, Hyperion, 2002, p. 1.
17 George W Bush, *A Portrait of My Father*, New York, Crown, 1994, p. 71.
18 The Pale was that small part of Ireland around Dublin directly controlled by the English in the late Middle Ages. Those beyond it were considered "uncivilised". It's a pity our ancient Brehon laws were so misunderstood.

MARK 10 MTHS + Rex

It's ironic that having grown up in an enterprise that grew grass to fatten beef cattle, I now make my living selling grass that won't grow.

As a child I loved Lego, building forts out of straw bales and making sandcastles on holidays. I always loved nature and instantly feel more relaxed when I go out into a forest or across the fields.

Unless it's a golf course.

Then I tend to tense up quite a bit.

Essentially I'm an outdoors person. Although, it took quite a while to realise that.

Because Dad was a cattle dealer he was, by necessity, off farm quite a lot. I ended up with plenty of responsibility at an early age – driving tractors, operating machinery, moving and feeding cattle and coordinating contractors (silage cutting, corn harvesting and such). So in many ways my current role running Sanctuary was a natural progression.

But first I had lots of mistakes to make and wrong turns to take.

In 1986 my father sold the family farm. I was 18 and had absolutely no objection. Farming was such bloody hard work. I was the second eldest of seven, with three brothers and three sisters, and he was downsizing in order to fund expensive college education for all his children. I embarked on a diploma in marketing and administration in the College of Marketing and Design. Boy, did I love the student lifestyle. Occasional lectures didn't interfere in any way with either rugby or socialising. Long summers were spent in Munich, Boston and Berlin.

I graduated in 1989 when there were virtually no jobs in recession-hit Ireland. Some 32 of my 39 classmates emigrated. I joined them, ending up in Australia for a spell. I blagged my way into the marketing department of the State Rail Authority (mind-numbingly boring, although my immediate boss, a statistician, was an actual Sri Lankan princess) and worked in a bar in Kings Cross on weekends. Plus I did a little bit of gardening in my late Uncle Jim's place overlooking Sydney Harbour. Please don't mention funnel-web spiders to me!

Soon enough I was back in Dublin for a final year of an advanced diploma with the promise of a Trinity College degree. I was elected class representative for what turned out to be a dramatic graduation. For once I knuckled down and sailed through. But the prestigious degree never materialised, perhaps ultimately a blessing in disguise. More on this later.

In parallel with our course we studied for professional membership of the

Institute of Chartered Secretaries and Administrators (ICSA). Somehow I got the professional qualification and even got the institute's tie. I never had occasion to wear it, however, and pursued anything else rather than following that particular path. Surely it would all come in handy once I figured out the nature of my calling.

I was in Berlin in 1989 but missed the mother of all parties by weeks when the wall and entire Iron Curtain came crashing down. I had been offered an additional 12 month contract with Ford Plastics (where I had bluffed my way into the IT department. Lotus 1-2-3 Impress anyone?) but turned it down in order to participate in the final trial for the Irish U21s rugby team back in Lansdowne Road in Dublin.

I had had the honour of playing for successful Leinster under-19s, -20s and -21s sides, but was only on the Possibles against the pProbables for the national squad. I will draw a discreet veil over how it went, but suffice it to say that I was picked, and as the East Berliners poured westward, I toured Italy representing my country. It was the eve of professionalism in the sport. As a second-row forward at only 6' 4", I'm not sure whether to blame my height or a fondness for wine, women and song, not to mention cigarettes, but that's as far as I ever got, aside from a couple of seasons on the Irish colleges side. Several of my erstwhile teammates went on to have long and distinguished professional careers with the Irish senior team.

The real world

Back in the real world I discovered a couple of things about myself. I have a healthy disrespect for authority (hence perhaps my blatant attack on the lawn-loving status quo). I'm most definitely *not* a morning person. I regard happy, chirpy early risers with deep suspicion. What is wrong with them? What do they want from me? In fairness I was never lazy and once I got going on something I deemed worthwhile, I was like a dog with a bone and wouldn't stop (hey, I even got this blessed book finished in the end).

The other thing was that, despite having been asked to do a few jobs in people's gardens, it never dawned on me that I have some kind of innate skill that not everyone shares. If I have a superpower, it's being able to look at a space, regardless of what state it might be in, and visualise what it *could* be. My parents had bought a derelict cottage with a large overgrown garden in Naas and I spent months repairing broken-down stone walls and clearing the jungle, laying it out beautifully according to my green-fingered mother's instructions.

Naw … still it didn't dawn on me what I could be good at.

To this day it gives me immense satisfaction to transform perceived chaos into some kind of order. My next book will delve into some of my design philosophies in that regard. Hint: it involves sacred geometry.

My Rome, however, was not built in a day.

After a year or two of glamorous stints behind bars (the drinking kind, not the metal ones), on building sites and in an abattoir, I ended up back in Germany still trying to master the language. I got onto a government-run graduate business programme to study and gain work experience. I studied for a few months in Heidelberg, played rugby and, for beer money, worked part time with a crew contracted to the City Parks Department. We mostly built stone walls and terraces on the hills overlooking the Student Prince's castle. Thereafter I was sent to a small meat packing company in rural Northern Germany where, for once, there were far fewer English speakers. The downside was the 6 a.m. starts, the upside was the 2.2 litre Opel Omega company car they possibly foolishly gave me. There are no speed limits on German autobahns.

Returning to Ireland I had a notion of working for Irish beef exporters selling into Germany. So back I went to work for the local abattoir where my father still sent his fattened-up cattle. Unfortunately with EEC price support mechanisms called 'Intervention', the industry was more interested in selling into cold storage or to dodgy Iraqi and Libyan markets (fun guys like Gaddafi and Saddam) than developing value-added markets on the continent. The subsequent beef tribunal did not help. Not unlike myself they were following the path of least resistance.

I switched to another local food company and worked hard. Or so I thought. After 364 days I was unceremoniously sacked (any longer and it would have been legally more difficult to get rid of me). I was quite bitter about the trumped-up reasons for expulsion, but looking back I realise I was not at all politically savvy, having trodden on too many sensitive toes.

At a loss, I seriously contemplated re-emigrating. However, I decided I'd aim for a nice warm office, a computer on my desk and my own car. After lots of painful rejections I found myself as a sales support engineer for a specialist gas company with all of the above. Strangely I found myself wistfully looking out the windows at the landscapers maintaining the grounds, seemingly without a care in the world.

I was in danger of becoming a jack of all trades and a master of none. After a couple of years virtually 'running the show' there, I threatened to leave unless they gave me a sales rep role on the road. 'Well Mark, we'll be sorry to see you go.'

Another valuable life lesson right there. Bluff called. Nobody is indispensable.

Next I clocked up another 364 days as a sales rep calling into hardware stores all over Leinster. I had no clue about most of the stuff I was selling. I opened new accounts left, right and centre but didn't hit too many other targets.

In desperation, by 1997, I had spent a few tough but satisfying months working for a local landscaping company. Strictly temporary, I told myself. Winter came, things went quiet, I caught a flu and they too let me go.

An epiphany

Then, as per page nine, San Francisco beckoned.

Maybe I'm a bit slow as I had done landscaping jobs casually for family and friends back home, but it had never occurred to me that it could be something more. Until then I considered it somehow beneath me if I'm honest. Loads of the guests at my boss's party, no doubt familiar with the disaster zone the garden had previously been, admired my work. On the US West Coast there is a real 'can do' attitude. Reinventing oneself is not at all frowned upon. The penny eventually dropped.

I chose to become a landscaper.

Overnight.

And loved it.

I begged and borrowed some tools, commandeered my sister's car and was soon earning good clean money by getting my hands dirty, crisscrossing the city tidying up properties. The foggy, friendly Bay Area is well known for its gardens, so it is a great spot to learn my trade. I spent time in garden centres, hanging around Golden Gate Park's botanical gardens, attending talks and exhibitions. I read gardening books and made mistakes.

Yes, this career path should have dawned on me far earlier.

After all, with a farming background and being naturally fit and strong all I really had to do was get over myself and kick on. But not before suffering through more than one long dark teatime of the soul. [ref. Douglas Adams].

I was always ambitious and demanding of myself but for years it was entirely wasted. There was never a lack of ideas, only a lack of execution and work satisfaction. A tough, happy-go-lucky rugby player on the outside, I mostly kept my worries to myself. My best buddy Mick helped me through some tough times of self-doubt. There was more than a little foolish pride. I had considered manual labour beneath me, what with all the (unused) letters after my name. I was like Darcy in Jane Austin's *Pride and Prejudice*, only I lacked his fortune.

I would have to make my own.

Happy and all though I found my lot in California, my past was to catch up with my present and project me into the future – and back to Ireland.

Years earlier, in my capacity as elected college class rep, we had taken a collective legal action against the Department of Education and our college for failing to award us our promised degrees. To cut a sob story short our day in court finally beckoned and I headed back to Ireland to see it through. After all, I had led the walkout at our graduation ceremony in protest. Plus, my visa had run out.

After an elaborate game of chicken, our barrister eventually settled on the steps of the High Court. We agreed on a compensation settlement that excluded our degrees, which 'could not be retrospectively awarded', but included a modest sum by way of making up for potential lost earnings. Happy days.

Ireland has become a highly litigious society which I abhor (all the more so as an employer) but this was a genuine case. Our class tangibly suffered in the job market as a result of alleged administrative negligence and many faced unemployment or emigration in the days before the Celtic Tiger got up and running.

But now I was back and this time, like Hannibal Smith from *The A-Team*, I had a plan coming together.

It was 1999, the world was my oyster and I now had a windfall lump sum in my back pocket, more than enough to get the show on the road.

As Ireland was not yet a rich country, gardening work was predominantly a DIY affair. When I first told people I was a landscaper, I got some glazed looks …

'Oh, a market gardener?'

No, I'm not bloody growing tomatoes – I'm transforming people's gardens!

'Ooh …'

With long unused marketing skills I designed some business cards and flyers, bought a second-hand Volkswagen van and, hey presto, overnight I was a self-employed landscaper back in the auld sod. I'd never been happier.

I would be no slave to convention. My destiny was, at last, in my own hands. Soon Niall, a buddy of mine unhappy in his job, quit and joined me. We became OAK Landscaping (O'Loughlin And Kavanagh). More than just a mow, blow and go outfit, we designed and created quite elaborate hardscaped gardens and soon added a couple of employees.

Close, but no cigar

Now Niall was a talented man, hardworking, resourceful and great with people. Together we pioneered an entirely new side business, importing and erecting Finnish (and later Estonian) log cabins. Everyone said we'd fail as nobody would ever pay so much for a 'glorified garden shed'.

We sold over 30 cabins in about 18 months. Then we got stiffed by a Northern builder for a large amount and it sickened us. Here was another very valuable lesson learned the hard way. Having found and fulfilled a niche need – in this case log cabins – we then let it all go. From having first-mover advantage and no competition, we failed to press on following a financial setback and now there's a dozen companies selling and erecting log cabins in Ireland. Good luck to them but I could have been the 'Log Cabin Man'.

It's not a mistake I'll ever make again. Around the same time Niall and I parted company. I said Niall *was* a very talented man – he later developed a serious illness and has since passed away. RIP, old buddy.

On my own again there was no question of not persevering in the landscaping business. I came up with 'Sanctuary Landscapes' as I saw my mission as making gardens a place of refuge and joy. It seemed to resonate and I quickly got busy again, but this time carrying debt from the 'divorce' and having to do uncomfortable things, like VAT returns, previously shared with my business partner. Yet another learning curve.

A major plus of being one's own boss is that I could disappear during the quietest month or so of winter. I usually choose somewhere warm, cheap and far, far away. I returned to San Francisco for New Year's Eve in 1999 on my way to tour around South America.

The following year I visited Mexico and Cuba with my girlfriend, Anne. While in Havana I managed to get an appointment with the State's cigar exporting company. Sadly, with my dodgy Spanish I failed to negotiate an agency for Ireland. '*No puedo amigo.*' It all went through their London office.

'But like you, we are a separate independent country – we too fought off the oppressors. Your offices are on Calle *O'Reilly* for God's sake'.

He was sympathetic but '*Lo siento.*' No harm in trying I guess.

Myself and Anne came back engaged.

My rugby swansong

Soon after we were married, I almost died. It was after my last ever rugby match, a lowly J3 Leinster Towns Cup final against our old rival Carlow. Despite having broken my left thumb in the first 10 minutes, I played the full game, egged on by Paddy, my second-row partner (and now my accountant). On the bus home, I got hoarse from the singsong while drinking beer and champagne from the cup, which I could barely hold.

The next day in hospital was less fun. The hangover didn't help. I needed an operation to put in some metal pins to repair the damage. I wish I could say it went smoothly.

It didn't.

After waking up from the operation I couldn't help but notice that the only part of the cast on my arm that mattered, the bit around my thumb, had failed to harden. Eventually I was taken by a junior doctor (seriously) into a broom storage cupboard to get replastered.

Anne and I decided to use the opportunity of me being out of action to take off for a couple of weeks' holiday. But first, with my arm in a sling, I went back, unwisely, to finish off a stone folly I'd been working on. It was folly alright.

The pain started somewhere over the south of France. By the time we landed in Turkey I'd started to drink brandy to numb it. The transfer to Northern Cyprus, our destination, was a bit of a blur but by the time we got to our hotel I'd finished the bottle and had munched all the painkillers we could find. To no avail.

The local hospital was far from a five star establishment. I'd no Turkish — well, apart from 'İki bira lütfen' (two beers please) — and they had little English but I was seen by a chain-smoking doctor within minutes. He instantly sent me for an X-ray. We grabbed the X-rays the minute they were printed and went straight back in to see him.

'Tut, tut, tut,' he said. Without ceremony, he produced a mini saw from a drawer on his desk and proceeded to saw off a square of plaster over the thumb.

Pop!

The little square sprung away over his desk and smelly puss and blood first shot then oozed out of my badly infected wound. I nearly fainted with relief. My ordeal was far from over, however.

I was confined to bed in a room without windows or air conditioning, on a cocktail of intravenous antibiotics for the duration of our two-week stay. Poor Anne had the job of minding me and keeping me sane. Sunbathing was low on the agenda.

My hero, the Turkish consultant, believed I was now his Irish counterpart's problem so he left the metal pins in and the rest of the cast in situ. My entire arm was now badly swollen and the pain continued. A few days later, in desperation, Anne liberated a serrated knife from the resort's restaurant and she administered some relief. Eh, to my swollen hand. As the entire hospital's staff were cheering on their mainland countrymen in the soccer World Cup semi-finals down the corridor, we took turns at slowly carving through my cast.

By right, I should have got an air ambulance home but one doesn't necessarily think straight when in dire circumstances. Despite arrangements to the contrary, on arrival back to hospital in Ireland we were directed to await readmission via accident and emergency. Being a weekend night, it was more like a war zone. It was full of drunks clogging up the system. Having travelled thousands of miles and still as sick as a dog, I was left on a chair for hours. Matters only came to a head when I said, 'Fuck this, I'm going home.' I got halfway towards the door when the room started to spin, slowly at first, and then I took an unscheduled nap.

I've had some bad dreams in my time but what happened next took the biscuit. Later that night, after Anne went home to get some much-needed rest, leaving me in the intensive care ward on yet another powerful antibiotic to treat my severe sepsis, I awoke to a bit of commotion.

The night nurse and porter were struggling to hold up the guy from the bed opposite me. He was hanging by the neck with his dressing gown cord. I was in no position to even move, let alone help, as this suicide attempt unfolded a few feet away. My recall is sketchy and it could have been a fevered dream but I suspect I heard or saw the guy go about trying to hang himself but I literally could do nothing about it. Miraculously he was spotted and saved. For the moment, at least. Having just been given a terminal diagnosis, he'd had enough. I clearly remember the night nurse coming in the next morning and, in true Irish fashion, giving out yards to him. Having scolded him firmly, she made him faithfully promise not to try pulling a stunt like that ever again or it would be straight to the psych ward.

Over the following few weeks, the man and I became friends and companions. Only I was getting better and he was not. A couple of months following my discharge, he passed away. RIP. It could have been me.

In 25 years playing rugby, it was my first and last broken bone. We'd seen no beaches in Northern Cyprus but the stone folly turned out great.

Boy, those Towns Cup medals are hard won.

After the thumb drama I went back to work but it took me several months to fully recover and get my vitality back. It was a worrying time. No work equals no income. That's the vulnerability of self-employment. I realised I needed to somehow scale up. I needed a team.

The following January my best buddy Mick invited me to join him in sunny Florida for a spot of golf. For him, it was a working holiday as he was in the golf merchandise game and was attending the annual PGA golf expo. I tagged along and, you guessed it, something I saw there became *the* fork in the road.

Next up, how I made it as Ireland's biggest grass dealer.

Chapter 5

Becoming the Fake Grass Man

'An ounce of commerce is worth a tonne of work'
~ Anonymous Polish granddad

At the Orlando PGA Merchandise Show my buddy Mick was busy sourcing products and attending meetings. All I wanted was January sunshine as I strolled around the convention centre, hands in pockets, wondering when our tee time was, yearning to get back to the pool for a spell.

Then I spotted something that stopped me in my tracks. An artificial putting green. I was actually far more taken with the very real looking artificial grass fringe around it. Intrigued, I found myself circling back to it a few times. As I chatted to the exhibitors, cogs and wheels began whirring in my brain.

At last.

I had my eureka moment.

This is it.

This was the future. My future.

In a moment of clarity I realised that Sanctuary Landscapes could become Sanctuary Synthetics. If I were to offer any career advice, it would be to search for something you enjoy doing. Find it *before* you take on too many responsibilities. As the saying goes, don't let the grass grow under your feet. I'd love to say I went to Florida keeping a sharp eye out for business opportunities. I didn't. But at this critical juncture in my career I stood staring, in tee shirt and shorts, excitement building in my breast.

Naturally enough I immediately procrastinated.

I could see the potential and did feck all about it but the idea wouldn't go away. Back home watching RTÉ's *The Late Late Show*, I got the final kick up the arse I needed. One evening the host interviewed a guy I knew about his new company Classic Decks. He was bringing the concept home from America and timber decking quickly became an unlikely but lasting craze in rain-sodden Ireland. Another time, Gay Byrne had his audience laughing heartily at some guy called Geoff Read who was promoting Ballygowan – bottled Irish water. What a preposterous concept. After all, perfectly good water comes straight out of our taps in this country. Plus it's free. Who'd ever pay for that? Lots of people, it turned out. The guy has since become a multimillionaire.

Screw it, let's do it.

Less talk, more action.

Myself and trusty sidekick Krzystof set up a stand at the 2002 Ideal Home Show in the RDS (Royal Dublin Society) and proudly launched Sanctuary Synthetics, with the tagline 'Artificial garden grass and greens'.

Boy, how people laughed.

'Ha, ha, shur, that's like trying to sell sand to the Arabs, son,' said one passer-by.

'You might as well try selling ice to Eskimos,'[19] chimed another.

It's the one thing we have plenty of in Ireland (besides rainwater) – grass, and *it* grows for free.

'Who the hell would ever want plastic grass? Ho ho ho!'

Was my epiphany a mirage?

This reaction counterintuitively galvanised me. A strong reception is better than being entirely ignored, right? Thankfully there was enough guarded curiosity to balance out the jovial and hostile reactions. Having abandoned the log cabin business prematurely I was *not* letting go this time.

We would be Ireland's very first specialists in the heretofore undiscovered domestic artificial grass niche. A pariah to some, I had no difficulty being a maverick. We had 'first-mover' advantage with all the opportunities and challenges that that entailed.

Brain over brawn

One fine day I had my sleeves rolled up and was digging in a garden when Pavel, employee number two, was musing about business and quoted his grandfather saying, 'An ounce of commerce is worth a tonne of work.' I had never heard that before and it hit home with me big time.

It was all very well doing manual work, selling my time for pay, but in order to build the business for the long term I had to get smarter. With our first child on the way I realised I would have to somehow work shorter hours but make more money. Brawn alone would not suffice. That very day I dropped my shovel, sat into the van, got on the mobile and started quoting and planning for the next

19 Some find the term 'Eskimo' offensive. More correctly, it should be 'Inuit' or 'Yupik'.

job, and the job after that. I chased payments and drew up designs. Basically I had to figure out how to become the Fake Grass Man.

They say a prophet is never recognised in his own land.

I can testify to that. My own wife, although supportive, was unconvinced. As mentioned, our own garden would be my first trial installation. Thereafter I could look people in the eye and tell them I had it myself. For posterity I videoed it and that video has garnered over 300,000 views on YouTube. It worked a treat and Anne is, as I said, now a firm convert. The first of many. My kids grew up on it.

An added bonus was that when I came home tired from work there was never an unkempt lawn lurking and demanding attention. It just sat there, minding its own business and looking good.

I had my own business to mind. The day I informed my long-standing grass-maintenance clients that my services were no longer available was simultaneously scary, exhilarating and liberating. After all this was half my income. My new business mentor Blaise Brosnan made me question everything I was doing. In the cold light of day pivoting the business made sense. I realised that with relatively few barriers to entry, low skill levels and no real training required any eejit could and did enter the market as a 'landscaper'. Hell, I did it myself. An enterprising kid pushing a borrowed lawnmower door to door could undercut any outfit doing the same thing. A rudimentary back of an envelope analysis showed I was only treading water financially. It was time to face some harsh truths and pursue my new specialist direction with conviction.

Except I'd painstakingly built up the maintenance side of the business. I'd gained the loyalty and trust of my regular clients, private householders, businesses and housing estate residents' associations (the politics of dealing with the latter would challenge a UN high commissioner). But it was time to say goodbye. Not wanting to leave them in the lurch, I approached a bigger competitor and simply handed my rounds over to him. I politely informed my customers, naturally offering them the opportunity to get a synthetic lawn instead. One lady immediately commissioned me thereby doubling my portfolio of completed installations. At the end of that year that competitor sent me a cheque out of the blue as a thank you. Which was nice. He had what I didn't, economies of scale and the ability to quickly fix broken machinery in-house. Funnily enough, a couple of years later he got me to install an artificial lawn in his own garden. I guess he could no longer face into maintaining his own lawn after mowing all bloody week.

Suddenly I had a couple of days a week to fill. Instead of being busy not making money, I was free to develop the synthetic grass business. I was well aware of people's biggest frustrations when it came to their gardens. The grass grew too quickly, was too wet, too mucky, they could never use it, they were too busy. Now I had a no-brainer solution. All I had to do was educate them as to its existence, overcome their objections and persuade them to invest. Having given away my grass cutting business there was a certain appeal to laying grass that would never grow.

I had the courage of my convictions and pressed on. In their pursuit of bigger juicy projects, the sports grass companies largely ignored the domestic market, leaving the field wide open for me. Thanks, guys. If it makes you feel any better, I have turned away umpteen requests to do sports pitches over the years.

The next step was to upgrade administration. It went from the front seat of my van to an attic office conversion. I soon outgrew that and over one weekend myself and Krzystof built a log cabin (you'll recall I had done this before) in my parents' back garden. This became our first proper headquarters. Then I hired someone for secretarial backup. That was a big leap forward.

'Oh, they have the internet on computers now' [20]
~ Homer Simpson

When I was in San Francisco in 1998 I recall the city being plastered with billboards for eBay, whatever that was. To visit a friend in LA I went online and booked a ticketless flight with Northwest Airlines (a model soon successfully copied by Ireland's Ryanair, now Europe's biggest airline). This whole internet thing seemed to be taking off.

In my early days as a landscaper I would check my emails about once a month, whether I was expecting one or not. Thanks to my buddy Shea of WebBuddy.ie I was one of the first to abandon the Golden (Yellow) Pages and launch a half decent website complete with before and after picture galleries. He helped me grasp the principles of online promotion and importantly how to keep Google happy.

High and dry

By now the Celtic Tiger was beginning to roar. Getting someone in to do the garden at last became a thing and by the time the Great Recession struck in 2008 we were strong enough to survive relatively comfortably. Many other

20 'Das Bus', *The Simpsons,* created by James L Brooks, Matt Groening and Sam Simon, Twentieth Century Fox Home Entertainment, Inc., episode aired on 15 February 1998.

landscapers went bust or were forced to scale back dramatically. Property values in Ireland halved over a very short and traumatic period of time.

In September of that year I turned 40. The previous day in the US Lehman Brothers had filed for chapter 11 bankruptcy protection – following 158 years of trading, with revenues of $19 billion and profits of $4 billion in 2006 – and this led to a big personal decision. To quit drinking. What caused this epiphany? My determination to drive the business on. Besides, I'd probably already drunk my lifetime's allocation. Plus hangovers and small children don't mix. Alcohol, although fun, is an addictive, poisonous, depressant drug. I've been on the wagon for over a dozen years now and it hasn't hurt my productivity one bit. Thankfully there was no lasting drain bamage. I do allow myself the occasional hot whiskey (purely for medicinal reasons) and I never refuse a glass of champagne. That's just rude.

All duck or no dinner

At this point I was still hedging my bets to some extent. Artificial grass still only constituted part of our income. We also held several lucrative long-term maintenance contracts with multinational supermarket chains. Due to the economic turmoil they understandably squeezed us hard. Much to their shock and chagrin I politely declined to re-quote downwards and walked away. This halved our turnover overnight in the midst of the worst global recession since 1929.

It was the making of us.

We were now 100 per cent artificial grass specialists – it was to be all duck or no dinner. With belts tightened none of our team had to be laid off. We simply plugged away relentlessly. We invested a high percentage of revenues into marketing (see Chapter 9). Sales grew steadily year on year as the popularity of artificial grass increased. The word was out. As the pioneer I got to set the mystical 'market rate' which others have since either followed or sought to undercut.

I couldn't have done it on my own. Mary, our long-standing office manager, and Dominic, now sales director, came on board. Employing people possibly a bit smarter than yourself certainly pays dividends. They brought experience from other sectors, a fresh perspective, work ethic and professionalism, but they still have time to have some fun on the job. It established a company ethos which others have subsequently bought into.

Thankfully we have low staff turnover though some change is inevitable. Recruitment being yet another skill to master.

An honest ad for an honest job

Below is our one page 'ad' as posted on our various social media feeds. The cost was precisely zero. It went viral locally and led to an almost overwhelming number of applicants. Queues formed outside our Grassland HQ. The moral of the story? It pays to come at things from a different angle. We were really targeting the Mammies and it worked a treat. No gilding of the lily.

Summary Job 2018 - An honest ad for an honest job

Helpers wanted - living in or near Naas !

Failed your exams ? Can't get a J1 visa ? Don't fancy going abroad ?

Why not amaze your parents and even offer them a bit of rent money (for the first time ever !) ?

Earn the wherewithal to book an expensive restaurant to take out that person you're secretly stalking on Facebook / Insta or buy the clothes that you like.

Want to loose weight, get fit and work on your (farmers) tan ? – Save on gym fees.

Not afraid of outdoor work ? Aware manual labour is not, in fact, a Spanish musician?

Join us at Sanctuary Synthetics and eventually you'll look good in that tight t-shirt again.

In addition we'll help you practice at real life i.e. working for a living * (unless AI takes over and robots will do it all for us)

The job – what to expect and the remuneration package: Be warned, it's a 7am start which can interfere with mid-week socialising. Doing unpredictable overtime (@€14 / hour net) and volunteering for the odd Saturday is expected. Please expect to get wet. Quite often, it's an occupational hazard. This is Ireland after all and you had your chance to go to San Diego but didn't pursue it. On the plus side you get to boost your self-esteem, learn to swear in Polish and listen to music all day . Having the craic is permitted, being impolite to Customers is not. Each job comes with a free logo'ed t-shirt, gloves and your own shovel (** OK it's likely to be communal shovels)

There's free parking in our HQ Grassland for bikes. Expect to clear €70 net per day (that's €350 per week for the benefit of those doing an arts degree) plus plenty of extra on overtime. That way you'll save loads coz you won't have any time to spend it.

We know it's not a fortune. However if you stay off the smashed avo toast, 3 months wages would add up to almost enough for car insurance for a year. Or indeed for college registration fees with some left over for a good weekend in the mud at Electric Picnic to celebrate finishing up with us.

All we ask in exchange is an honest days work. The landscaping world and artificial lawn installations demands physicality and steel toe capped work boots. Some sweat may be involved, plus the odd blister and eventually you and the wheelbarrow will be as one. Yes you will physically tired in the evening but you are unlikely to be mentally stressed and studies show pints go down especially well having truly earned them.

If you've read this far, this opportunity could be for you (or if you are the Mammy or Daddy then this is for your offspring who sleep in far too long and spend far too much time /money staring into their feckin mobile phones !) It it's NOT for you then hide this quick before your parents see it.

Otherwise step up and give us a shout. Don't expect us to actually ready CV's and expect no formal interview process. Just call into Grassland (Naas – Google us !), say Hi to the girls in the office and leave us your number. But be quick. We only need about 3 people. Free trial days are available (remuneration upon satisfactory performance).

It's not for everyone. There's no shame in trying and walking away – maybe you can serve food or get really good at computer games instead. Maybe working in a supermarket is not as soul destroying as they say.

So, come to Grassland, transform a different garden every day and if you survive the summer, write your own reference and we'll sign it for you ☺ **Regards, Mark (MD- Sanctuary Synthetics GRASSLAND, Naas, Co Kildare Tel: 045 901970)**

Market conditions

Ireland is a small, open economy. The property market had gone bonkers in the early 2000s so it was particularly badly hit by the recession. A virtual freeze on consumer spending resulted and, humiliatingly, the IMF (International Monetary Fund) was called in. Massive ECB (European Central Bank) loans were issued to save the reckless and now failing banks, foisting future taxpayers with a massive repayments burden. Many family homes were threatened with repossession. Bank branches closed. The public were angry but the closure of one branch nearby helped us furnish our new headquarters.

I had always had an aversion to working for builders and developers I didn't know and trust, so mercifully we were not overly exposed to that sector. Construction virtually ceased for several years. In forthcoming chapters we'll see how my small business navigated through the morass.

As Vinnie Jones (Bullet-Tooth Tony in *Snatch*) said, 'It's been emotional.'[21] Regrets, I've had a few. Then again who hasn't? In over two decades of self-employment in the landscaping industry I was never sorry I took this road. It has led me, often via tortuous routes, to overcome challenges I'd never anticipated. Documenting the highs and lows in my blog www.thefakegrassman.com, I talk about the fear, the pressures and the joy. Let me preface the following by getting one thing straight. The privilege and responsibility of going into people's private gardens, creating and transforming their space, and thus hopefully transforming their home lives, is a great honour. Plus they give you money to do it. How cool is that?

'Trust in Allah but tie your camel'
~ Traditional Bedouin saying

To fully appreciate what it took to get where we are today and the makings of the Fake Grass Man, I need to acknowledge money problems, legal issues, arson attacks, crashes and thefts to name but a few.

I'll spare you the gory details and linger no longer with the heartache that comes with running a business. Becoming the fake grass mogul was not easy, but as outlined below I love it when a plan comes together. You'll have noticed my superhero cartoon avatar on the cover but what's my superpower? Answer: vision. The ability to see how a garden is and knowing what it could be. This also extends to derelict old factories.

21 *Lock, Stock and Two Smoking Barrels*, Director Guy Ritchie, Gramercy Pictures (I), 1998.

The birth of Grassland

'The time to buy is when there's blood in the streets'
~ The first Baron Rothschild

The Republic of Ireland has a population of just over 5 million. We can add another two upon reunification with the North someday. Relatively speaking it's a small place and everyone knows who's who. So with the economic crash of 2008 things got a bit awkward. The bankers, lawyers, politicians and property developers all moved in the same circles, golfing and socialising together. When the party ended there was hell to pay. The circles were no longer golden. In a few short months Anglo Irish Bank, Ireland's second largest, collapsed along with property prices.

The government, bullied by the ECB, panicked and issued sweeping bank guarantees, even covering unsecured bondholders, ultimately costing beleaguered taxpayers €64,000,000,000. That's a lot of zeros. NAMA, the National Asset Management Agency, was tasked with taking bad loans off the balance sheets of the surviving hamstrung banks which resulted in very few people controlling the destiny of many. Perversely the same accountancy firms who had signed off on what proved to be rather dodgy balance sheets now acted for NAMA and their receivers. These guys found themselves controlling vast property empires and with the market in turmoil they could decide what deals to make and with whom.

'So what?' I hear you ask.

Well, it was in this context that, having survived the initial shock, I decided to take the Baron's advice. Now was the time to buy. Renting is dead money so I started to look in earnest. On the plus side there was a vast amount of commercial property allegedly 'on the market' but in reality little of it was *actually* for sale. You see, if an empty factory valued at say €750,000 pre-crash, now suddenly in receivership, was sold for €300,000, then the financiers would actualise a huge €450,000 loss. Far better to leave it languishing on the books at an inflated paper value, thus propping up tattered balance sheets. It became a waiting game. On occasions when a sale was actually forced, a small cohort of money men (possibly buddies of the lawyers and receivers?) got the inside track and swooped in to pick up the bargains.

Swimming with sharks[22]

Into this world of sharp suits and sharper practices I stepped. A total novice. I was, however, armed with a pre-approved loan from the bank on the strength of my solid accounts and history. Lovely jubbly. All I had to do was find a place, put in my bid and away we go.

Slowly discerning the unwritten rules of the game I tried to leverage any and all relationships. Over a couple of years many promising properties came and went. Several were for sale but not really for sale. Nobody ever gave *me* a nod or a wink.

One perfect place was both nearby and affordable but the county council effectively blocked the sale saying they were owed a six figure sum in development levies from the property's long-bust developer. 'Yes, but he's long gone. I'll reopen the place, operate there, pay taxes and employ local people' – unemployment having jumped from under 4 to over 16 per cent (300,000 of our youngest and brightest having had to suddenly emigrate to America, Canada and Australia) – yeah, no thanks. They were content to leave the place idle. Recently I drove past. Tumbleweed. The 'For Sale' sign is still up though.

Remember, I was continuing my stressful search while struggling in an adverse business climate. My hair got greyer. Then at last I found a warehouse and offices with ample yard space in an industrial estate at the right price. Having twisted a few arms, I managed to have my bid accepted and deposit taken. Brilliant! As I made my plans to move in, things started to drag on. And on. And on. The liquidators blamed the estate agents who blamed the lawyers.

Like a dog with a bone I persevered, knowing I had a bargain. The roof blew off in a storm; I made sure it got fixed. I pulled every trick in the book, doorstepping the suits, banging heads together with a growing folder of correspondence.

Eventually I got a closing date.

Unfortunately for me the unscrupulous previous owner, who had overstretched himself a tad, did not want to see it sold, deluding himself that he could somehow regain his lost empire. In the week before closing the deal, a series of unfortunate events mysteriously unfolded. By an amazing coincidence the unit, having lain idle for years, was broken into and occupied by a bunch of unsavoury characters. They even went to the trouble of changing the locks once they had gained squatting access. In fairness the property manager got the gardaí involved and the intruders were persuaded to move on. No prosecutions ensued.

22 I swam with sharks off Durban, South Africa, a few years ago. With no cage. It was possibly foolhardy but we fed the sharks first. I was careful to stick close to a fatter lad than me, figuring I could outswim him if it came to it.

A local detective kept me abreast of developments off the record. Twenty-four-hour security was put in place but things escalated. On successive nights leading up to closing day a gang of thugs in balaclavas attacked the place, smashing windows, banging doors, almost scaring the poor security guard to death.

I had a lot of time and energy invested in getting this over the line. We were bursting at the seams, both in the log cabin office and our rented warehouse nearby. We badly needed to amalgamate the operation into a single larger space. If I were a younger, single man God knows what I would have done.

As it was, I walked away, broken-hearted.

The thugs, and their anonymous employer, had won. Game over. It was eventually sold as part of a much larger lot (what the receivers and estate agents wanted all along) to a big American fund. It's someone else's problem now. This was a particularly low point for me as we desperately needed to move, not least for staff well-being and health and safety. By now the economic recovery was well underway. No more property bargains.

I was back in limbo with zero irons in the fire.

In my desperation I looked further afield despite desperately not wanting a commute. My mother, God rest her, kept saying, 'What's for you won't pass you by.' I was doubtful. Then she died, quite suddenly, in January 2013.

Three years later, almost to the day, I received the keys to what I immediately christened 'Grassland'. I had been sorely tested but in the end it turned out she was right.

This book was largely written in my secret office. Like the wardrobe in CS Lewis's Narnia, behind a large cabinet in the corner of my office there's a narrow hidden door through which I occasionally disappear.

A sucker for self-help books, I read Rhonda Byrne's 'The Secret' which quotes W Clement Stone: 'What the mind can conceive it can achieve.' Grassland was long a dream before becoming a reality. I know it's only bricks and mortar but it has been a labour of love and it is now my pride and joy.

A former paint factory, it had lain derelict for years before we managed to acquire it. To say it was ramshackle and overgrown would be an understatement. On almost an acre of ground near the town centre of Naas it had 10,000 square feet of warehousing, some of which even had a roof.

'There are decades when nothing happens and there
are weeks when decades happen'
~ commonly attributed to Vladimir Lenin

63

This particular property was not even up for sale.

I spotted the place while looking at another nearby warehouse which had supposedly gone on the market the day before. Later I learned that that deal had been done *before* the 'for sale' sign went up. The sign was just for optics.

Luckily for me an abandoned place opposite piqued my interest. I managed to gain access – don't ask – and myself and Dominic, our sales director, had a good poke around. There would be a mountain of work to be done to get the place operational and we were not getting our hopes up but it was worth a shot.

I tracked down the owner. Conveniently it turned out he was a friend of my father (one of the advantages of small town living, right there). Over the phone I told him I was interested in buying the place. A week later we met in a pub in my home village, did a bit of haggling and shook hands on a deal. No lawyers, no estate agents, no hassle.

Well, naturally there was some hassle but not with the vendor. It was a matter of good luck and even better timing. As simple as that. The bank could see the great synergies and cost savings that amalgamating our operation would yield. Having a place where potential customers could come to see our wares, where we could bulk buy and store everything, a workshop, internal and external display areas, good yard space, parking and room to build bespoke office space made great sense. Besides, we had been pre-approved for a good bit more money than we initially needed.

Then they said no.

I had paid a deposit in good faith and mentally had already moved in. After all the previous disappointments if mountains had to be moved, then moved they would be. Everything stacked up on paper but the bank, horribly spooked by the legacy of the recession, insisted on every last *i* being dotted and *t* crossed. Unfortunately their solicitors baulked due to a relatively minor leasehold/ freehold technicality. I quickly became an expert on aspects of property law, trawling through deeds and legal tomes. To no avail. Without a crystal clear title their hands were tied, it couldn't be financed.

Having gone through hell and high water to get to this point I ploughed on regardless. Every cent of my savings over many years including post office and credit union accounts, even cashing in my prize bonds, would only get me so far. Any and all spare cash flow from the business was marshalled. Still not enough. Dominic produced a rabbit from a hat with a big deposit for a substantial school job he had been chasing. That helped. In the end I got another loan from a different bank for a 'home extension' (I can write that now as every penny has

The Birth of Grassland

since been repaid in full) which just about got us over the line.

Less than a month later the bank called me. To paraphrase: 'Hey, now that you own the property, we'd be happy to refinance it for you.' Talk about offering you an umbrella when the sun is shining. My answer was a curt 'no thanks'. Within 12 months, at a cost of about €5,000 in legal fees, the leasehold/freehold technicality was fully cleared up and we had 100 per cent freehold ownership of the entire property.

Now all we had to do was put up roofs, fix the leaks where there was a roof, replace and reinforce all the structural steels (someone had cut off and removed most of the structural RSJ steels, probably to sell for scrap), put in skylights, clear out lorry loads of detritus including paint making goo and chemicals, chop away bushes and trees growing internally and externally, weld the gates back on, de-rust and paint same, spray foam insulate all the roofs, power hose literally everything everywhere, remove and replace overgrown gutters, unblock all the surface drainage, replace all the perimeter fencing, plant perimeter hedges, replace and put in windows, replant and paint all internal and external walls, install storage racking, put in external storage bays, create parking spaces, treat and paint the floors, buy steel storage containers, build walls and lean-tos, construct shelters and a few other bits and pieces.

For the first couple of months I was too scared to go into what were, allegedly, the toilets. Eeeeuck … totally overgrown, with spiders and creepy crawlies aplenty. I wouldn't even send my mother-in-law into the place! Eventually we cleared that too, unblocking all the sewerage, replaced everything and tiled it all up.

We needed to divide up the yard space so we liberated two huge concrete pipes which had lain abandoned in a ditch, then stood them upright and clad them in synthetic grass, forming instant gate pillars in the middle of the yard. Next I filled them with topsoil and planted a large beech tree in each. Either side we made a raised bed from old railway sleepers, in which we planted a Photinia (red robin) hedge. Behind this we erected metal fence panels (and gates) that we had been paid to remove from a school. A collection of pots, all inherited from customers, were planted up with mostly rescued plants, and the boundary was almost complete. Finally we installed a nice pedestrian gate rescued from a skip.

This was just one mini project among many. All done in our 'spare' time while keeping the grass business show on the road. As I write, six years after first walking in the gate, I can see where we just finished concreting the last of the yard space. We've completed all the drainage work and constructed a plinth for our diesel tank. This is surrounded by high wooden uprights onto which we clad our synthetic hedging (see Chapter 9 on the HidBin) thereby hiding it from opportunistic thieves. Bulk buying saves money plus all the hassle and lost time fuelling up the fleet off site.

Our most recent project was prompted by Brexit. We converted an existing change in levels into a truck loading bay complete with hydraulic ramp. This now allows us to receive container deliveries direct from Rotterdam bypassing the UK entirely. For a €7,000 investment this will save us €50,000 per annum and result in more predictable delivery times. Slowly, step by step, we have moulded the place into a bespoke, efficient operational HQ.

Getting hooked up

Did I mention we initially had no water. Or electricity. Or lights. We had no phones, no phone lines and, you guessed it, no internet. No matter as we initially had no offices either.

Notwithstanding all of this we promptly received a hefty rates bill for €10,000 from the local council within weeks of taking possession. No inefficiency there I noticed. I had to plead my predicament – that we were far from fully operational – in order to get a six-month moratorium before commencing payments. The fact that we were right beside the council's award winning €100 million offices might not have helped. All they had to do was look out the window at us.

Getting power? Not a problem. After all, the ESB has a substation within the property boundaries. We just had to pay the reconnection fee, in advance, and wait. And wait. Due to deregulation the semi-state power company had to spin off its networks so different outfits had to come separately to do different jobs. We had all the joy of trying to coordinate them as well as us having to dig trenches through our newly cleaned and concreted car park. Then we had to strip out all the old wiring and rewire the lot with kilometres of cables. We sourced second-hand former airport car park lights and constructed mountings for them so that, especially during winter time, our crews could load safely in darkness.

Water was a priority. Water butts fed by roof run-off yielded only so much. Thanks to the recession and the intervention of the IMF a new water utility, Irish Water, had been established. Not wanting to actually fire anybody, the water departments of individual county councils remained in parallel. Irish Water didn't want to know, 'Ask your council.' The council suggested talking to Irish Water. So we fell firmly between two stools. Faced with this intolerable dilemma we improvised. I took out my old divining rods and tracked down where the old pipe works were buried. As a paint making factory it would once have used a lot of water. Following the line to the nearest junction outside we promptly dug a hole and connected it up ourselves. Someday the water company will realise it. Or not. Fine, bill us then. Meanwhile we have the water we need and tried, in vain, to pay for.

Then we sought phone lines. While there were telephone poles in the vicinity, there were no wires. The phone company, with a bit of cajoling, came and hooked us up. Internet, no problem. 'You have five megs.'

'Is that all? We're in the town centre, right beside the county council HQ, for God's sake.'

'Sorry, that's the best we can do,' was the answer.

Well, their first answer. Not good enough. Mary, our office manager, got on the case. She pulled some strings and a van came down the very next day. 'What seems to be the problem?' I followed the driver down to the junction box on the street outside, watched him poke about for a couple of minutes and he declared, 'There you go.' We had jumped to 50 megs.

Not that that was any good to us without an actual office on-site.

Now, in tandem with running the business we were able to do a lot of the work transforming Grassland ourselves. Tommy, now promoted to warehouse, yard and fleet manager, was a dab hand at many things including plumbing. The contractors we did use, electricians, roofers, steel workers, welders and so on, were often relatives or friends so thankfully we weren't always charged top dollar.

To get around planning permission, we dedicated most of the first bay of the warehouse to internal office space. Or the 'home office' as I like to call it, so called as it's built to look like the facade of a regular house complete with wallpaper bricks and slate tiles on the fake roof. The theory being that the grass display in front would then look more like a garden.

I sketched out the look I wanted, laying it out according to our workflows and showed the team. Dominic, looking ahead as always, said what about future-proofing it? Why not put in a second floor and make your bungalow a two-storey? It would be tight and we'd have to work around steel roof trusses *in situ* but we managed to incorporate them and even make them a 'design feature'. There was lots of improvisation along the way. Hence my 'secret' office. We since added 'extension' to accommodate Keith, our new sales guy.

A fancy glass balcony upstairs was on my wish list but it would have cost

€1,200 per linear metre and it was over 12 metres long. We couldn't blow the budget. There was no budget. Instead we bought toughened glass for €300 from the local glazier and constructed a timber frame for the panes. Next we clad the timbers in a nice bright artificial grass, added a couple of Grassland stickers to the glass and got a bespoke balcony for very little cash.

In order for the 'home office' not to dominate the adjacent display area, I insisted on lots of windows and glass doors, hopefully striking the correct balance within the bay. Adorning the walls are pics of some of our award winning Bloom show gardens and medals, our Best in Show Certificate and our Chamber of Commerce SME of the Year award.

The board room features a huge solid oak table and chairs we picked up for a song. A toy store at the other end of town had gone up in flames and the furniture store next door had a flash sale, having suffered (minimal) smoke damage. It conveys a solid, established look. Behind it is a stone wall, again adding an air of permanency in what, essentially, was a timber office complex.

I recently hosted a Chinese sales delegation. They were on the last leg of an extensive tour of European grass companies and said it was the most impressive grass company HQ they had seen. Still didn't buy from them though. Maybe they were impressed with the sign over my door, in Mandarin, saying 'Welcome to Sanctuary'. At last we had a home with funky internal and external display areas. I know one shouldn't get overly sentimental in business but it's a place into which I poured my heart and soul.

A place I'm proud of.

They say if you build a better mousetrap, the world will beat a path to your door. Not true. Going out on a financial limb to have a fancy HQ, notwithstanding the fact that we accomplished the lot on a shoestring, is all very well but in reality we still had to go out into the marketplace to sell our wares. Nobody cares, I get that. The market is very fair. One gets measured and rewarded on one's output; on what we do when we drive *out* the gates every morning. With that in mind, I will show you just how we persuaded the public to come to Grassland.

Sofa so good, as the furniture salesman said. Now it's high time to explore the ecological credentials of synthetic lawns. I'm painfully aware that by sticking my head above the parapet I will be attacked with gusto. Funnily enough, although tut-tutted at by many in the gardening world, it's hardly ever raised as a concern by our customers. I've done my research. I guess my conclusions will be obvious but the next chapter lays out the facts as I see them and you can decide for yourself.

Chapter 6

How green is artifical grass anyway?

'Farewell, happy fields where joy forever dwells: hail, horrors, hail'
~ John Milton, *Paradise Lost*

Lolling about on the lawn of Kill House as a kid, my earliest memories were watching the clouds drift past, smelling freshly cut grass, blowing the tops off clocks (dandelion seed heads) and making daisy chains as butterflies wafted about, an airplane droning overhead. Time seemed to go by far more slowly back then. I'm still chasing that feeling today. I think we all are. Perhaps the recent worldwide Covid-19 lockdowns have helped many of us to observe and reconnect with nature. Both CO_2 emissions and life itself seemed to slow.

A travesty?

Leo Tolstoy said, 'One of the first conditions of happiness is that the link between man and nature shall not be broken.' Since fake grass is seen as symbolic of our distance from nature, I well understand the hostility towards it. How do I square my livelihood with my own environmental concerns? Is it really worse than what it's replacing?

For starters we got kicked out of Eden. Humankind has long had no choice but to hunt, farm and build cities. A blind man (like Milton) can see that. By definition our existence and activities disrupt nature. Remember Chapter 1, real lawns don't exist in nature either. Another chapter will explore the pros and cons more generally but let's first look at its eco-credentials and see if fake grass is actually hastening the end of the world.

Turf war

Horticulture Connected magazine published an article I once wrote defending synthetic grass along with opposing arguments by gardening writer Eugene Higgins cleverly titled 'Sward fight'.[23] He condemns it as 'a crime of biblical

23 Eugene Higgins and Mark O'Loughlin, 'Sward Fight', Horticulture Connected, Vol. 5/2, 4 August 2018, pp. 49–51, https://horticultureconnected.ie/horticulture-connected-print/2018/ summer/insight-summer/sward-fight/.

SWARDFIGHT

We're using a lot more artificial grass than we used to. It's on pitches, playgrounds, balconies, rooftops, gardens, road verges and everywhere in between. It's a phenomenon and the jury is out on whether it's a good thing or not. To help articulate this debate in public we decided to invite two well-known and vocal garden professionals to share their side of the story.

Many thanks to Mark and Eugene for sharing their insights. We'll be picking this debate up online afterwards, so keep an eye on *horticultureConnected.ie*.

NOT SO FAKE NEWS

Mark O'Loughlin, owner and operator of Sanctuary Synthetics, presents his perspective on why using synthetic grass may well be a sustainable option for the future.

"In my 17 years importing and installing synthetic grass, I've never tried to change anyone's mind. In our marketing I bring its existence to people's attention, lay out the benefits and let people vote with their feet. Fear not, concerned readers; of the 270,000 households in our Republic, we've only converted about 5,000 which leaves plenty left to go.

I should mention, we've transformed the grass for another couple of thousand trade customers including hotels, pubs, balconies, graves, and a few hundred national schools and crèches. Oh, and don't let me forget the 24m² we donated to Mayo mountain rescue team, which is installed half way up Croagh Patrick. A popular picnic spot when not a first aid station, I'm told.

OK, so it's plastic versus grass. I get it. But as our tagline says, *'No more muck, no more mowing, no more maintenance.'* Well, very little maintenance, comparatively speaking. Think about that for a minute. No more 40 hours needed per annum with a petrol mower, giving off higher CO_2 emissions than cars. No more no catalytic converters needed.

No rotten smelly cuttings dumped behind the shrubs or stewing in the wheelie bin. No pesticides required. Glyphosate anyone? No fertilisers required. And no floor cleaners either. That's a significant reduction in chemical use and pollution over the lifespan of a lawn.

I can hear you shouting at the page, "Mark, c'mon, it's fake." Indeed it is, but its appearance is continually improving. My Dutch suppliers - remember they will be first to be flooded when global warming kicks in, dykes notwithstanding - have an impressively lean and waste free manufacturing process.

"Yeah, but Mark, it's fake, it's not a natural thing like grass." Hmmm, a natural lawn? Now there's an oxymoron. The beloved natural lawn is not natural at all. It's a high maintenance, wasteful, energy and chemical hungry monoculture whose genesis lies in expressions of power and wealth over nature. Something which filtered through the English Parks Movement and into the psyche of the European populous and beyond. Lawns are the default garden element, an unnatural and labour intensive affliction. A natural lawn is a meadow.

I will make a concession; artificial grass is not biodegradable. No surprises there. But why single artificial grass out? Take a close look at modern gardens...the steel, the concrete, the reconstituted paving, the tarmac, the resin bound gravel, the pressure treated, chemical laden timbers.

Beyond the muck and the plants, very little is biodegradable, and unlike many modern artificial grasses, they're not even recyclable. As technology improves, all artificial grass will be recyclable. More on that later.

In an ideal world we'd all be living some contemporary version of the Good Life, producing our own food and living harmoniously with our environment. We don't live in an ideal world. We live increasingly busy lives, are time poor and have ever smaller houses with shrinking gardens. Mow the lawn? Ha, you'd be lucky to have space for one let alone the time to mow it. By the time the average homeowner flops onto their couch at the end of the week - before they are called to do kids' drop offs, organise parties, sports events and countless other free time demands – they have no energy or inclination to mow the lawn. For most it's easier to draw the curtains and turn their backs on the garden. From this perspective, it could be argued that lawns discourage garden use, their endlessly demanding nature a cause of resentment. We take the demands away, allowing our customers to enjoy their gardens without the hassle. I'm always amazed how many of our customers really get into gardening once the onerous mowing tasks are removed. On that note, it has been interesting to see how Bloom designers are increasingly using artificial grass in combination with excellent planting. Yes, its fake but it's encouraging a whole new generation of people to use their gardens.

Please be aware I'm not defending Astro turf. We specialise in next generation multi-play surfaces and non-infill landscape grasses (the ones that don't use rubber granules). I've always had reservations about rubber granules but that's a debate for another day. We waste nothing. Offcuts become grave or balcony coverings. Smaller pieces become hairy green door or car mats, or samples. The rest is donated to and snapped up by Recreate Ireland to be recycled by kids and artists for arts and crafts.

I'm sure Eugene has spotted that artificial grass is a single use plastic. A by-product of the oil refining process, it is extruded onto spools of thread and woven into rolls of grass by the same machines that make carpets. Regrettably it is currently difficult to recycle. However, our grasses last twice as long as a typical Astro turf pitch, on average 20-25 years. After that, it's landfill. But several manufacturers have come up with grasses that are both recycled (minimum 90%) and recyclable. They are currently at a premium price. We've tried promoting this but so far with limited success. I think it needs government action to encourage uptake.

Meanwhile, I sleep quite soundly at night. Before sitting down to write this piece I leafed through our 'book of testimonials'. The gratitude and satisfaction of past customers and their happy children are affirmation and motivation enough for me. Why not come to Grassland, our Naas HQ, and see for yourself?" ✳

MARK O'LOUGHLIN, can be contacted at his office on 045 901 970, on his mobile at 086 833 3255 or via email at mark@sanctuarysynthetics.ie. You can also contact him through his website at www.sanctuarysynthetics.ie and also on FaceBook at www.facebook.com/sanctuarysynthetics

"Beyond the muck and the plants, very little is biodegradable, and unlike many modern artificial grasses, they're not even recyclable"

73

THE TRUTH, NATURALLY

Eugene Higgins explains why we need to turn our backs on plastic grass and embrace what comes naturally. "When I started out in landscaping in 2000, I wanted to trade under a name that would define my desire to take a more modern approach to gardening. I needed a simple phrase that would sum up the ethos of what I was about, and so Colour Green was born, a simple, short trading name and for me, a moral guideline too. I applied simple rules: no weedkiller where possible, less chemical based products, a no-no to slug pellets, and most importantly no plastic in the gardens I designed

Synthetic grass was not something I ever envisaged as being part of the typical garden. For me, gardens are oases, where people and nature thrive. The idea of introducing an artificial version of grass is a garden crime of biblical proportions. The original concept of artificial grass was first devised in the early 1950s and was brought to the market by the Chemstrand Company. Interestingly, it changed name to Monsanto, and let's face it, there are a few folks out there who see that company as having its own biblical connotations. The Ford Foundation also got involved. They had admirable aspirations in the 1960s to create year-round urban recreational zones that would allow children to play on more gentle surfaces than Tarmac and concrete. The crowning glory of this process was in 1966 when when the AstroTurf Dome in Houston USA was opened.

The future of this concept was bright and looked brilliantly futuristic, but we were naive. However, as we know, both time and reflection bring wisdom, and now plastic in all its forms is finally being recognised as a potential cause for ecological collapse. As a society, we have finally woken up and are now realising how the the fragile habitat we share with nature is being poisoned, strangled or choked into destruction. Our reckless disregard for the place we live in and for future generations is catching up with us.

Artificial grass is just part of this Doomsday story, but it's a significant part. Synthetic grass may look and feel like the real thing. Some people simply can't get past the fact that it's plastic based. It is hailed by those who advocate it for for its water-saving benefits, but artificial turf has its own environmental drawbacks. It is a petroleum-based product that creates pollution and waste in the manufacturing process. And, while it is often made partially with recycled materials, it is not biodegradable. The vast majority of artificial grass will end up in landfill after its expected lifespan of 15-20 years. I use the word 'expected' because most materials used in the humid climate of Ireland rarely last as long as they should. I noticed a huge amount of actual grass poking up through an artificial lawn recently. That may have been down to poor installation but it speaks to its performance in Ireland. Secretly, I was delighted.

Critics point to synthetic turf as an environmental heater. It absorbs heat and feels hot to the touch in direct sun. Pet owners give synthetic grass mixed reviews. It does not absorb animal waste, but is permeable so liquids pass through to the ground underneath. Some suppliers have reported a surge in business in recent years, with one company seeing a year-on-year increase of 50% since 2010. If this trend continues then there is a serious threat to the country's wildlife that relies on gardens as a valuable food source.

Artificial grass provides no benefit to wildlife. Experts say its popularity will only increase the decline in bird, insect and mammal populations across the country. Reflect on that when you make your next lawn choice. Grass lawns also matter in terms of the greenhouse effect. Plants convert carbon dioxide into oxygen. If you remove lawns, then you remove a significant carbon sink and oxygen producer. It's negative for the environment no matter what way you cut it, or install it for that matter. Tim Rumball, editor of Amateur Gardening magazine has been quoted as saying, "This trend could even affect the atmosphere, as plants convert carbon dioxide into oxygen and a lack of natural grassland could affect the carbon levels in the atmosphere."

Remember, when grass grows longer it attracts insects. If you have an artificial lawn these insects will be depleted and the whole of the food network will be affected, especially birds that rely on insects for their diet. Natural lawns also provide an interface between the atmosphere and the rhizosphere. Covering over the ground slowly chokes the soil beneath. Although it is typically designed to allow water to percolate through, because there is no root action the materials below often become compacted, leaving water to be displaced. You will find bees burrowing into natural lawns, which are a mix of grass seeds. Other insects will be in there too, and also worms which are incredibly important in terms of the ability of the soil to absorb nutrients and keep it structured, so that when you have heavy rain or drought you have a soil system which can cope. In an increasingly hard landscaped world, every bit of green is vital. To hand over our lawns is an abomination. An affront to nature from its own custodians.

Did you ever lift up a piece of grass and read the ingredients? No, of course not. Me neither. I do suggest you read the ingredients of artificial grass before you propose to use it. The padding is often made of recycled tyres, which keeps them out of landfill, but the petroleum-based artificial grass materials are complex chemical creations, the products of intensive and energy hungry manufacturing processes

Finally, I'd like you to consider Amy Griffin, a college soccer coach in Seattle, who sparked a national conversation in the USA with her suspicions about the number of current and former soccer goalkeepers who had developed blood and other rare cancers. She points to all the goalkeepers that have played on artificial grass infilled with recycled rubber tyre crumbs, and to the fact that the recycled rubber tyres in question, according to the Environmental Protection Agency, can contain heavy metals, polycyclic aromatic hydrocarbons, carbon black and other known cancer-causing chemicals.

My message to Ireland's landscapers, gardeners and specifiers is to really consider the options. The people who will feel the impact of your decisions the most are the next generation." ✳

EUGENE HIGGINS is a garden writer and broadcaster. His CV includes The Mail on Sunday, Newstalk, The Afternoon Show, BBC's Room For Improvement and ITV's 'Glorious Gardens'. He is currently developing Garden Café, a radio programme he describes as the Top Gear type experience for gardeners.
Email: *eugezne@colourgreen.ie; www.eugenehiggins.ie*

74

proportions'. This chapter constitutes my riposte to many people's gripes.

What could be greener than grass?

In truth, making the correct eco-friendly choices can be incredibly complex. The government recently announced a ban on single-use (plastic-lined) coffee cups. A small but welcome step. Ireland was the first country to introduce a hefty charge on the plastic bags previously handed out freely by all shops. Since then one sees far fewer flapping in tree branches and caught in ditches.

Confession time. I fully supported the measure. Paper bags, although not as strong, are commonly used in the US and seem a good alternative. But oh no, Irish shoppers are now encouraged to buy a cotton or canvas 'bag for life' instead. So what's the problem? Two things: one, I have failed to get into the habit of bringing said 'bag for life' with me on each shopping trip. Therefore we have ended up with an entire press full of (expensive) bags, more than enough for several lifetimes. And two, according to a Danish Ministry of Environment and Food study, their assessment is that the cotton shopping bag alternative has a carbon footprint of between 130 and 180 times that of a plastic one. So, even if you used the same plastic bag five or six times, you'd have to use the cotton alternative a thousand times before reaching an ecological break-even point.

Like many plastic items, plastic grass is incredibly useful and long-lasting. The problem goes way deeper than this one product. Our current environmental problems are a reflection of our capitalistic culture of disposability. How is built-in obsolescence even allowed? That's a rhetorical question. Could it be a reflection on our collective laziness, our short attention spans, busy urbanised lives and distance from nature?

How bad is it if a copy of the real thing, essentially a giant plastic rug, tempts humankind back into the great outdoors, starting with the back garden?

I was in San Francisco just after that city banned smoking in bars, shock horror. That would *never* happen back home, I wrongly thought. Turns out Ireland was soon to be the *first country* in the world to ban smoking in pubs and indeed all indoor public areas. Moreover, it was enforced and obeyed. Many other countries subsequently copied our regulations.

So even as a small country we can lead by example.

Unfortunately we are laggards in Ireland, thus far, as regards climate change regulations and performance. This is disappointing for the Emerald Isle as a good eco story would surely help tourism as well as helping to save the world. Indeed our grass-fed beef cattle herd is demonstrably more content and ethically preferable to factory lots, yet their methane farts somewhat skew our national emissions stats. Despite progress with renewables like wind, we are still far too reliant on oil-generated energy.

As we lack our own coal and other natural resources, the Industrial Revolution, with the exception of the greater Belfast region, largely passed Ireland by. Now as an advanced nation specialising in tech and pharma, we ought to be leaders not laggards. Like Denmark with wind, and Germany with solar, the Emerald Isle ought to be at the cutting edge of renewables such as wave and tidal energy.

Trump's legacy cannot last and I choose to be optimistic rather than fatalistic about the chances of mitigating the worst effects of human-made climate change and creating a sustainable future for humankind, my children and all the creatures that have, thus far, survived.

Like it or not, technology will be our main tool. As Barry Commoner said, 'The proper use of science is not to conquer nature but to live in it.' One thing is for certain though, change is inevitable and as an entrepreneur it's my job to see around corners. That's why I'm staying in the synthetic grass business. On balance I'm comfortable with what we are doing. Let me explain.

Not my niche, not my problem

Let's get one thing out of the way. Like my sward fight opponent Eugene above, I won't defend 3G and 4G crumb rubber sports pitches for a moment. If I may be so bold, I predict that they will someday be banned outright.

First of all, no one seems to have figured out what to do with the huge bulk of plastic and latex at the end of its useful life, often only about 10 years long. Hiding or exporting it is simply a cover up.

Secondly, like smoking, the obvious hazards of which the tobacco industry was in denial about for years, they may eventually be phased out on health grounds. These little balls of chopped-up rubber are great for ballast and cushioning impact but if old tyres are classified as toxic waste, how can zillions of tiny granules of the very same material be OK? Advocates argue that the rubber is treated and washed with all metals extracted but although preliminary studies by the Environmental Protection Agency (EPA) say there's no health risk, heavy metals and volatile and semi-volatile compounds have been found in the black rubber specks. Several of these compounds – including cadmium, benzene, nickel, chromium and arsenic – are known carcinogens. They are not micro-beads but this odious toxic ex-car tyre infill is not great. There are similar concerns about the rubber crumb used as mulch in children's playgrounds, particularly about carbon black nanoparticle dust being aspirated into young lungs. The industry will say it recommends only virgin plastic infill be used and it is currently experimenting with alternative organic infill materials such as cocoa shells and chemical free wood grains but with limited success so far. Meanwhile, it's a cheap way of getting rid of used tyres.

Great and cheap for some. Even if you are conscientious enough to drive a hybrid or electric car, depending on mileage, you'll go through about 20 tyres over 5 years and 40 of them over a decade. They all have to end up somewhere. Worryingly, a German study says a midsized electric passenger car must drive 219,000 km before it outperforms a corresponding diesel in terms of CO_2 emissions. The problem being that passenger cars only do an average of 180,000 km and EV batteries don't last long enough to achieve this distance in the first place. So a green delusion really. Roll on hydrogen. My daily commute to Grassland takes minutes. In summer I sometimes cycle.

We stock and sell a more expensive alternative non-infill sports grass which we believe will gain more traction over time. So far it has not got FIFA's or UEFA's formal 'blessing'. Either the industry comes up with alternatives fast or Astro will go by the wayside, with new hybrid pitches dominating the future (see Chapter 17).

No greenwashing
My own specialty, you will know by now, is synthetic grass primarily for lawns. Please understand the distinction between it and Astro. I do not wish for it to be sullied alongside infill sports grasses or to be tarred with the same brush.

The big picture
Artificial grass is made from plastic. We've established that.

Plastic is an undeniably useful and versatile substance, long-lasting, pliable and easily shaped. Chapter 5 told you that the components of artificial grass are sourced from the oil refining process. It is ubiquitous and has been a boon for humankind in the last half century. What did you brush your teeth with this morning? What was the toothpaste tube made of? Look around you right now. It's everywhere.

Unfortunately, after its useful life, because it typically takes so long to biodegrade, it also causes pollution. There have, however, been promising recent developments in research into plastic-eating enzymes.

Plastic was first polymerised in 1951 by German and Italian petroleum scientists using a hydrocarbon resin. By 2020 according to a *Financial Times* report it's estimated that 8.3 billion tonnes of this thermoplastic polymer resin will have been produced. Its feedstock monomers can be produced from coal, gas, oil or sometimes even plants. Typically it starts to degrade in landfill after 20–30 years or it can be combusted leaving energy, CO_2 and water afterwards. Too much carbon dioxide, for anyone living under a rock for a long time, is a major cause of global warming.

The open-minded reader will, however, acknowledge that there is a big difference between single-use once-off plastics (straws, coffee cups, beer can binders, water bottles and most of the contents of your Christmas crackers) and a product that will be in constant use for, say, two decades, like my own lawn.

What would a now retired 'Graduate' Benjamin Braddock (Dustin Hoffman) tell us about the general plastics industry he entered in the late 1960s?

He'd probably admit that despite industry-sponsored propaganda to the contrary, the vast majority of plastic is still not recycled. The figure is possibly as low as 10 per cent. It was never economically viable to keep plastics out of landfill, and oil lobbyists in Washington and elsewhere made sure that legislators didn't interfere with their profitable production of virgin plastics. Think about it. Why would producers invest in costly recycling when it's cheaper to make it out of oil than gathered-up old trash. The recycled stuff is competition. The recyclable symbol (a triangle of green arrows) is mostly window dressing. The producers are the polluters and they must be forced to act.

For as long as humankind continues to use oil, virgin plastic yarns will be used to produce synthetic grass. As we wean ourselves off petrol and diesel (hopefully via hydrogen rather than hybrid or battery-powered vehicles) manufacturers will have to switch to using recycled plastics, of which there is a plentiful supply, or simply find some other way. Could today's landfills be the mines of the future?

As a business which is always looking to get ahead of the curve we launched a new ecograss made from 80 per cent recycled materials and which is virtually the same price as regular artificial grass with minimal difference in appearance and performance. Sadly there has been little public interest to date but we are determined to continue to push and promote it. Dominic even designed a recycled garden for Bloom. Just as we pioneered artificial grass in our domestic market in the first place, educating our potential customers as to the existence and advantages of synthetic grass, we now intend to do the same for the recycled alternative. There is now an almost 90 per cent recycled *and* 100 percent recyclable synthetic grass available. I'm certain that this is the future. Perhaps one day there will be hemp-based artificial lawns (hint, hint to innovative engineers and manufacturers).

The birds and the bees

Back to nature.

All growing plants, including grass, produce oxygen – a medium-sized lawn allegedly produces enough for a family of four – but when all the maintenance is taken into account lawns are responsible for way more greenhouse gases than actual oxygen. I maintain that environmentalists who attack inorganic artificial lawns are missing the point and are going after the wrong target, protecting an obvious shibboleth. Paving, tarmac and most other hardscaping materials in your garden are inorganic too. 'Well, I have gravel in *my* garden,' some smugly say. Dig a bit deeper. Literally. You'll most likely find a plastic sheeting layer underneath.

I contend that climate change activists and concerned eco-warriors are barking up the wrong tree, so to speak, picking on an easy and highly visible target. How about you go after the serious offenders, say 'Big Oil', corrupt politicians or lobbyists for example. According to one *Guardian* newspaper article in the UK, construction accounts for 60 per cent of *all* materials used, one-third of all waste and 45 per cent of all CO_2 emissions. Go picket a building site. Or protest intensive farming, the disappearing rainforests and relentless pursuit of GDP growth. Here's another juicy target instead, folks. I recently heard that the US military causes more pollution in a year than 120 entire countries combined. Could be true. Oh, and increase investment in female education in the developing world, which will help curb exponential population growth. That might help. Maybe persuade the Vatican to OK the use of condoms (what are *they* made from again?).

Rolling in the clover

Hopefully I've already established in Chapter 1 that real lawns suck. Before giving you truly astonishing stats on lawn care, consider the following fun fact: over a million pounds (in weight) of pesticides (including herbicides) are used on precious US lawns every year. Now before you start quoting 'lies, damned lies, and statistics' to me (commonly attributed to Benjamin Disraeli), let's have some context. Thanks to our friends at Monsanto (ironically where artificial grass was developed in the first place) and others, you will be aware that modern agriculture relies heavily on the use of such human-made chemicals. How do you think the amount used in our lovely gardens compares to agricultural usage?

Half as much? Nope.

Around the same? No.

Twice as much? Not even close.

Five times as many chemicals as in the fields? Keep going.

The depressing answer is *ten* times that amount is deployed in our gardens. Verify that for yourself. This figure convinced me that our alternative, despite its flaws, is in fact a much better alternative. To 'control' our precious lawns we have been programmed to blindly traipse down to the hardware shop spending fortunes to keep these multinational corporations in clover. If you think that is a trite analogy, consider this.

Trifolium repens (clover) is a legume – in the same family as peas, beans and peanuts. It has long been domesticated for ground cover and livestock forage. In 1747 Benjamin Franklin praised its value in improving pastures. Among the biological services this bee-friendly plant provides is fixing atmospheric nitrogen into soil fertilizer, drawing up trace minerals making both the soil and grasses more disease resistant. An article on lawnstarter.com reports that up until several decades ago clover was actually a standard part of grass seed mixes. Killing it was not always in vogue.

One day it simply got branded a weed. What made this foot-traffic-resistant grass-friendly companion suddenly deserving of eradication? The aggressive marketing of chemical companies of course. You see, their herbicides won't kill grass but they do kill clovers. So now it's the enemy.

Here's another fun fact: the dreaded dandelion is from the sunflower family. All parts are edible and are high in vitamins K and A. Dandelions were long seen as extremely beneficial – up until the 1800s people would actually remove grass to plant them. Before herbicides were invented and promoted people accepted dandelions and clover and other flowers as the inevitable mix in their lawns. The *real* problem is not the lawn per se but all the petrochemicals and water used to keep it as a 'weed' free green monoculture.

Biodiversity is of course a must, but please don't lump all the responsibility onto John and Joan Smith in their three-bed semi-detached way out in the suburbs. Enough with the guilt trip already. Maybe start with diversifying intensive agricultural practices. Much of the 'civilised' world is already covered in vast tracts of concrete, asphalt and hard surfaces.

That horse has bolted.

Could it be that critics are trying to close the stable door on artificial grass because the mere notion offends them, rather than on sound ecological grounds? Maybe investigate the burning down of rainforests. How about addressing these issues rather than the modernising of small urban lawns? It's true that having a fake lawn inhibits burrowing insects, but I'm pretty sure they are not to blame for the worrying decline in insect populations. Recently published studies conducted in nature reserves in Germany prove the worrying decline. As it happens the Germans have not really gone for artificial lawns to date, so no real correlation there. Personally I'd be looking more closely at their giant chemical companies. What are some of their products made for? Oh yeah, *real* lawns.

Lawns are nature living under a totalitarian regime

I say let's be more democratic. One of my main contentions is that you can still be a gardener while having a synthetic grass lawn. I suspect people's obsession with order and conformity in their gardens stems from being largely disconnected from nature. American writer Michael Pollan declares, '[real] lawns are nature purged of sex or death'.[24]

Natural turf has been praised for its ability to sequester carbon dioxide but I've already shown you that cutting it more than negates any potential benefits. Keeping a real lawn demands time and equipment. Mowers, strimmers and scarifiers, all of which emit greenhouse gases in their use as well as their manufacture. According to the EPA in the US, a petrol push lawnmower emits more pollution in an hour than 11 cars. It states typical usage of a petrol mower over a year creates the same amount of greenhouse gas as driving a car for more than 2,050 miles. Reportedly and shockingly petrol powered lawnmowers make up 5 % of air pollution in the US.

According to a recent article in *The Irish Times* advocating going electric in the garden, research carried out in Sweden found that a four horsepower petrol lawnmower caused the same amount of pollution in one hour as a car would if driven 93 miles.[25] What about a ride-on mower I hear you ask? As many as 34 cars. Consider their end-of-life destination too.

On a more visceral level, when is the last time you smelled the decomposing stink of rotten grass cuttings and effluent, often lurking in obscure corners of gardens, leaching away. Newsflash, folks – that pong is a greenhouse gas emission. 'But I put all my clippings in the brown bin for recycling' you will virtuously protest. Yeah, also mostly going to landfill where decomposition and fumes will inevitably result. The EPA in the US reports that in 2009 alone 33.2

24 Michael Pollan, 'Why Mow', *Second Nature: A Gardener's Education*, New York, Grove Press, 1991, p. 62.
25 Barry McCall and Sandra O'Connell, 'Don't Preheat the Oven, and 24 other Ways to Save the Planet from Home', *The Irish Times*, 11 January 2020, www.irishtimes.com/life-and-style/homes-and-property/don-t-preheat-the-oven-and-24-other-ways-to-save-the-planet-from-home-1.4132982.

million tonnes of trimmings were generated. And before you say it, sure, fake lawns also need some maintenance and aftercare. True, but by comparison it only takes a tiny fraction of the time, energy and effort required by the old-fashioned ones.

Consider the environmental implications of that barbecue you hosted on Saturday evening, partly to show off your newly manicured lawn. The CO_2 emissions from your barbecue combined with those of the meat consumed average out as the equivalent of a 90 mile car journey.

Water

Do not throw the baby out with the bath water.

Just to be clear, synthetic grass in this instance is the baby, and the bath water is muddied with chemical pollutants. Unlike our neighbours across the Irish Sea, Ireland has no missile silos, no nuclear deterrent or power plants. But it could be that we are very well armed with the most precious resource over which many say World War III will be fought.

Not oil.

Water.

We've got rivers, full aquifers, lakes and springs aplenty, thanks to our latitude and proximity to the North Atlantic and no shortage of rainwater. I may have mentioned that before. It seems like an infinite resource.

Yet despite all this we had to introduce our first ever nationwide *hose pipe ban* during a warm dry spell in the summer of 2018. While this rare, sunny weather was most welcome, on another level it was a foreboding taste of the challenges of climate change that might well be on the way.

Such drought periods are not such a big issue so far in the temperate zones, both here and in the UK. In the south of the continent just as in the southern US and elsewhere, drought is certainly a bigger deal. In Europe, Mediterranean plants are undeniably marching north due to climate change. So on water conservation grounds alone the fact is that artificial lawns are most useful. The demands of real lawns on the other hand constitute an environmental nightmare in some places. As awareness of the need for water conservation increases, expect restrictions or the outright banning of the use of precious water for lawn irrigation.

Ireland recently had mass protests against imposing water charges in this country. Water usage awareness and wastage has entered public consciousness for the first time ever. Expensive sprinkler systems are standard throughout the US and elsewhere (no need for them in Ireland ... sigh). According to UK company Hitechturf it was estimated that in the warm summer of 2017 a whopping 75 percent of British residential water was used for lawn irrigation.

US EPA figures in 2015 (the most recent,relevant figures I could find) say American lawns soak up 9 billion (not million, *billion*) gallons (not pints, not litres but *gallons*) of expensively treated and filtered drinkable water per day (not per year or month or even week).

Of the 320 gallons of water the average American household uses per day, 192 gallons, a shocking two-thirds, are dedicated to the irrigation of their lawns.

The Association of Synthetic Grass Installers (ASGI) website quotes the following US statistics:

- 91 million households have a lawn and at least some landscaping.
- 78 million of these use pesticides, fertilisers and herbicides.
- 90 million pounds of herbicides are used annually.
- 1.2 million tons of synthetic commercially produced fertilisers are used on lawns annually.
- 210 million tons of pesticides are used on lawns annually.

A 2004 national survey revealed that only 5 million US homeowners (i.e. a small percentage) claimed *organic* lawn practices. What's the worldwide picture?

A biological desert

Real lawns are monocultures. Biological deserts.

Now, at last, there are the beginnings of a public outcry.

According to Megan Garber's definitive 'The Life and Death of the American Lawn' article in *The Atlantic*, the appearance of the hashtag #Droughtshaming shows signs of a shift in public consciousness.[26] Slowly an anti-lawn sentiment is growing in tandem with environmental awareness. Increasingly activists are calling for a radical rethink of our entrenched aesthetic views.

Heretofore, keeping a healthy green lawn has been a civic duty, a bow to expected conformity and the collective responsibility of homeowners. In one high-profile example of changed attitudes actor Tom Selleck got #Droughtshamed in California. Moreover he was forced to settle a lawsuit taken by his home county's municipal water district for taking copious amounts of water to nourish

26 Megan Garber, 'The Life and Death of the American Lawn', *The Atlantic*, 28 August 2015, www.theatlantic.com/entertainment/archive/2015/08/the-american-lawn-a-eulogy/402745/.

his avocado farm and expansive lawns during a drought period. This shift in approach is even more surprising than learning that Magnum PI (subsequently promoted to NY police commissioner) is now an avocado farmer.

Brown is the new green

Subsequently California Governor Jerry Brown issued an executive order in response to their periodic droughts mandating that citizens reduce their water consumption by 25 per cent. Given that California has an estimated 12.2 million lawns that use 2.4 billion gallons daily, it's hardly a big surprise. 'We are in a new era,' he explained. 'The idea of your nice little green grass getting lots of water every day, that's going to be a thing of the past.'[27]

Could the love affair with real lawns be over?

Poor Tom Selleck thought he was doing the right thing, keeping his lawn well-watered and in tip top condition, obeying convention. Many US homeowner associations (HOAs) have local ordinances strictly mandating residents to keep a proper lawn. Indeed municipalities also have strict guidelines on how exactly a lawn should be maintained. Look it up. It's often an offence not to keep it mowed. Many have been fined. Some were jailed. So much for the land of freedom and liberty. Little wonder that in F Scott Fitzgerald's *The Great Gatsby* Jay is so troubled by his dastardly neighbour Nick's failure to properly maintain his lawn that he sends up his own gardener to sort it, thus restoring order and harmony to their shared pastoral space.

The problem is that of the 116 million American households around 75 per cent have a yard or lawn. I'm sure they are individually modest in size. But added all together? In a *Harvard Magazine* article Nell Porter Brown reports on an analysis of NASA satellite data. This showed that lawn turf covers almost 50,000 square miles of American land. That's three times more than the next biggest crop, which is corn. US Department of Agriculture figures confirm this. Let that sink in for a moment. That's 2 percent of the surface area of continental US. *The Washington Post* reported that Delaware is made up of 10 per cent lawn. Connecticut and Rhode Island are 20 per cent. Massachusetts and New Jersey are similar.

So what you ask? In one 'sustainable landscaping' report the EPA says three million tons of synthetic fertilizers and 70 million pounds of herbicides are dumped

27 Darryl Fears, 'Calif. Governor Orders Statewide Mandatory Water Restrictions', *The Washington Post*, 1 April 2015, www.washingtonpost.com/national/health-science/calif-governor-orders-statewide-mandatory-water-restrictions/2015/04/01/3495867a-d89e-11e4-8103-fa84725dbf9d_story.html.

on American lawns every year. Worse still, they say between 40 and 70 percent of these chemicals find their way into the local water systems. Permaculture advocate Bill Mollison said that 'The American lawn uses more resources than any other agricultural industry in the world. It uses more phosphates than India, and puts on more poisons than any other form of agriculture.'[28]

The US, with over 30 million acres of lawns alone, has over twice the area as Russia has in gardens. The US spends $25 billion a year on lawn care. Those dastardly Russian gardeners reportedly produce 40 percent of all their food.

Suspended animation

Consider the state of this symbol of prestige, these polluted artificial representations of nature. The cruel fact is we don't allow the grass to get tall enough to go to seed but we also water and feed it just enough to keep it from going dormant.

We don't let it die and we don't let it grow or reproduce. Constant mowing is a zen-like pursuit but I'm not sure Buddha would entirely approve. Life, especially for the incessantly cut grass, is suffering. Lorrie Otto was one of the founders of the US movement known as the Wild Ones. She condemned lawns as 'sterile', 'monotonous', 'flagrantly wasteful' and 'really evil'. Strong words. But when you really think about it are they not rather preposterous?

It doesn't have to be this way. No watering and no mowing = a carbon footprint win. I really like how Arianne Shahvisi put it recently in her book "The Lawn Problem". She says natural lawns are tidily demarcated, closely cropped, monocultural, pesticide-coated, water greedy green stubble. She adds that maintaining a block of land on which no food grows, no animal feeds and no carbon is stored is absurd.

Artificial grass is only one possible alternative. With my designer's hat on I can assure you there are lots of other practical solutions, as outlined below. You can combine my product with other materials, planting and layouts. In many southern US cities taxpayers now get generous rebates for installing artificial grass thus saving water. The concept of Xeriscaping is an acknowledgement of the ecosystemic realities of the new century. It's the process of gardening that reduces or eliminates the need for supplemental water for irrigation. It is popular in regions without plentiful water supply and uses succulents, cacti, drought tolerant trees and typically lots of stones and pebbles.

28 Bill Mollison with Reny Mia Slay, *Introduction to Permaculture*, 2nd ed., Tasmania, Tagari Publications, p. 111.

Rewilding

Leave the lawn alone, let it go to seed. Then maybe give your garden 'a Mohican' – simply mow a path through it to get to your shed/utilities/seating area. Think laterally, let Mother Nature reclaim at least some of your space. How about introducing some big rocks, some mounds and a couple of trees. Wildflower seeds grow particularly well on barren ground. Combine rocks with gravel and plant alpines and perennials. Let bulbs appear annually. Don't kill the moss. Nature abhors a vacuum and in time beauty will naturally return. You don't have to devote the entire garden to this but you could give nature some space, even if it's only some raised beds.

I'm a fan of Irish garden designer Mary Reynolds. Ever since she created the naturalistic Celtic garden that wowed Prince Charles and won Gold in Chelsea (the story of her journey has since been made into a rather charming film *Dare To Be Wild*), her philosophy has evolved and she has since written a bestseller on rewilding called *The Garden Awakening*.

Japanese botanist Akira Miyawaki's pop-up native mini forests become 30 times more dense and have 100 times more biodiversity than conventional planting.

I happen to think both are absolutely right and that this is the way forward for society. Plant more trees. Everywhere. Left to her own devices and with sufficient time undisturbed, Mother Nature will naturally select those species most suited to prevailing conditions anyway.

As part of our company's CO_2 alleviation efforts we've long been corporate supporters of the Native Woodland Trust which does great work propagating and promoting native forests in Ireland. We've been privileged to work with them to set up a new nursery in the nearby Wicklow mountains to grow thousands of rare and threatened species ready for reforestation nationwide. Grassland itself is full of plants and flowers.

Unfortunately I cannot agree with Mary and Akira when it comes to small suburban gardens, however. What they advocate is appropriate for parks, public spaces and the countryside but I'm afraid it's just not practical in garden spaces not much bigger than the footprint of their actual houses.

I live in a town.

In a housing estate.

So do over 90 per cent of *our* domestic customers and the majority of the population. There is limited outdoor space to begin with. Given the competing demands of families, kids, pets, clothes lines, wheelie bins, swings, slides, sheds, mortgages, jobs and endless commitments I'm leaning more towards practicality.

In this instance, towards plastic.

Yes, I know it's not natural. It's a bit weird at first and people are rightly sceptical. But the bottom line is it works.

Recycling – the rubber hits the road

Our world currently generates 2 billion tonnes of solid waste every year.

Most decent artificial grass lawns will, if properly installed, and with reasonable aftercare, easily last over 20 years. Thereafter, yes, they may end up in landfill, as most grass cuttings already do. But artificial grass *can* be made from recycled plastic, melted down and repurposed. Unfortunately due to the current combination of the backing and the plastic grass, most artificial grass is presently difficult to recycle. Not impossible, but tricky and thus prohibitively expensive.

Until now, mere lip service has been paid to the need to properly recycle such large volumes of material. A recent Dutch public TV documentary, *Zembla*, exposed several companies that falsely claimed to recycle fake grass and instead were found to have stacked it in towering piles. After similar discoveries in Norway their minister for the environment announced tighter controls. Unfortunately for now there appears to be zero capacity to properly recycle it in the US. Some of its 'recycled' turf has been found in Malaysia.

This is slowly changing and progressive suppliers have changed the backing to allow it to be both recycled *and* recyclable.

The harsh reality is that no 'closed-loop' process exists yet. A cradle to grave system is needed and that grave can no longer be a hole in the ground. Incineration is not the answer either.

Leading yarn manufacturer TenCate for example has just partnered with the first 'circular' artificial grass plant in the Netherlands: GBN Artificial Grass Recycling BV. This initiative makes it possible for municipalities, sports clubs and other organisations to have end-of-life synthetic turf (mostly pitches) processed in a sustainable manner. The used infill and turf from a single sports field can weigh up to half a million pounds. Its goal? To produce high-quality raw materials for re-use in industry and in the construction of new artificial grass fields. Until now there have only been a couple of plants in Europe, notably Denmark, capable of this. This welcome development, while well overdue, will begin to lessen the environmental impact of the industry. Its stated ambition is 'to create a fully circular artificial grass process globally'.[29]

The absence of action to date threatens to damage both the industry and Planet Earth. My hope is that by virtue of such innovation and leadership in conjunction with inevitably tightening legislation, people can continue to enjoy the benefits of both artificial sports and leisure grass in a guilt-free fashion. Look, I'm just trying to make a living here, alright?

Don't hate the player, hate the game.

I believe fake grass is a relatively environmentally friendly, ergonomically pleasing and economically sound investment. A greener way, if you will. Naysayers say it doesn't feed anyone but the owner's ego. I say that this misses the point. Chapter 11 considers the future of the product and includes my call to both governments and the public about what should be done. Hint: mandate recycled raw materials *and* recyclability.

Don't just take my word on its credentials as a viable alternative though. To quote (undomesticated) fictional character Jack Reacher:

> *Yard work summed up the whole futile procedure. First you spend a lot of time and money making the grass grow, just so you can spend a lot of time and money cutting it down a little while later. You curse about it getting too long and you sprinkle expensive water on it all summer, and expensive chemicals all fall.*[30]

To elaborate more on artificial grass's potential it's time to look far more closely at *all* the pros and cons, its advantages and disadvantages. But before that you need to understand its utility. One of the things I love about my job is that no two days are ever the same. You see, when it comes to artificial grass there's a huge and surprising variety of applications. Let's take a quick look.

---

29 Comment attributed to TenCate CEO Michael Vogel. See www.recyclinginternational.com/plastics/artificial-grass-recycling/26295/.
30 Lee Child, *Tripwire*, 1st ed., London, Bantam Books, 1999/2011, p. 99.

Chapter 7

Multiple uses

Whenever I hire someone new I always promise them one thing – variety. People are often bemused at how successful we are. 'Surely it's just a quirky niche market?' they ask, failing to see its vast potential. In fact we are quite diversified having found, explored and created several distinct market segments as one flows to the next. Almost from the cradle to the grave. Moreover, it's far less seasonal than one might assume. One of the real joys of working with fake grass is its sheer versatility.

You know by now there's way more to it than AstroTurf for sports pitches.

The next best known application is of course domestic lawns. But that's far from the full story.

Take the childcare sector for example, starting with kindergartens and crèches. My perception grew in tandem with the arrival of my own children. From the moment they were crawling I was able to look people in the eye and say yes, it's perfectly safe and practical for smallies. The owner of Apple Tree Crèche & Montessori, where my own pair attended, asked me to sort out her facility. Far better to have my own kids and their little friends out playing on nice soft and safe synthetic grass than the existing hard concrete yard. Seventeen years later it's still in daily use, generations of kids having benefited from the investment.

Inspired by cartoons I persuaded a responsive crèche owner to add 'puddles' of blue grass in her otherwise boring play area. I installed a series of splashes cutting out the green and gluing the blue shape into position. That was the start of a learning curve that has been extensively copied ever since. My colleague Dominic has since pushed the concept a lot farther.

Primary schools

Admittedly I was also not cognisant of the possibilities for primary schools until my kids got a bit older. Imagine my surprise when my daughter reported they were *not allowed to run* in their own schoolyard. During breaks they could only *walk* about. WTF? This, despite growing awareness of endemic childhood obesity. You couldn't make it up.

Upon investigation I discovered that, particularly in urban areas, boards of management are terrified of being sued should little Johnny or Mary injure themselves on their watch. In my day this was regarded as part of growing up. One cannot legislate for all accidents and banning running has consequences too. When children's natural exuberance is suppressed, they can't burn off energy, are more fidgety and less able to concentrate when back in class. What are break times supposed to be for, one wonders?

So I made it my mission to do something about it.

This was genuinely more of an emotional reaction than a commercial decision targeting a new market. Artificial grass, I reasoned, would make schoolyards softer and safer thus allowing proper play. Besides, most schoolyards are drab, grey and in dire need of brightening up.

But can't the children just play on real grass, I hear you ask. Yeah … no.

Most schools do indeed have large green areas. But think about it. The academic year goes from September through to June so it's only during the initial and final month that the ground *might* be dry enough to use, otherwise you are looking at a muck fest.

The schools' solution? *Keep off the grass.*

Jesus wept.

PE (physical education) is way down the priorities list for school budgets, gyms often being pitifully small and wholly inappropriate. So I made the principal of my kids' school an offer she couldn't refuse – a large 'trial' area, for free. She declined. 'Too weird', 'too new', 'too much of a gamble' was the reaction. I was disappointed but undeterred.

Given it was an unproven market I baulked at paying several thousand euro for a tiny stand at the annual principals' conference. Instead we tried a spot of guerrilla marketing, parking our most colourful van at the main entrance for the duration. Next, without permission (seeking forgiveness after the fact being sometimes easier) we proceeded to drop leaflets on windscreens in the car park and managed to get most done before being told to clear off by security. Observing from a safe distance we saw them half-heartedly remove a few, soon giving up and retiring back to the lobby. Job done.

As a result we got about a dozen enquiries, some commenting they were sorry they didn't spot our stand inside. Not to worry. Our first couple of schoolyard conversions ensued and suddenly we were in business.

Schools were well aware of the sports grass companies who would convert playing fields into AstroTurf pitches albeit for several hundred thousand euro.

Holy Cross Before & After

Carysford Before & After

Cork Presentation Before & After

Swords National School

St Louis National School   St Joseph's Waterford

Rathfarnham   St Peter and Paul's Balbriggan

We focused instead on existing hard yards which were cheaper to convert as well as doing whatever size fitted the budget. Armed with pictures and more importantly glowing testimonials ('The first-aid box is now hardly ever used', 'Best decision I ever made') we soon rolled out a shiny brochure featuring coloured grass, running tracks, shock-pads and bespoke shapes. This satisfying work now represents over one-quarter of our entire turnover. We have done about 200 schools and our mission is far from accomplished.

Play areas/playgrounds

As we saw in Chapter 3, the Ford Foundation's work to make urban playgrounds safer in the late 1950s was the spark that started the entire industry.

Many public playgrounds just have grass or bark mulch. When I say grass I really mean mud given that with any foot traffic at all, the ground becomes bald and visiting children inevitably get covered in mud. The sprinkling of a few inches of bark mulch is not much better. By definition it biodegrades, meaning it needs constant topping up. Another solution is rubber tiles. Depending on their quality and how well they are laid, these too can deteriorate, becoming worn and uneven. A more expensive option is wetpour, a spongy substance that absorbs impact and comes in different colours. It works well but is prone to becoming worn and dangerously slippy with frost. On occasion, to save expense, we have simply covered over such surfaces, thereby retaining the shock absorption of what's already *in situ*. Shockpads, often made from recycled rubber and carpet underlay in varying thicknesses, with several different levels of critical fall height, can be added. This is often a legal safety requirement.

Special needs

Some schools are now adding specialist ASD units, keeping more children in mainstream education. Other schools cater for children with a visual or hearing impairment or who have a physical or learning disability and who are in need of particular support. A nice, bright, soft and safe tactile outdoor or indoor surface is just what the doctor ordered, so to speak. We are proud to be able to contribute to their care.

We have learned plenty over the years and have successfully designed and installed several safe sensory gardens for various special schools and even won awards for them (see Chapter 10). Thanks to the networking of happy principals our services are increasingly sought after. Our team take great pride in this work. It's especially lovely to watch the children's reactions when we unveil their new safe play zones. TV programme *DIY SOS* can't get enough of it. Sales director Dominic has taken a special interest in this sector and has been interviewed on national TV about his work with special needs schools.

Pets

'*Who let the dogs out?*'
~ Baha Men

Apart from children, people's pets (mainly dogs) are a main driver of domestic synthetic grass sales. The big question being 'Is it dog friendly?' The short answer is yes.

To prove it we donated some to the Dublin Society for Prevention of Cruelty to Animals (DSPCA) dog shelter HQ in the foothills of the Dublin mountains. Over 50 dogs joyfully play on it daily. We also installed it in the training centre for Guide Dogs who later asked us to quote for a much larger training area. I take that as a sign that they are pleased with what they already bought.

We've installed our grass in many boarding kennels nationwide. The owners are delighted with the results. Our furry friends love playing, stretching and scratching on it and they go back to their owners clean and happy. It turns out there's never any damage to the grass when there are loads of dogs on it. It's usually only when there's a single dog (or pup), possibly left alone for long periods, that frustration sets in and the grass can be attacked.

One day before Christmas, following years of unsuccessful lobbying, my wife and I were summoned into the kitchen by our kids, then about eight and nine, instructed to sit down and asked to hear them out. They proceeded to produce €250 *in cash* – their entire pooled savings. They then showed us pictures of puppies for sale and they told us how they had researched different breeds (with the clandestine help of an aunt) and found the ideal pet. Next came promises of how they would feed, walk and mind said animal and even pick up the poo if only we would finally agree to getting a dog. Don't forget, dear parents, we already have a synthetic lawn so there won't be any issue there. How could we possibly refuse?

Actually, if either of them ever read this it might serve as a reminder of all their promises that fateful day. Especially the picking up of the poo bit. So off we drove to County Wicklow to look at a litter of three-month-old little fluffy brown and white puppies.

They were a designer breed – cavachons. A cross between a Cavalier King Charles spaniel and a bichon frise – the perfect house pet. Predictably we were all smitten. They have non-shed coats and a chilled-out temperament. We brought home a little brown and white guy who instantly become the fifth member of the family. Naming our kids was way easier than naming the new dog. We eventually settled on 'Darcy'.[31] Over the years he never damaged a blade of grass, but as a pup he destroyed every chair and table leg in the kitchen, relentlessly chewing as his teeth matured. If an adorable ball of fluff can single-handedly destroy 20 wooden legs (one table, four chairs), the truth is any dog is certainly capable of damaging grass if so inclined.

Dog friendly not dog proof
Honesty is the best policy so this is what we tell our customers: 99 times out of 100 there'll be no issues whatsoever. However, there's a small chance your dog will pull or rip up some grass and damage it. Luckily it can be fixed, repaired or replaced. We usually fix it at a discounted rate or even free of charge the first time around for goodwill purposes but after that sorry, tough, we did warn you that it's *not* completely bulletproof. You need to be more vigilant. If you are both at work, your kids off at school and the dog is left all alone (they are pack animals and crave company), then boredom and frustration will inevitably lead to damaged furniture, plants or even your beautiful new artificial grass lawn. Don't believe vendors who tell you otherwise. We sell on the basis that our grasses are 100 per cent dog friendly as opposed to 100 per cent dog proof.

Dog sh*t
The next bone of contention (see what I did there? … never mind) is dog poo. Getting it on one's shoes is everyone's pet hate. It stinks. It's very unhygienic and if it comes in contact with the eyes, it can even lead to blindness. For our sales guys out visiting gardens, it's a dreaded occupational hazard. No matter how careful they are when measuring up, they often tread in doggie do-do. It's usually hidden behind tufts of grass or between the blades and you can be miles away before sniffing that dreaded pong in the jeep. Put it this way, all the crews go through a lot of offcuts for vehicle floor mats.

---

31 Darcy is not named after the moody rich dude in Jane Austen's *Pride and Prejudice* but, rather, after the retired Irish international rugby centre Gordon D'Arcy. I met Gordon one day and told him we'd named our dog after him. 'I bet you've never had anyone say that to you before,' I said. 'I've heard it before,' he answered, a bit nonplussed, before walking off. A couple of years later, I did his garden.

The good news for dog owners with artificial grass is that it's an even surface that doesn't continually grow so any and all poo is immediately obvious. We recommend the stronger mid- to high-end quality grasses for dog owners. Some owners are concerned that the longer piles of higher-end grasses will make it more difficult to pick up solid waste. Not so. Even at 40mm and 50mm they are still considerably shorter than real grass. Once spotted it's simple (if a touch unpleasant) to remove. If particularly runny (yuck) it's a bigger job but it can still be washed off. More fibre in the diet from now on please. My pooper scooper works great on fake grass and even automatically squirts deodorant and sanitising liquid at the same time. To be honest we (and when I say 'we' I mainly mean me, despite earlier promises to the contrary) usually ignore it during the week and sort it on a Friday evening or Saturday morning so it's spic and span for the weekend.

What about pee?
Don't fret, it won't discolour fake grass. Typically dogs will pee against something, say a wall, tree trunk or a stationary postal worker's leg, instead of on an open lawn. Remember, the bigger the dog, the bigger the bladder. With a permeable sub-base and porous grass, the wee drains away. The copious rainwater we have in Ireland, in case you didn't know, helps wash it away. But in hot countries or during hot spells here, the odour may become obvious. We sell non-biological anti-bacterial spray but household disinfectants work just fine too. Diluted white vinegar acts to neutralise the odour, a possible side effect being that your lawn could then smell like a plate of chips. Ideally do not add regular sand as this will soak up and help crystallise the uric acid making things worse. Silica sand or copper slag works better. More recently a pet-friendly infill technology has become available. Durafill sand reportedly withstands both animal urine, breaking down the ammonia, and the elements. It works by preventing the growth of spores and bacteria on the surface. In any case we advocate periodic disinfection as pathogens are not broken down by natural processes in the same manner as in natural turf. As a by-product of the push for more sustainable recyclable grass some now have a non-latex backing which doesn't trap the uric acid. Finally you can buy a bag of Zeolite pet odor infill which will neutralize ammonia and kill bacteria.

Alternatively, make them do their business down at the park rather than in your garden. Just remember to bring along your poo bags.

TIP Although a weed membrane is sometimes used in synthetic lawn installations, I would recommend not using one if you have a dog. It can act as an unwelcome barrier trapping the urine, hindering the drainage process and making the smell potentially worse.

What about digging?

We've seen that, if determined enough, a dog might just succeed in ripping through fake grass, so the trick is to monitor their behaviour and teach them not to. Specialist products and even pepper can be applied to discourage this. Perhaps retain a separate designated digging area if that's what they really like to do. Where's their favourite spot? Where did they hide that bone?

If you have retained beds within the garden, they will naturally dig there instead. If soil gets flung onto the grass sweep it off periodically, otherwise it becomes matted and more difficult to remove.

TIP Your dog's urine will have soaked down several inches under the surface. For your cleaning agent to be effective, it must be applied in sufficient volumes to penetrate to the same depth. So, don't apply sparingly. Shake and mix well before use. Finally, don't apply bio-enzyme cleaners on very hot days. The heat could kill the odour-killing bacteria before it even gets to work.

Hospitality

Nobody would have believed that by 2004 we would become the first country in the world to ban smoking in pubs. Because we don't generally get great weather, a new industry was spawned overnight: the construction of smoking areas, aka beer gardens, with very specific regulations regarding ventilation and the amount of shelter allowable. I made a bit of a short-term killing importing and installing infrared outdoor heaters. More importantly we've installed our grasses in lots of them. Time for a topical but lamentably bad joke.

Did you hear the Irish have invented a new low maintenance grass?

You just soak the seed in whiskey and it comes up already half cut.

Boom, boom. Told you it was bad.

What better way to advertise our grass and prove its durability and versatility than to display it in public? It's great getting paid to put it in pubs, clubs, hotels, restaurants and cafés. Often used on street fronts, rooftops, balconies, smoking areas and in garden areas, it's a practical, safe non-slip solution that beautifies any area.

The normal guarantee period does not apply, however, given the heavy traffic and abuse these areas might be expected to endure. Think cigarette butts, spilled alcohol, mushed food and puke. Publicans are happy enough to get a few years out of such a surface before replacement. We certainly recommend a sand infill to act as a fire retardant.

We've installed in places from the mundane to the outright funky, including stairs, walls, ceilings, signage and more. We usually make sure to pop up our name plaque in such places so curious punters can find out who installed this fancy new-fangled plastic grass. 'Maybe we could get this at home?' Music to my ears. Although, I quickly learned to remove my mobile number and only include the office landline. I got one too many late-night drunken slurred enquiries. 'Do youse do dis eh, dat fake … hic … bleedin' eh, whatchamacallit, AstroTurf do ye? Whaat duz it … how much duz it cost n anyway … hic?'

Kelly's Resort Hotel & Spa in Rosslare in Ireland's sunny south-east has been a popular family destination for generations. The hotel overlooks a long sandy beach. In fact it's just down the coast from the spot where Steven Spielberg shot the Normandy beach invasion scene for *Saving Private Ryan*.

The views of the beach were rather spoiled by the unedifying vista of a low flat roof with skylights, utilities, air conditioning units and miles of power cables. We covered the lot, giving guests a much more aesthetically pleasing view. It worked a treat and we were invited back to do more balconies and redo their 18 hole mini golf course.

Many of Kelly's guests were thus introduced to our product for the first time and it inevitably occurred to some that it could be an option in their own homes. We were then able to thank them for the business by donating grass to an adult autistic centre with which he was involved and our warehouse manager, Tommy, kindly installed it for them.

It doesn't always all go so smoothly. We were once commissioned to solve a problem for a McDonald's drive-through where they had scruffy grass verges around their restaurant. We did our thing and the franchise holder was very pleased. A few days later I met him to get paid. In fairness to the guy he wrote the cheque with no quibbles. As he handed it to me he announced, 'Now rip it all back out again and restore natural grass please.' It seems HQ had a big issue with plastic grass being used outside their restaurants. I will make no comment on the irony of that, but we duly obliged. Much of the grass was recycled, being relaid elsewhere.

In another hotel, an installation we did literally turned to shit. We had successfully installed over 120m² in the outside smoking area of their nightclub. After about 10 years I got a call. 'It's destroyed, come and replace ASAP.' It transpired that after heavy rain, the adjacent river burst its banks and lots of smelly raw sewage polluted the whole area.

I was delighted.

The lads, not so much. The hotel's insurance paid for it. Our crew had the unpleasant task of ripping out the old stuff but the new grass is in now and I still refer prospects from the area to see it.

Events

Back in the early noughties a local racetrack hosted a big music festival called Oxegen. One year we put in some grass which I wanted to photograph in use, only I had no ticket. Instead myself and my brother put on yellow bibs, jumped into my black Isuzu jeep and headed for the concert. My wife was pregnant with our first child and I had just bought a yellow 'nee-naw' flashing light (like the magnetic one Starsky and Hutch had on their Gran Torino) which I planned to use if we had to rush to the maternity hospital. I popped it on the roof of the jeep which as yet had no sign writing on it and we drove past the main entrance straight to the crew, ambulance, garda-only gate. A security guy waved us to a halt and by the time I had my window half rolled down he declared, fag dangling from his mouth, 'There's still room to park right around behind the main stage, lads.' 'Cheers, buddy' and off we drove. Better still, much later a gang of friends piled back into the jeep and whizzed along the services road, past a long tailback of traffic leaving the venue. When we got as far as the exit, the gardaí kindly stopped all other traffic to let us out. 'Thanks, fellas.' We made the pub before closing time. Not sure if I ever got those photos of concert goers enjoying the grass.

By virtue of our longevity and reputation we are often the first port of call for organisers and event companies when it comes to concerts, seminars, trade shows and all kinds of events nationwide.

Despite tight deadlines, chaotic setups and often limited budgets, there's often a great buzz in being involved 'backstage' so to speak. We are past masters at negotiating the chaos of set-up day. Trade shows have long appreciated the value of using synthetic grass for both individual stands and common areas. Ironically we often get more business attending such shows from the other exhibitors rather than from the general public. Many companies come to us again and again to grass up their stands. I imagine by now some of their employees have entire gardens fitted with grass that 'disappeared' after previous shows.

Our grass adorns the large studio-side balconies of national radio stations Newstalk and Today FM, where they do photo shoots with high-profile guests.

We've teamed up with big beer brands for some of their events, including Guinness and Carlsberg. We've even covered the top storey of a city centre multi storey car park with grass, mocking it up to look like a soccer stadium.

The Ford Motor Company (where it all began, you will recall) got us to do lots of temporary pitches in dealership car parks during the UEFA European Football Championship.

We even installed a 'rugby pitch' on the main stage at the 3Arena in Dublin.

Our grass is regularly on the famous *The Late Late Toy Show* set.

And we covered life-sized elephants for charity at the Electric Picnic.

Corporates

There's been a bit of a craze, especially among food companies and breweries, to adorn boardrooms with artificial grass.

Innocent drinks were very early adopters and their fleets of friendly grass-and-flower-covered delivery vans have brought them attention internationally. We covered their entire Irish fleet along with their boardroom in their 'Fruit Towers' HQ. Paddy Power bookmakers got similar treatment.

We've covered the foyer of a Sports TV company, made to look like a pitch, and the lobby of Bord Bia. We did an entire rooftop for Bord Gáis. They had a fancy rooftop garden with expansive and expensive hardwood decking and walkways. Sadly for them (not for me) the health and safety people came along and said – no, sorry, too slippy. Access denied. Until we came along.

We put our grass outside the famous Ambassador cinema on Dublin's O'Connell Street. Such was the success of a 'temporary' installation at the entrance to the Children's Science Museum that it's still there, nine years later.

Lots of tech companies have their European headquarters in Ireland. Google, Facebook and LinkedIn have all bought our products. It's true, they do have pinball machines, beanbags, slides and all you'd expect from adult playground-themed workplace.

Bloom Fringe Festival

Roof of multi-storey car park, St Stephen's Green shopping centre

South Anne Street, Dublin   Ivy Gardens, Dublin

Pop-up in Dublin 2

In The Gym

Black grass

Retail

Our fake grass has regularly appeared in many shop front displays, including Kildare Village outlet shopping destination. Honda used our synthetic hedging and grass for its displays. A modelling agency used our grass on the catwalk for a fashion show. As I recall there were no shortages of volunteers for that particular installation.

We worked with a mobile phone company to deck out all its outlets, covering the floor to look like mini pitches to mark its sponsorship of Irish rugby.

Lifestyle Sports is Ireland's leading sports retailer. What better surface on which to try on and admire your new boots than fake grass? We've installed it throughout their branch network.

A dentist's chain got us to do its entrances, perhaps serving as a welcome distraction to the horrors awaiting within. Supermarket chains such as Tesco, Aldi and Lidl have been our customers. We also supplied grass to health food start-up The Happy Pear long before it grew into the brand phenomenon it is today.

Gyms

When I lived in California back in the late 1990s I noticed everyone was either a health nut or, shall we say, somewhat overweight. Increasingly I see the same here in Ireland. We've had an explosion of new gyms nationwide and many use our schools grass for working out and pushing prowlers on. It's tough enough to take abuse and soft enough to be practical. As it comes in a variety of colours, we can do line markings, tracks and logos so we've become the go-to guys for several fitness chains. Now if only I could motivate myself to use one of these fine establishments myself, I'd be a lot better off.

Local authorities

A few years ago a county council quantity surveyor enthusiastically specified that we lay a narrow meridian strip for a new motorway project. It would have been miles of work. Never happened. While the general public quickly got with the programme, I can count on one hand the amount of projects we've done for local authorities. So far.

Why are most roundabouts planted with real grass? Who thinks it's a good idea to use something that never stops growing and needs constant mowing to keep it looking respectable? Let's get maintenance crews to dodge across the traffic with rotating metal blades flying around spewing out grass cuttings.

Synthetic grass has been extensively used around the circuits of Formula One racing tracks. We've done the meridians and island beds of car parks where it's impossible for anything to grow anyway.

Perhaps it's fear of vandalism. In the early days we had just completed a big play area for a crèche in County Offaly. The owners were delighted and couldn't wait for the kids' reaction the following Monday morning. Unfortunately that weekend some scumbags broke in and thought it would be hilarious to spray paint obscenities all over the lovely new surface. We got the 'help' phone call first thing that Monday morning.

Within an hour my lads, stopping at the hardware store en route, were able to successfully remove all traces of the paint and the kids were out playing on it by lunchtime.

Another exasperated phone call came in after the school holidays from a principal's office. Some yobs had decided to burn a couple of plastic traffic cones in the middle of the yard. No problem. We simply cut out the affected areas, including the blobs of ex-traffic cones, and glued in replacement pieces of matching grass so normal play could quickly resume.

Waterford City Council is more enlightened. A decade ago a brave city architect called us about an urban renewal scheme they had underway. She thought artificial grass might be the solution.

The environs of a housing estate were badly in need of renovation. Part of the project was a central 'green area' intersection. When we first saw it, it was hopelessly neglected and overgrown. The 'green area' was strewn with old shopping trolleys, broken bikes, tyres, car batteries and mountains of beer cans and bottles. It took some courage for me to even venture in and measure up the area.

When I followed up on my quotation, the price was not the issue. Rather she queried how it might withstand vandalism. Anxious to progress the project and confident in its resilience I offered a two-year written guarantee that 'any damage for any reason would be immediately repaired or replaced'. This did the trick and we were soon underway.

We subcontracted the clearance work. Upon my arrival on the first morning I found the local work crew laughing heartily. They were already halfway through clearing the first area with their JCB digger. Reportedly I had just missed a local young lad who had frantically waved at them to stop digging. In a panic he searched around the now barren soil.

'Did any of yiz see the plastic bag I left here?'

'Sorry, son, 'fraid not,' they replied. 'Why, what was in it?'

'Me pills … little white pills.'

'Eh?'

'Where the f**k did it all go?'

'Well, the first load has already gone off to the city dump, pal.'

And with a curse he jumped back on his bike and peddled furiously down the hill in the direction of the city dump, presumably to see if he could rescue his stash of illicit contraband.

We'll never know what happened next but I suspect it can't have ended well for him. His suppliers are unlikely to have been impressed. Let that be a lesson to all.

TIP

Always be careful where you stash your stuff.

We pressed on with the job. Within a week we had completed the installation, often watched by the bemused local youths.

'Here, can we play soccer on dat?'

'Sure you can,' I answered, 'maybe just wait till we're finished please.'

The architect never did have to call us back. I'm told the area is still in daily use and the local kids regularly clear any litter away themselves so they can have a kick about.

Rooftops and balconies

Typically it's easier to install our grass onto a hard surface. The drainage will already have been taken care of so the grass is simply secured in place.

We've installed on tiny apartment balconies as well as massive hotel rooftops, fancy office block terraces and penthouse gardens. What better spaces to use for health and well-being of staff, customers and private citizens, allowing for container gardening, sunbathing, fag breaks, clothes drying and generally chilling out.

Don't worry be happy

One day we were busy doing a new office block roof terrace when one of the lads spotted something across the way. Something that was probably not supposed to be seen. No, it's not what you are thinking, rather he spotted what he reckoned was a row of nicely mature marijuana plants in the south-facing windows of the building opposite. A pair of binoculars brought in the next day settled the bet. It was indeed a well-tended mini-plantation. It must be said there's a wealth of misused horticultural skills out there. We simply had a laugh and worked away. I said let them worry about their grass and let us worry about ours.

A holy show

Speaking of the challenges of getting our grass high up, I'm reminded of the time our grass ended up atop Ireland's sacred mountain.

On the edge of Ireland's western seaboard, along the Wild Atlantic Way in County Mayo sits a solitary mountain, Croagh Patrick, aka the Reek. It overlooks the spectacular Clew Bay with its hundreds of tiny islands. According to tradition, St Patrick, Ireland's patron saint (the dude who got rid of all the snakes and converted us to Christianity, more on him later) fasted and prayed on the summit for 40 days circa 441AD. Well before him it had been a pagan place of pilgrimage for over 5000 years.

So where better to install 30m² of our artificial grass?

A sacrilegious desecration, some might say.

Indeed.

But it was all for a worthy cause. You see, on the last Sunday of July is the annual Reek Sunday ceremony when thousands of the faithful make the precarious climb, often barefooted, to attend Mass at the top. It can be particularly treacherous in inclement weather conditions. A landscaper customer approached us in early summer 2015 seeking our assistance. He explained he was a volunteer with the local mountain rescue team. Annually they set up a first aid station near the top of the mountain to treat climbers and worshippers for cuts, abrasions, hypothermia and worse. So we gladly donated a roll of our Sanctuary grass and I joked that they would need a helicopter to get it up there. He replied they had one on standby.

So coming up to Reek Sunday that year we got the grass to the base on a windy day to find the rescue helicopter had been called away on an urgent mission. Thus a large team had to haul it all up the hard way. It was carefully laid and secured on a pre-prepared rare flat section of ground. Their treatment centre, an elaborate tent, was to be pitched on top. Unfortunately that year the weather was so bad the mountain rescue team advised the bishop and the authorities to cancel the pilgrimage. Undeterred, several hundred of the faithful made the climb anyway. Reportedly there were many injuries. I called Conor

Trip to Croagh Patrick

Croagh Patrick: to climb or to golf?

 MAYO MOUNTAIN RESCUE TEAM

4th August 2015

Dear Mark,

The Mayo Mountain Rescue Team would like to thank you for your support with our Annual Reek Sunday operations.

The Annual Reek Sunday pilgrimage is the busiest day on the MMRT calendar with multiple rescues and numerous Mountain Rescue teams from around the country coming to assist us.

The provision of synthetic grass on the base of our medical tent during our Reek Sunday operations will make it more comfortable and secure for those who work at this location during Reek Sunday.

Once again many thanks for your help.

a few days later to see how they got on. 'Well,' he said, 'the first aid tent blew away!' Oh dear.

But the grass survived intact. It remains there to this day and is used periodically not only by the team as a platform for evacuations and treatment but also by climbers for a picnic and a little rest, its aesthetic incongruity belying its utility.

Sadly our discreet if impious 'Sanctuary Synthetics' signage was soon vandalised and is no more, no doubt a sight some vexed pilgrims could simply not tolerate. Personally I delight in the existence of our small island of green, invaluable to so many, in such a bleak, rocky and holy landscape. I get pics and selfies from the spot sent by friends and acquaintances who correctly leap to the conclusion it must have been the Fake Grass Man's work.

Golf

It was the growing popularity of that weird new Scottish game, hitting a little ball into small faraway holes with sticks, that led to the first formal scientific research into what were the best grass types to use. There are 6,000 known species of grass. For a long time people had to make do with whatever happened to grow locally. In 1924 the Royal and Ancient Golf Club of Saint Andrews first decreed that research be undertaken. Evolution, as we have seen, never stops.

What exactly is it, I wonder, that draws us out into the open air onto these neatly mown expanses of fairways and greens? 'Golf is a good walk spoiled,' as the saying goes, and what's with the questionable clothes? I'm brutal at it and I'm still addicted. As the popularity of the game really took off in the 1970s, (hence perhaps the dodgy gear), the US Department of Agriculture helped develop tougher grass varieties. In 1968 a golf club in Westchester county, New York, first installed artificial grass on its tees to the 'complete satisfaction' of its members.

As previously mentioned, the first time I properly noticed fake grass was around the perimeter of a synthetic putting green at the PGA golf show in Orlando, Florida in 2001. It's no exaggeration to say that this discovery changed my life. Besides artificial lawns we in Sanctuary now install top quality bespoke non-infill synthetic putting greens all over Ireland. These are engineered to perform and play with the speed and feel of real golf greens, only without all the expense and hassle of constant maintenance.

There's an old adage that says you 'drive for show and putt for dough'. Taking out the big dog driver and belting the ball miles down the fairway is certainly fun (assuming you hit said fairway) but any pro will tell you around the putting green is where it's really at. Statistics show that the average golfer uses up 45 per cent of their strokes on or immediately around the green during a typical game. Thus synthetic home putting greens, which allow for more practice, are becoming increasingly popular. In Ireland, north and south, lots of parents dream of their kid becoming the next Rory McIlroy … or Shane Lowry or Pádraig Harrington or Darren Clarke or Graeme McDowell. All recent major winners from Ireland.

Having used my own garden for our first synthetic lawn installation, I kindly offered to put in our first synthetic putting green, complete with small mound and even smaller bunker into my parents' garden. A proof of concept, if you will. Practice makes perfect after all. My father and I had previously tried (and failed) to cultivate a natural green. It was well below par … never mind.

To my delight, both my parents, avid golfers, regularly used it. Eighteen years later it's still used and now the grandchildren love it. OK, admittedly the smallies equally love playing in the sand bunker with a bucket and spade. Fun for all the family. Unless there's a putting competition for money. Then it gets serious. It's in use all year round and helps 'get your eye in' before going out to play, ultimately helping to lower one's handicap. Plus they are custom made to fit your area, requiring zero chemicals for upkeep and make an attractive focal point, giving visitors something to do while you get the barbecue going. You get a consistent ball speed (we do our own stimpmeter tests) but there's one major disadvantage that I can personally testify to. When you miss that crucial putt, your playing partners may tend to slag you even more if they know you have your own personal putting green at home. Or at work. Maybe just don't tell them.

A couple of years ago we installed a modest synthetic putting green set into a larger synthetic lawn along with some raised beds for a golf pro. Only recently he told me he needs me back. 'Oh no, what's wrong?' I asked. 'Nothing. I need you to do the same again in my new, slightly bigger garden ASAP'. Phew! It transpired he had just traded up and, despite a flat property market, his house sold within a week, allowing him to do the deal for his new place.

Design aesthetics and functionality
Whether for DIY or pros, the budget and size of the available area will dictate the layout and the appropriate number of holes.

The first consideration is to ascertain if it's for putting only *or* for both putting and chipping. Essentially there are two types: infill and non-infill. The

The author's parents' house: first ever install

Shrewsbury Road

Druid's Glen

former will take a chip from distance and give a truer bounce and the latter is more for putting and only very short chips. The infill greens require periodic maintenance and topping up, however. We in Sanctuary focus exclusively on the non-infill variety. Much less hassle and besides, most suburban back gardens will not allow a chip from more than a few yards.

As regards aesthetics it's this author's firm opinion that including a fringe of regular (longer) artificial grass around the green, combined with rounding the edges of the more expensive putting surface, greatly enhances the utility and appearance of the area. From a functionality point of view it makes little sense to have your putting green abut a wall, bed or edge as it's wasteful given that there may be no room to swing your putter. By all means incorporate existing structures into your layout, for example rocks, trees or shrubs, but be careful it doesn't become more like crazy golf. Adding even a metre or so of fringe leaves more room to play and makes it look far more natural. Indeed, adding two layers of fringe grass, with descending pile heights, can match the look of a transitioning fairway, replicating first and second cuts.

What does it cost?

Much more than regular artificial grass. Over 50 per cent more in fact. The dense specialist surface costs more to make and although the build-up is the same as ordinary fake grass it can be more time consuming to lay, thus higher labour charges. Right now expect to pay in excess of €125 per m^2 including VAT. So a $4 \times 5 = 20m^2$ will cost about €2,500. Don't forget the necessary accessories: cups and pins and even caps to close off the holes when not in use (handy when toddlers are about).

Issues to remember

Firstly many will expect to be able to pitch onto their greens from a distance. Unscrupulous salespeople are often quick to say, 'No problem.' However, if it's a non-infill putting surface, chipping from any more than 10 or 12 yards away *is* a problem. Remember a real putting green surface is usually firm, sometimes moist, to assist with a soft landing. Hence the appearance of divots and the constant necessity for pitch repairing (it's hugely satisfying having to repair same after a nice high controlled wedge shot – for the greenkeepers, not so much). However, with a synthetic putting green this, by definition, cannot happen. It will be a harder landing, probably with a bigger bounce and carry. It's good to be aware of this in advance when deciding on and laying out your own home putting green. As an embarrassingly high handicapper myself, I can live with this limitation. We have a modest demo green within our Grassland HQ display area and it's proven a super refuge for timeouts during a busy day.

Many golfers will have notions so it can take a whole lot longer to install by the time the greens are contoured to their preference with undulations and breaks.

One rule of thumb: the smaller the green, the flatter it should be. It's important to have the immediate six inches surrounding the cup dead flat, regardless of client's requests. Most practice should be on the flat. Only if one can consistently sink them is it time to consider incorporating undulations and breaks. Check out Chapter 15 for advice on how to install a synthetic putting green.

Our experience

Over the years we've had the privilege of being involved in many interesting high-profile golf-related projects, both domestic and commercial. We've installed it in driving ranges, on penthouse rooftops and in some of the most expensive properties in the country (put it this way, on the Monopoly board they would be on Shrewsbury road in Dublin, or Mayfair in London). We repurposed a disused infinity pond overlooking the beautiful Wicklow mountains.

We have a presence in several pro shops and golf retail outlets including the premises of Ireland's most renowned 'fitter' who splits his time between here and some place called Augusta National in Georgia. Only modesty and pressure on space prevent me from reproducing his flattering testimonial here.

We've installed at my home club of Palmerstown House Estate, as well as a 200m² putting green overlooking the wild Atlantic in the exclusive and magnificent Old Head Golf Links in Kinsale. The word is that when it was being developed locals lobbied to have the approach roads improved. 'No need,' said the developers, 'all of our golfers will be coming in by helicopter.' When Tiger Woods was asked to name one of the holes he simply suggested 'Wow'.

Thirty years ago my uncle died and left the farm to my aunt and his several children. Rather than the eldest just continuing to farm they collectively decided to turn it into a golf course. Thus Highfield Golf and Country Club was born. Later it became apparent they needed a bigger club house. At the time I was importing log cabins from Finland and Estonia. In a throwaway remark I suggested they should get a giant log cabin instead. A year later a team was over from Canada constructing a unique clubhouse where one has to tee off from the roof onto the first fairway. It was designed around a practice putting green courtyard. Happily (for me) real grass was too difficult to keep – due to insufficient light – so I was commissioned to install a large synthetic green. More than 15 years later it's still in daily use, I'm happy to say.

We've installed in hotels and pubs, for example an 18-hole mini course for the patrons of busy west Dublin pub The Old Mill, as well as rejuvenating the course in Kelly's Hotel in Rosslare

For the corporate world we've done outdoor and indoor, temporary and permanent putting greens for meetings, events and headquarters, notably one on the top floor of the trendy new Ryanair HQ at Dublin airport. Although, and I'm sure Michael O'Leary will forgive me for saying so, I suspect that being seen actually using it, while possibly beneficial for one's game, might not be terribly beneficial for one's career prospects with the airline.

Of all the golf-related work we have done, however, our involvement in one of the world's most prestigious golf events, the Ryder Cup, must take pride of place. Ireland's hosting of the biannual event for the first time, in 2006, was a pretty big deal and was, I think, the climax of the Celtic Tiger years. The tournament was played close to Naas in the K Club, County Kildare.

I've always been a sucker for getting our grass in front of the public at every opportunity. In suburban back gardens, hardly anybody, except family and friends, sees it. So, imagine my delight when I got a call to design and install a synthetic putting green and more for the prestigious Ryder Cup. What an opportunity.

It involved two main projects.

First, two double-decker buses had to be covered from top to bottom in artificial grass. We'd covered several vans in our own fleet at this stage so how hard could it be? The buses were to advertise the sponsor, O2, and ferry people to the venue. We figured out the technicalities but the deadline was so tight we had to pull an all-nighter to finish. Thousands of mostly middle-class golfers, our ideal target customers, were to ride in the buses.

With all hands on deck, the first bus was completed by teatime. The second would surely be easier and covered faster, no? It was time for breakfast by the time we were done. A few hours for the glue to dry and the hairy green buses were ready to roll.

The second project was to bling out a railway station. The closest station to the K Club is Leixlip Louisa Bridge, from where our hairy green buses were to ferry patrons to the golf tournament. Sure, how hard could the blinging out be? Quite hard, as it turned out. With trains of 1,000 tonnes plus thundering past at 80 mph every few minutes, health and safety was a bit of a concern. The idea was to give arriving passengers a golf course feel by covering the platform edges and walls in grass and laying a putting green in the car park. The grass had to be sufficiently secure but completely removable afterwards, as if we'd never been there.

The green was a piece of cake. Since it was just for show we laid straight onto the tarmac with a longer 'fairway' fringe grass. We simply cut out four-inch circles and the tarmac made them look just like holes. We then made a curved section, added some sand and, hey presto, there was your bunker.

I borrowed a couple of pins from my cousin's golf club in Highfield and secured them by (secretly) drilling a couple of small holes in the tarmac. I then glued the sponsor's logo to the flags and both the sponsor and the public were suitably impressed.

The platform was another matter entirely. Iarnród Éireann, the state rail authority, understandably had what seemed like the entire health and safety department on our case. Dudes with clipboards and frowns followed us around. Yellow safety vests were no good – they had to be orange. Was our grass fire-certified? There could be no trip hazards whatsoever so the grass had to be heavily glued. But it also had to be removable without a trace immediately after the Ryder Cup ended. Again we managed it, getting plenty of curious looks during the process.

Europe won that year, I'm glad to say. I was lucky enough to get hold of a few tickets and was able to invite my then grass supplier, a golf nut, over as a thank you for having educated us. It rained so hard the event was nearly abandoned. The spectators didn't mind, though. I was on a balcony overlooking the 16th when Tiger Woods conceded to the recently bereaved Darren Clarke (from Northern Ireland). It was sensational and the Guinness flowed.

The following week, we were back on our knees using scrapers, elbow grease and (when the clipboard men were not looking) blow torches to try to remove all traces of the green glue from the black platforms. Well, almost all traces because some bits were simply impossible to get rid of. But Krzystof had a bright idea. We just painted the last few bits black and walked away. Quickly.

The Ryder Cup is coming back to Ireland in 2027, this time to JP McManus's magnificent Adare Manor, County Limerick. I can't wait. I once birdied the 18th there. Got on the green in two over the river.

I'll conclude with my favourite piece of advice which some readers will understand perfectly: the secret to golf is to play it as if it's just a game.

Hospitals, hospices and care of older adults

I want to tell you a quick yarn.

Back in 2002 I was in the UK visiting my then supplier Anthony. Based outside Blackpool, his company were leading pioneers in their market, having had the foresight to develop a strong internet presence. Anthony mentioned they had been called back to an installation only recently completed down the M6 in Liverpool. They had to rip out a perfectly good back garden artificial lawn for an older lady.

'Oh dear, what was the problem?' I asked. Seemingly her grown-up children, living abroad or in London, had clubbed together to surprise her by having a brand new synthetic lawn installed while she was in hospital getting a new hip.

On her return, all was well, and the invoice was promptly paid. Then less than a month later Anthony's office got a call. 'She's not happy and wants it restored to natural grass … Sorry about that.'

It transpired that Fred, her gardener odd-jobber, who came fortnightly, had been invited inside for tea, biscuits and questioning.

'I love the progress you are making with the flowerbeds and all, Fred,' she said, 'but why have I not heard the lawnmower working during your last couple of visits?'

'Eh …' Fred replied '… no need anymore.'

'Why ever not?'

'Well, 'cause the grass is artificial!'

She hadn't noticed and nearly choked on her bourbon cream.

As it was meant as a surprise no one in her family had mentioned it since. Unfortunately, instead of delight there was disgust. They got Anthony to belatedly and painstakingly explain what it was, how it was made, all its benefits. Never mind that Fred now had more time to do some actual gardening instead of just managing the lawn. Whatever would the neighbours think? Their mother insisted on having her old lawn back. So Anthony obliged, selling off her unwanted synthetic lawn at a discount elsewhere and poor old Fred had to get the lawnmower back into action.

Moral of the story – and something I luckily learned early on – synthetic grass is *not* for everybody. Oh, and maybe check with the recipient(s) in advance of giving it as a gift.

We have done several 'quick while my spouse is away' surprise lawns and putting greens over the years without issue. Thankfully we find it's increasingly accepted as a labour-saving solution with our older customers who look beyond tradition.

In the same way soft and safe artificial grass is effective for small children, it's also ideal for older adults with mobility difficulties. Many hospital designs include courtyards, a good way to allow light into buildings but a nightmare to grow a decent lawn. We've been commissioned to replace several of these so patients and staff can enjoy the best of both worlds. Besides laying safe and maintenance-free lawns for retirement and nursing homes we have incorporated bowling greens and putting greens which have proven popular. We've worked in Dublin's largest hospice installing a non-slip wheelchair- and Zimmer frame-friendly short grass walkway.

We recently installed a large circular lawn complete with a red path and border – their design, not ours – for an Alzheimer's care centre. Only afterwards they 'forgot' to pay and had to be reminded a couple of times.

There's an innovative project called McAuley Place in the heart of Naas, County Kildare, which allows for independent living for older adults, with on-site nursing help, situated right beside the shops, schools and, importantly for many, the church. As it happens, the complex, donated by the Sisters of Mercy, adjoins my parents' garden. For several years we operated our office from a log cabin there, watching the renovations. Besides making a couple of modest financial donations, I was anxious to somehow help in the transformation of the old convent buildings.

As a teetotaller I usually endeavour to have some kind of a healthy, alcohol-free activity before our annual Christmas party. So I volunteered our services to the manager. In front of the apartment building is a large courtyard of grey uninspiring brick paving. In front of the entrance were two large beds with, you guessed it, matching grey pebble stones and a few planters that the residents lovingly maintained. I always considered the stone surface impractical, unsafe and dull. As usual the last aspect of a project to be considered is the garden, often with the last of the budget. They gratefully accepted our offer and the founding director insisted on giving all 16 Sanctuary volunteers a hearty breakfast and an inspiring talk before work commenced.

With a nod to equality and to give our office staff a better understanding of the ins and outs of hands-on installation the women were delighted to muck in with the men. As you can imagine the craic was 90. With several manholes and utilities to negotiate it was technically challenging, but encouraged by the bemused residents we made light work of it. Besides, we had a deadline. We needed to get home, showered and changed to reassemble in Lawlor's Hotel across the way to start our Christmas party.

Then the old 'While you are here, you wouldn't just ...' request once again reared its ugly head. Each of the 40 plus individual apartments had a small timber floored balcony. This became slippery when wet, so dangerous for many.

'Mark, ye are doing a great job here. The residents love the look of the fake grass, you wouldn't just ...?'

Clearly there was no hint of hostility towards that 'plastic grass' from the residents who could see what a difference it would make. So we scrambled to get access to every single dwelling over four floors, digging deep into our reserves of energy and offcuts. In for a penny, in for a pound.

The entire exercise cost me thousands, both in materials, grass and the opportunity cost of a day's labour for the entire firm. But balanced against the facts that we were giving back to the community in a practical way, enhancing the Sanctuary staff team spirit, breaking down some role barriers and about going on the beer in good conscience, it was well worth it. It rained most of that day. We hardly noticed.

With my marketing hat on it was no harm either. There have since been TV cameras down looking at the complex as a care model to be replicated elsewhere in the country. Not to mention the fact that our work is clearly visible from the main entrance of the Catholic church. Only now, if people glance over, they possibly assume it's simply a well-kept grass area and think no more of it. Plus we were featured in the local newspaper.

We've installed in several public and private hospitals including Crumlin's children's hospital. I'm glad to say we've been specified for the new two billion euro national children's hospital in Dublin, currently under construction. That's in the unlikely event they have any money left by the time we are needed.

Funerals (a grave situation)

Let me tell you a story about the day we got things dead wrong.

It's the reason why we only *supply* grass for graves and politely decline requests to install it. It's not only due to the small size of the jobs.

In the foothills of the Dublin Wicklow mountains lies Bohernabreena. There's not much there but they do have a large and well-populated graveyard. Back in the early days, before we instituted the above policy we accepted a commission. Reportedly all went well at the grave and on the following Monday our office rang the relative.

> **Office:** 'Hi, we were just calling to see if you'd like to fix up for the artificial grass put on that grave.'

123

Customer: 'Sure, no problem, we'll pay just as soon as it's done.'
Short pause.
Office: 'Eh, it was done last Friday.'
Customer: 'Well, I was up there on Saturday and it most certainly was not done.'
Office: 'But we've a photo of it here and it's done.'
Customer: 'What's the name on the grave?'
Office: 'John A. Murphy.' (The name is changed to protect the identity of real persons, living or dead.)
Customer: 'Well, our grandfather was John B. Murphy. Row 9, on the right, as we told you.'
Office: … Silence.

It turns out John A. Murphy was in row 6, rather than row 9, and on the right. As were many other Murphys, a common Irish surname.

Customer: 'Just call me when it's done.' Hangs up.

Which was fair enough. Not being able to contact John A. Murphy or his surviving relatives, given where he was (what were we to do – leave a note?), we drove back to the graveyard, reversed the installation, restoring the shiny green pebble, which mercifully hadn't been disposed of, and did the correct John Murphy's grave. We hoped.

This is why we shy away from such work.

It's a dead loss.

Although, I have personally done my mother's and grandparents' graves.

One final thing. Why do we bury the dead underneath lawn grass anyway? Why not in a forest? Maybe that's why artificial grass, besides all the obvious benefits, somehow seems appropriate. It's not alive either.

Just a thought.

Even in death, dear reader, there is no escaping artificial grass.

We supply grass to funeral directors to assist in tidy and dignified burials and also to bereaved families to cover over the grave plots. It's cheaper than coloured gravel, weed free and neat and tidy.

I love this business as we never get stiffed (see what I did there?). Customers are never not going to pay. The pangs of guilt when visiting the grave would surely be too much.

Sometimes we sympathetically listen to poignant stories spontaneously volunteered by these customers about their dearly departed. All in a day's work.

We supply the Glasnevin Trust, which operates the country's most famous graveyard, the final resting place of the rich and famous, rebel leaders, poets and politicians. It's surrounded by high stone walls and watch towers. These were built in the nineteenth century to guard against the phenomenon of body snatching. Fresh cadavers would be dug up in secret and sold so that medical students could work on them. Nowadays they tell me it's our grass that gets stolen, possibly by local descendants of the erstwhile body snatchers, probably to adorn the balconies of the various flat complexes nearby. *Plus* ça *change.*

Insider secret: thanks to the fact that many regular installations result in unavoidable offcuts, and because this 'waste' must be paid for, we often get to sell the same piece twice. Such offcuts often fit single graves. Knowing that, dear reader, should you be so heartless, you can haggle away for a cheaper cover for the final resting place of your dearly departed.

The weird and the wonderful

I once thought that putting artificial grass around the base of a tree along a footpath was clever and innovative. Since then I've discovered the true versatility of our product and now I want to share some of the more quirky uses. It's why I love my field so much. In Sanctuary we have done more than our fair share of innovating. I like to think we've helped put the *art* back into artificial grass. Rather than describing it, check out the pics on page 150 and 168.

We remain fascinated with the many ways synthetic grass ends up getting used. Please send us *your* ideas. Meanwhile, next up are the pros and cons.

Chapter 8

Pros and cons

A freshly mown lawn is surely a thing of great beauty and comfort. I think we can all agree on that. The colour green, at approximately 550 nanometres, is in the middle of the visible spectrum and certifiably the easiest for the retina to perceive. Lolling about on a manicured lawn is one of life's simple pleasures. I'm here to tell you that from my own experience and the feedback of thousands of happy customers, it's the same on a synthetic version, only you get to sit and watch the grass *not* grow.

There's a bunch of reasons why people might think twice and I'll be as frank as possible in addressing them. In truth I want to put some people off the idea. If you've read this far, chances are you are not entirely hostile to the concept. If you've just landed here via a casual page flick and you feel your eyebrows raised or frowning, then please just flick off. It's worth repeating: a fake lawn is not for everyone. I only want willing prospects. They make for happier customers. I'm simply not engaging with the haters. But if you like the idea of reclaiming precious free time please read on.

Ten reasons to consider switching to artificial grass

Let's start with 10 reasons to consider breaking taboo and saying bye-bye to your 'real' lawn:

1. Your existing lawn is a lifetime sentence of servitude
Let's conservatively estimate, assuming no rain, it takes only 45 minutes to cut your grass, including taking out the mower, fuelling it up, sweeping up afterwards and dumping the cuttings. This excludes time spent psyching yourself up to do it. Multiply this by once every 10 days, depending on how particular one is about lawn care, for a growing season of say nine months (now noticeably longer than when I started out only two decades ago). That's conservatively north of 20 hours' toil per annum, excluding any and other gardening jobs. Starting at 9 a.m. on a Monday morning of a normal working week you'll be non-stop mowing until Wednesday lunchtime. Over the term of your 35 year

mortgage that's 18 working weeks, in excess of four entire months shackled to your mower. Rather you than me, buddy.

Indeed according to the American Time Use Survey the average American homeowner spends about 70 hours a year on lawn and garden care. A CBS News poll in November 2011 found that for one in three Americans mowing the grass was their least favourite chore ranked even lower than raking leaves and shovelling snow. I've no comparable Irish data but draw your own conclusions.

2. Unsuitable lawn grasses
Outside the temperate zones huge swathes of the world are entirely unsuited to the unaided growth of traditional lawn grasses.

3. Real lawns are not good for the environment
As we saw in Chapter 6, fertilisers and pesticides have proven toxic to birds, insects and, once washed into watersheds, to fish and river life. They can be carcinogenic and endocrine disrupting. Plus monocultural lawns lack clover, food and nesting materials for wildlife.

4. Less machinery
Besides the endless hours of maintenance demanded by your lawn-manicuring regime, remember the machinery required.

Principally but not exclusively the ubiquitous lawnmower comes at a high cost in terms of air *and* noise pollution. Plus you need a shed in which to store it. Either it'll have a long, dangly knotted electrical lead (easily tripoverable) or you'll need a petrol can too. Then you'll likely need mechanical engineering skills and a strong right arm to pull the starter cord. If I had a euro for every time one broke off in my hand, I'd have certainly well over a tenner. Battery-powered tools, quieter and less prone to breakdowns, are thankfully gaining in popularity nowadays.

A University of California, Irvine study concluded that having real lawns, rather than counteracting greenhouse gas emissions, actually contributes to nitrous oxide and CO_2 in the atmosphere. Remember two-stroke mowers don't have catalytic converters fitted as standard. Figures from the EPA in the US estimated that 800 million gallons of petrol are used cutting grass *per annum*. That figure includes a shocking 17 million gallons of estimated spillage. You've done it, haven't you? I certainly have. It's impossible to know when it's full, especially if using a funnel. That's a lot of hands, shoes, patios and lawns doused in highly flammable liquid. It actually adds up to more than the infamous Exxon Valdez spill off Alaska. Every year. In American gardens alone.

5. Costs

This will vary from country to country. Besides the labour (and opportunity cost) mentioned above just how much is a new mower? Let's say €350 for something half decent. Then consider the other accoutrements: the petrol (both spilled and used) and storage shed for same.

As an aside my friend runs a successful steel garden shed company. They cost two or three times the price of the traditional 'Barna' wooden shed but last a lifetime. Trees in Ireland grow very quickly due to our damp climate. Thus commercial timber tends to be soft so steel is better and despite a higher initial outlay the return on investment is far better. So it is with fake grass.

6. Where, oh where, to put the cuttings?

Over time a serious volume of grass cuttings accumulates. On farms this is saved for winter fodder as silage or hay. Many people, you know who you are, simply hide it behind a bush or tree where it slowly breaks down but not without heating up, leaching liquids and smelling to high heaven, especially when disturbed.

But it can be composted, I hear you cry. Indeed. Despite good intentions the vast majority of people can't make composting work. They have waaay too much unwanted grass versus other compostables to make up the correct balance. Fresh cut grass has high moisture and nitrogen content and when clumped together, no anaerobic action takes place. Hence the notorious odour problems. Let's face it, people have neither the time, space, knowledge, discipline nor stomach to compost effectively. Many of our customers have tried and failed. Having been begged to take them away, we could sell big (plastic!) second-hand composters if they were not so smelly and infested with creepy crawlies.

Ah, the old chestnut 'While you are here, you wouldn't just …' – those dreaded words no tradesperson wants to hear. I know a lad who keeps a laminated list in his breast pocket which he produces with a flourish upon hearing those words. He consults it carefully. 'Certainly, madam.' It details his charges for extras, for example €20 to remove and dispose of that old Christmas tree stuffed behind the shed, €25 for broken patio furniture and so on.

'But we've got a council/private refuse collection 'brown' bin that is collected fortnightly.' Indeed. So even more trucks on the roads belching exhaust fumes and consuming fossil fuels. Out of sight is out of mind. Do you fill plastic bags with your grass cuttings or just toss it straight into the wheelie bin/trash can? Either way heavy gunky green slime results.

7. Real lawns are frankly not much use to Mother Nature

It's kind of cruel when you think about it. Grass is never allowed to mature and flower and go to seed as nature intended due to the incessant cropping. Hence the birds and bees fly right on by. 'Natural' lawns demand ongoing input. Concentrate instead on your plants, not the grass. Get some bird feeders. Sow some lavender.

8. You can make better use of the space

In this author's opinion gardening should not be all about pushing a noisy and dangerous machine (think of the horrific statistics on blade injuries) up and down in straight lines. Rather the rewards are to be found in spending time on your roses, the herb garden, planting bulbs, growing perennials and picking and arranging them for the vase in the hall. Watching stuff grow and mature. Experimenting. Learning.

9. Are there not enough grass and green areas already?

Certainly that's the case in Ireland anyway. In the UK and other urbanised societies there are surely enough pitches and parkland open to the public without fencing off more little square patches and obsessing over them.

10. Replace it with what?

Lots of our customers are sheepish about even showing us what they have. Many have more moss and weeds and mud than blades of grass. This is typically due to overuse or damp, shady conditions.

That's what you usually get when you buy a suburban house, with 1.2m high cavity block walls or softwood timber fences surrounding your typically rectangular back garden. Maybe instead of attacking the moss with ferrous sulphate which makes it black and ugly just leave it alone.

As you now know, having read thus far, it's too simplistic to claim artificial lawns are an environmental disaster. I say it's a rather lazy accusation.

So save time and effort.

Save the planet.

Go kill a lawn today.

Summary of the advantages of artificial grass

In no particular order:

- It's aesthetically pleasing. It's green and serene and available in many different hues. Up to 40 shades of green apparently. Not to be confused with '50 shades of grey', a less well written but admittedly far kinkier book than this one. Possibly also sold more copies.
- It is strong and durable compared to real grass which often has bare patches from constant use. It can handle wheelchairs, playing children, heavy foot traffic and even car wheels (my wife somehow parks half her car on our front lawn all the time).
- The lawnmower will become surplus to requirements. Sell it. One statistic I came across in my research is that they cause 5 percent of US air pollution.
- Due to the fact that there is no more mowing and also thanks to the fact that artificial grass actually absorbs noise, it's lovely and quiet, thus eliminating noise pollution.
- It's safe and non-toxic as no fertilisers, chemicals or weed killer sprays are required. In turn they cannot leach and contaminate the water table.
- It is environmentally friendly as it saves a huge amount of watering. Plus the stone base material acts as a bio-filtration system for rainwater soaking back into the water table.
- No more back-breaking weeding.
- Well OK, there might be the odd weed that gets seeded from above, windborne or from bird poo, but they are rare, easily spotted and easily removed.
- Plastic fantastic. It's long-lasting – easily over two decades if not abused.
- Serious time saved. Instead of struggling to maintain the perfect lawn, spend your time gardening or chilling.
- Easy to clean. If the wind and rain don't do it, a yard brush, vacuum cleaner or hose will.
- Fewer vermin. Roaming bears, rabbits, raccoons, urban foxes and so on will avoid your garden as there's no organic material or nutritional value in the fake grass.
- No fading. Once an issue but now colourfast for life with inbuilt UV inhibitors incorporated into the manufacturing process to protect the grass against the sunniest and most hostile conditions.

- It stays nice and flat but with the look and feel of a real lawn. Did I mention it doesn't grow?
- No digging (so no moles or gophers, not an issue in Ireland as we have neither). Dogs like it and rarely harm it.
- It's a valuable asset. It enhances the property's value and no doubt helps sell a house. My wife and I sold our first home last year. In a slowing market we got lots of offers thanks to our garden. The local estate agent's literature kept mentioning the grass, despite the fact it was installed 18 years previously. Property sections in newspapers and increasingly all those annoying TV property shows are making a big deal of it.
- Aesthetics: curb appeal. Hey, it looks nice.
- It's terribly versatile. Not only can it cover where your old lawn was, it can also be laid over decks, paths, steps, you name it.
- It discourages and provides no habitat for fleas, ticks, flies, wasps, etc.
- Good for those with allergies. People with asthma or cystic fibrosis or who are pollen sensitive or suffer from hay fever like it. There's no pollen or allergens. (Sanctuary has an ongoing 10 percent off deal with Cystic Fibrosis Ireland.)
- No more muddy footprints in your house or difficult-to-remove grass stains on your clothes.
- It's a nice, soft surface. Even without shockpad a good thick pile will absorb impact. With shock pad it can meet any required critical fall height requirements so visiting kids can't sue if they fall off your swing or slide.
- Erosion control. If soil is not there it cannot be washed away.
- It's perfect for dog runs and keeps pet areas sanitary. You can spot the poo much more easily for starters and it's easy to clean away.
- It's becoming a much more widely accepted solution. Once it was considered a bit weird but thanks to constant re-engineering the improved quality makes it economically attractive. Don't try to keep up with the Joneses. Be the Joneses.
- Job creation. It's a (relatively) new but growing industry.
- It's a lifestyle choice. As it demands little aftercare it frees up lots of time. Family time. So for working parents it's a godsend.
- For the disabled and older people no longer physically able to cut the grass it's a boon.
- It's a no-brainer for holiday home owners. I know people who drive hundreds of kilometres to the coast to their supposed place of sanctuary and relaxation to 'check on the place' but really it's to cut the grass. Just so neighbours

won't raise an eyebrow? Then they turn around and drive all the way back home again. Madness.

- It's perfect around swimming pools as a safe non-slip permeable ground cover beyond the splash area. Plus no mud, dirt or dust gets into the pool messing up the tranquil blue water.
- It's perfect for roof gardens. Its relatively light face-weight makes it a safe and practical solution.
- For some reason, presumably due to its uniform look, it always makes an area look bigger.
- It's great for events. Unlike on a real lawn, putting up a marquee is not an issue as when you've finished using the marquee the grass underneath won't be brown and dead. It allows one to have a pop-up garden anywhere, anytime.
- It spruces up spaces where it's just not practical or possible to have grass, for example the shaded passageway along the side of the house.
- It dries out quickly after rain. This can be hugely beneficial to crèches and primary schools. Teachers love the fact that they can let the kids out to play/ blow off steam much more often than before it was installed.
- It can be quickly and relatively cheaply installed over paving, concrete, tarmac and other hard surfaces.
- One can easily integrate lighting into it, including fibre optics which can look stunning.
- There is no need to be constantly reseeding your lawn in an effort to bring it back to its (long) past glory.
- It makes building snowmen easier and cleaner.

Okay, maybe I've gone far enough for now. Last one: Peace of mind. Mostly, once the satisfaction of having it newly installed has worn off, you'll simply take it for granted. Once in a while, opening the curtains on a sunny morning or perhaps when you hear a neighbour struggling to start their mower or you hear someone complaining about their unruly lawn, jealously looking at yours, you'll get a warm glow of satisfaction, safe in the knowledge that your lawn worries are over.

People tell me, 'Ooh, I'd miss the smell of freshly cut grass too much.'

It's reportedly many people's favourite smell. Well, you can always buy the fragrance of freshly cut grass in a spray or bottle. The one I bought online says:

'A pungent synthetic oil with fresh grass notes often meshed with jasmine, fresh hay and cyclamen with just a hint of sea breeze and aniseed, 100 percent phthalate free with zero percent Vanillin.'

But the unmistakable smell of newly mown grass and the resulting wooziness, although pleasant to humans – being linked to warm weather and convivial memories of being outside – is actually a distress signal. The process of chopping blades of grass leads to enzymes breaking down fats. Thereby producing organic compounds including ethanol, methanol and cis-3-hexanal, aka *leaf alcohol*. This has a very low odour threshold (the amount -0.25 parts per billion) required, so even the human nose can detect it. It seems the surviving grass is frantically trying to save itself from the injury so callously inflicted on it. The mower's blades have caused the grass blades to release these volatile organic compounds (GLVs) which not only stimulate the formation of new cells and act as antibiotics, preventing bacterial infection and inhibiting fungal growth, but also alert neighbouring plants of an imminent attack. This famous green odour is made up of oxygenated hydrocarbons including aldehydes and alcohols. By the way, this photochemical smog, so loved by all, *is considered a serious contributor to urban air pollution.*

Consider the following. My friend, garden designer Brian Burke, wrote a thoughtful essay for Woodies (the garden centre chain) and expressed his thoughts far more eloquently than I can:

> Kids no longer have the propensity of old to go outside and engage, the sad reality is that they need coaxing into doing so. The attractions need to be provided, it's not good enough to bemoan our kids' lack of resourcefulness while unquestioningly supplying them with everything they need to facilitate a sedentary lifestyle. Our kids have changed. The environment has changed. It is churlish and unfair to expect our kids today to embrace the lifestyle of *fadó, fadó* [long, long ago].
>
> During school holidays nine year old Jack will no longer head out the back door in the morning and reappear at teatime. We need to start embracing this reality and stop mythologising the 1980s and running our kids down for lack of inventiveness. If we want them outside we have to provide the sort of dynamic environment that will attract them. Transfer our average annual investment in console paraphernalia to the garden and we've made a great start … don't

let the Internet fill the void …

Consider also the Irish climate. Its impact will need to be carefully evaluated from two primary perspectives: the view from the inside outwards and year-round usability. The reality is that for substantial portions of the year we admire the garden through the double glass door from the living room …[32]

He goes on to say that when considering extended usability and the wish to see our children play outside far more, then artificial grass becomes a major element in facilitating year-round immersion. He argues that, although a lover of nature, recommending fake grass is not as paradoxical or counterintuitive as you might initially assume.

'The rise in the appeal of synthetic grass,' he says, 'exists at the confluence of several modern, and seemingly contradictory, imperatives of suburban family living.'

Couldn't have put it better myself, Brian.

'The debilitating effects of incessant screen exposure are inarguable,' he continues. As is the need for kids to be outside, the fact that in many cases both parents work and the fact that their packed schedules simply don't allow for cleaning muck off every internal surface and maintaining the lawn. 'Run all those factors through the design algorithm and what emerges? A pragmatic response to the ever-growing problem of how to make it a more attractive proposition for the kids to get off the couch and head outside. Ergo fake grass.'

Exactamundo.

I've observed this evolution of thought many times and have encouraged lots of professionals like Brian to stop being so po-faced about synthetic lawns. I've seen them struggle with their instincts, juggling their love of nature with the need to create pan-generational appeal and to make interesting, interactive immersive outside spaces. Hey, gardens are a waste of time and do not work if there's nobody out there.

Welcome to the dark side, Brian.

Consider the consequences of inaction

The facts have been presented but then you get distracted, some other expense comes up. 'I'll do it after the holidays/in the new year/when I get my bonus/after Covid-19 …' whatever. For some reason we don't spend on the outside what we

32 This extract and the following quotations by Brian Burke were written for a Woodies brochure.

routinely spend on the interior, for example on remodelling projects. Imagine what you could achieve outside with the budget for those new kitchen units? Is a different shade of enamel in the bathroom really worth it? Imagine no jungle to face into after your holiday or after a wet spell. Think of the peace and quiet afforded to you by having that chore gone forever. Think of the time you get back. Think of the rows that will no longer occur. Your lifestyle will change for the better.

Or not. It's up to you.

Hold that thought while we work through some 'yes, but ...' objections and possible downsides.

A dozen myths

This might be a good time to expose some of the myths about fake grass that seem to have gained traction recently.

It's toxic

This myth stems from the rubber infill used in AstroTurf/sports turf. As we've learned most crumb rubber comes from chopped-up old tyres with the metal bits removed by magnets in recycling plants. Yet heavy metals such as lead cannot be extracted in the same way. In fact the American Agency for Toxic Substances and Disease Registry found dozens of metals and volatile and semi-volatile organic compounds in the black rubber specs so no surprise that there are concerns about potential carcinogens. Could it be ingested or absorbed through cuts and abrasions? Recent reports of American soccer players, notably goalkeepers being diagnosed with a particular cancer (non-Hodgkin lymphoma) have raised suspicions but current studies insist there is not an elevated health risk. Further US (EPA and Centre for Disease Control) and EU research is ongoing. Any later editions of this book will detail any and all findings, whether adverse or favourable.

So for many, although a fake grass is a great shock absorber, the jury is still out on its acceptability for sports fields. Besides the abrasion injuries already discussed, there's a risk of picking up nasty infections such as MRSA, although pitches can be treated to prevent this. How many are actually being treated though?

This book is not written to answer these questions. I've merely asked them.

Don't worry about the sand infill. Sand is a naturally occurring material, typically washed and dried in a kiln in order to be more easily brushed in. Please don't let your perception of landscape grasses be tarred with the same 'sports grass' brush.

It's full of PFOA chemicals (aka C8)

Thanks to Mark Ruffalo's recent film 'Dark Waters', this is a new concern. Since the end of World War II waaay too many chemical compounds have been invented and abound in our environment. The increase in cancers since then can be no coincidence.

In this case more durable versions of synthetic turf are made from extruded plastic polymers that are moulded into the shape of grass blades when in molten form. Well, this perfluorooctanoic acid (PFOA) 'forever chemical' compound is used to help with it's extrusion. Think of KY Jelly in different circumstances. A bit like that.

First developed in the 1940s these fluorochemicals are commonly used in products such as flame retardants, non-stick pans, pizza boxes, clothing and furniture. PFOSs are known as forever chemicals because they never fully degrade. Ruffalo's film concludes with evidence that they are already basically everywhere, including in all our bodies. Now tests show that the synthetic grass blades themselves have traces of this toxic chemical. If at 70 parts per trillion or more they are considered by the EPA to be bad news in drinking water. The specific concern is that the grass fibres, once exposed to a certain level of abrasion, can ooze out some of these chemicals into the atmosphere or water table.

This author is not in a position to judge definitively. The extrusion process can work without them so they can and should be phased out. Compared to the rubber pellets problem and recycling challenges I don't consider it to be the biggest problem with artificial grass today.

It overheats in summer

Not really an issue in the Emerald Isle. Synthetic grass can get hot, I grant you. Less so than previous generations. Due to heat dissipation, synthetic grass surfaces absorb more sunlight than they reflect, thus causing the build-up and emission of heat. Natural grass reduces the surface temperature by absorbing the sun's heat during the day and releasing it slowly in the evening. This incidentally contributes to the urban heat island effect which creates more demand for air conditioning and increases air pollution (the solution is more trees).

Without the photosynthetic properties of natural grass there is no inbuilt auto cooldown process. If it's too hot don't walk on it in bare feet. Maybe wear flip flops – I draw the line at sandals. Hose it down. Beach sand or even concrete/asphalt paths are far more prone to causing third degree burns on feet.

It's too expensive
Or is it simply that you can't afford it? There are plenty of cheap products on the market but my advice is not to scrimp on it, or on the installation either. Quality grasses are excellent and long-lasting. Taking watering, environmental concerns and time saved into consideration it is quite easy to justify financially. Some estimate payback to be only three to five years.

It's not safe for children
Totally untrue. It's completely safe and significantly better than most alternatives. Think of it as an outdoor waterproof carpet. Are indoor carpets dangerous for kids? No. It's safe, soft and fun to play on with no grass stains on knees. We've installed it in hundreds of primary schools and crèches without incident. I rest my case.

It's not safe for dogs
As per above. My dog Darcy loves it, as do thousands of dogs in gardens we've done over the years. We get photos and feedback all the time. Not from the dogs. From their owners.
We installed it in the Irish Guide Dogs training centre in Cork city many years ago. The Dublin Society for Prevention of Cruelty to Animals (DSPCA) has 50 to 100 dogs playing on our grass without incident every day. Admittedly they use our non-biological anti-bacterial spray to get rid of the smell of urine. Loads of dog kennel owners buy our grass. They can't all be wrong.

It's bad for the environment
I refer you to the contents of this book so far. Plus most forthcoming chapters. Then make up your own mind.

It looks terrible/not real/fake/bad
Indeed. It didn't look great in the 1980s when on the fruit and veg shop displays, I'll give you that. It has come on in leaps and bounds since the Brady Bunch had it in their backyard, in all fairness. If badly installed or with visible joins, yes,

it can be a terrible eyesore. Lawn snobs scoff at the naffness of it but ask any family who once lived with a quagmire if they'd like their old lawn back.

It holds water
Eh, no it doesn't. Not if installed correctly.

It's hard to maintain
Patently untrue. Relative to a real lawn the requirement of an occasional brush up is insignificant. Property developers are churning out postage stamp-sized gardens with no space for a shed let alone a mower and often badly drained with very poor topsoil over heavily compacted clay. What are people to do? It's not a question of hating nature, rather a practical solution to making what outdoor space people have more usable.

It won't last
OK, that's true. But during its (conservatively estimated) 20-year-plus lifespan you'd have had to cut your lawn 540 times. In my 20 years in the business we've been paid to go back and replace an old synthetic lawn only twice. Once because all the kids had grown up and moved out and their small patch was looking tired, and the other time they just fancied one of our newer grasses instead. The lawn I installed in my last home, front and back, has been down over 19 years and despite constant use looks as verdant as the day we rolled it out.

Once it deteriorates that's it
Not quite. While a periodic brush and clean will prolong its life and keep it looking good for longer, at some point it may be worthwhile giving it a good once over. It can be power hosed – carefully, at an angle so as not to disturb the build-up underneath. It can be vigorously brushed, removing all the accumulated debris and it will be nicely spruced up for another while.

The disadvantages
Now, in the interests of fair play, let's take a proper comprehensive look at the cons.

Cons

Please forgive my little joke.

Of course, like everything there can be downsides. This book would be incomplete, fraudulent even, without addressing them. I realise the thought of retiring the lawnmower permanently is appealing but before you run out and tear up your lawn please understand all the ramifications and potential drawbacks. If you are married or a co-owner, it needs to be a joint decision. Another reason for having this book I guess. Now let's see what the lawn snobs are scoffing at.

Appearance
Be aware that your synthetic lawn won't change with the seasons. Sure, there'll be leaves on it in autumn and snow perhaps in winter but the colour underneath will not change. In summer dry spells your neighbours could have brown baked grass and your green one will stand out.

A *badly laid* lawn, say with visible joins or, worse, with the nap of the fibres not uniform, can stick out like a sore thumb. We'll look at these potential flaws in Chapter 15. Or worse, after all the trouble and expense of installing a nice artificial lawn *people don't even notice,* thus by definition they can't be impressed.

It's costly
Yep. There's no getting away from it. To do it right will cost a chunk of your hard-earned money. But remember when you buy quality you only wince once. Plus the pain of a poor quality purchase stays with you long after the smug satisfaction of a 'deal' has long evaporated. You get what you pay for. We'll come back to what price you can expect to pay later, in Chapter 14.

It's smelly
It can be. If you are worried that it might become a hotbed for bacteria it can be easily treated with eco-friendly biocides. On its own it's odourless but we all know that the pong of uric acid from dog isn't good. Dog wee on real lawns kills the grass, leaving lots of circular burned patches, but it won't damage the synthetic grass in any way. It's an easily solvable issue thankfully.

It's lots of work to keep it
Not by comparison to real grass. Just a bit of aftercare, the odd sweep or blast of a leaf blower (or even a vacuum cleaner) and Bob's your uncle. Leaves and loose debris ought to be cleaned off periodically, but not necessarily daily or even weekly. I often think a few leaves on the (fake) lawn make it more natural looking.

It flattens

True. Eventually. After heavy or prolonged use the fibres can be prone to flattening. Particularly where it is most walked upon, perhaps on the way to the clothes line or shed. Thus an occasional brush up (preferably with a stiff-bristled brush or a plastic rake, don't use metal) is recommended. It may not come back to 100 percent but I can honestly report that in my almost two decades of selling and installing grass I've never once had a complaint about this phenomenon. So in summary it can and does happen but I think people just accept it, or more likely over time don't notice. Perhaps by then they appreciate all the other benefits and don't really care.

It requires professional installation

Maybe. If you are handy and carefully follow instructions or say buy a book on the subject (thanks again!), you should be OK.

It can't feed wildlife

Thus hastening biodiversity collapse and threatening human food production. It's a Chernobyl for worms and wildlife. But can your frequently cut monocultural lawn do them much good either? It would need to be a diverse wildflower meadow to provide the basics, including nectar and pollen.

It's no good in the event of a zombie apocalypse

If civilisation collapses because our current consumerist capitalist culture depletes the earth's resources with overpopulation and climate change or maybe just because of a pandemic, it'll admittedly be more difficult to grow your own food with an artificial lawn (all the more reason to retain some of your topsoil to make planting beds).

141

Reversing the process is possible but costly. I refer here to removing the stone and putting back in good soil and not to saving the planet of course. Also possible but costly, I guess. Some customers think, 'Ah shur, we'll put it back to real grass when the kids grow up/move out.' Never happens. Anyway with zombies roaming the streets you mightn't have time to grow carrots. Besides, your starving neighbours will just nick them.

(Please don't misconstrue my facetiousness as callousness. If you didn't laugh you'd cry.)

It's degenerate counterfeit kitsch

Fake grass has long been derided by our green-fingered friends. But in retaliation I could say that 'real' lawns are in a permanent state of eerie suspended animation, bereft as they are of the chance to flower and go to seed. If you think about it, the constantly frustrated work of a living lawn is to self-destruct. It's alive but barely. Almost zombielike.

It creates run-off

Real grass allows rainwater to naturally seep down into the soil. With a proper base, synthetic grass allows the same thing to happen. Depending on the compaction of earth beneath the build-up, storm water run-off contributes to urban flooding. Concrete driveways and patios are far worse offenders. Fake grass then is part of the solution. The proper fix of course is planting more trees.

It kills soil microbes

We'd argue this often happens with heavy plant machinery as housing estates are under construction, either via compaction or excessive mounding. It's often the reason we get called in. At least the soil we remove is recycled and reused, either in the same garden or elsewhere.

It's vulnerable to attack by vermin

Perhaps, but it's rare. It's in far more danger from your puppy than from any unwanted and/or nocturnal animal visitors.

In the past we've had one or two issues with foxes. I personally suspect they are attracted to the smell of fresh glue. The worst they've ever done is either poo on it or dig the beds spreading soil over the grass. Like their canine cousins I guess they just like playing and rolling around on it.

Rats. Everybody hates rats. People with wooden decks probably host a family of them without knowing it. Only once have they chewed a hole in our grass.

Our last vermin take the biscuit, however. And when I say take the biscuit I mean literally take the biscuit, or chips or indeed sandwich. I'm referring, of course, to the dreaded seagulls. They seem to have a contempt for humanity bordering on sheer hostility. Having recently completed a Dublin city centre school, near the River Liffey, we had a large payment delayed because of them. Reportedly they would congregate daily on the roof at precisely 10.55 a.m. in advance of the 11 a.m. break so they could swoop down and rob the kids' snacks whenever the opportunity arose. The rotters!

But when they attacked our grass it got serious. Seemingly some were nesting nearby and they decided our loose fibres would make great nesting material. That's fine, they were welcome to them. But when we were finished and had brushed away all remaining loose debris and tidied up they kept pulling at the fresh joins with their beaks. We soon redid the joins and got paid – just in the nick of time before Covid-19 closed every school in the country – but they are an enemy to be reckoned with. Do not underestimate them.

It's plastic for God's sake!
Indeed, just like an awful lot of other things in this human-made environment we live in. Critics attack its sterility. They say it's dismal, inert and unchanging. Sure, but plastic is a ubiquitous, durable and versatile material. Yes, although it doesn't have to be, it's mostly petroleum-based. Hopefully someday soon it'll all be fully recycled and recyclable. Let's be honest, it's an inorganic surface that's made to look like grass. Is it, to play devil's advocate, really any more gross than covering a garden with stones, cobblelock brick, concrete paving slabs or tarmac? Don't forget that natural shiny porcelain paving you fancy is a product that requires particularly high energy manufacture and shipping.

It can give you a shock
Unlike Michael Jackson I hate getting even a mild electric shock. As kids growing up on the farm we used to have competitions to see who could keep hold of the electrified livestock fence the longest. I always lost. Or chickened out altogether.

But the answer is yes. This, although rare, can be an issue, as with a lot of floor covering. I avoid the supermarket as I always get a jolt from touching the metal trolley. Setting my hair on end and feeling my fillings tingle in my teeth is not my idea of fun. Non-infill grasses can, on occasion, be prone to the generation of static, especially in playgrounds with lots of movement (did you ever whip off an acrylic jumper in the dark?) when combined with metal (play) equipment and/or fencing. For example, sliding down even a plastic slide at speed can create an electric charge.

The solution/trick is to brush in kiln-dried sand, particularly around the perimeter, to alleviate it. But better still simply spraying on diluted off-the-shelf fabric softener works a treat. It acts in the same way as it does with clothing. Even one treatment, regardless of the size of the area, seems to last indefinitely. It's quick and cheap to repeat in any case. Others have experimented with earthing the grass with metal pins with mixed results. Forever Lawn, a UK supplier, has developed and patented a non-conductive polymeric compound infused into the grass which apparently helps dissipate static build-up in the first place.

It's another barrier between children and nature

Research shows that kids today suffer from 'nature deficit disorder'. They do need to be in touch with living greenery for optimum physical and mental health. But we believe it would be far better for the kids to be outside in the first place, even if it's on a fake lawn. Then they have some chance of observing nature, much better surely than playing Fortnite, FIFA, making faces on Tik-Tok or incessantly Snapchatting.

Anecdotally at least, we know people use their gardens far more after getting a fake lawn. You will find they plant and garden *more* as a result.

There can be weeds in fake grass

Yes, that's true, if the base is substandard or if they seed from above, just as weeds can seed in walls and concrete and anywhere else. At least in a fake lawn they are easily spotted and removed – either carefully by hand getting their roots and all or by spraying them. Salt, vinegar or chemicals, such as Roundup etc., will *not* damage the grass in any way.

In her 1962 book *Silent Spring* Rachel Carson explained that humans have an exceptionally narrow attitude towards nature. If we see utility in a plant it gets fostered; if deemed undesirable it is condemned to destruction. Thus our culture sees dandelions in a yard as a failure of citizenry. Once upon a time they were a valued source of medicine. With their really deep roots they are a curse to kill though.

There can be moss in fake grass

Also true but the same as above. It's less likely to appear if there is no sand infill in the grass. But in shady spots it can be inevitable eventually. Again, you can use sulphate of ammonia or simple elbow grease. Physically remove it or kill it and brush it off. If it's bad or well established you might have to do this a couple of times.

It's flammable

Not really. It will melt in the first instance rather than catch fire. It's widely used along airport runways and indeed on the margins of Formula One race tracks so it can't be particularly dangerous. If a hot coal falls from your barbecue, it will singe and damage your grass. So too can a lit cigarette blacken off a small area where it is carelessly thrown. In smoking areas of pubs, hotels and nightclubs, as mentioned, we either insist on brushing in kiln-dried sand that acts as a fire retardant or we specify a particular grass that has the official fire rating certification. The vast majority of synthetic grasses have a low rating whereas our 'Fair' grass, for example, has a Cfl s1 certification. We install it indoors for a variety of applications all the time.

It can melt in direct sunlight

No, it doesn't *but* beware of concentrated light. Synthetic grasses have a very high melting point at 200 plus degrees Fahrenheit. Reflective surfaces, say a window or a mirror, can generate heat in excess of that. So take note of west- and south-facing windows. A filter or sunscreen may need to be fitted. These inexpensive solutions also contribute to the energy efficiency of the house.

I've seen streaks of melted grass across a lawn where sunlight over the daylight hours bounces off an ornamental mirror in the garden. It's simple to stop it happening. Simply move or angle the mirror away.

TIP

When considering the effects of sunlight on your lawn, be wary of shiny chrome planters.

Another problem that arises is when you or your gardener simply lays down a chainsaw, hedge trimmer or whatever on top of the grass. If the engine is hot it will melt and mark the grass. Yes, a patch can be switched out but then it's new versus old so it won't initially look identical and it can be challenging to match up the batches.

Is a fake lawn really acceptable?

Many serious gardeners remain unconvinced. They are horrified and offended by its existence. Ordinary people, not zealous adherents to the cult of the lawn, possibly parents to several small children, are proving to be much more open-minded. They are voting with their wallets. A real lawn quickly turns into a quagmire in their world. I sometimes wonder if hostility is driven more by snobbery than genuine environmental concern?

Across the Irish Sea a prim and proper lawn is seen as part of England's heritage. It's one of the things that make us British, they say. Fake grass, they say, is naff and a blight on 'England's green and pleasant land'. Here in Ireland we have a slightly more relaxed attitude towards this particular pursuit of perfection. Perhaps it's a post-colonial thing. Advocates pour their heart and soul into the work, their rituals keeping it between 2.5cm and 4.5cm in height (or they would if they ever accepted the metric system). So some hesitancy and hostility is to be expected. In the UK alone billions of pounds are spent annually on lawn care. In the US it's tens of billions.

Maybe someday 'real' lawns will be frowned upon in the same way fake ones are today.

So there you have it. Ultimately it's up to you to decide.

But before that let me tell you how one lonely guy with a whacky new idea introduced it to the entire country, eventually making it big in the Emerald Isle.

Before & After

Before & After

Before & After

Chapter 9

Building a blooming business

*'Half the money I spend on advertising is wasted; the trouble is
I don't know which half'* [33]
~ John Wanamaker, marketing pioneer

They say every business person needs a good elevator pitch. When asked, I tell people I'm 'the Fake Grass Man' but their eyes glaze over a bit. Then I ask, have you ever seen any of our hairy green vans on the road and they invariably light up with 'Oh, yeah, is that you?!' As a guerrilla marketing exercise it's been highly effective. Running a fleet of lorries and vans is no picnic.

Pulling back the curtain

The first time we exhibited artificial grass we were laughed at. In retrospect those jokers did me a huge favour. It was either go home with my tail between my legs or use that public ridicule as motivation. Remember, people just want the product of your product. The benefits not the features. If artificial grass is the sausage, then getting your garden back and never mowing again is the sizzle.

In keeping with the 'how to' nature of this book I want to describe how we successfully marketed it in the Emerald Isle. How we zagged when others zigged. To be frank my biggest fear had always been the fear of selling. Well, that and going to the dentist. The solution? Do it anyway.

It took me a long time to get over myself, fear of rejection and foolish pride being the main blockers. I had sought out a sales rep job to get experience. In the end it was a simple change of mindset that did the trick. The answer? Don't sell. Instead just help people find what's right for them and then help them to make up their minds. In the case of artificial grass it's not so much the technical specifications of the grass or the installation methodology, the slickness of our service or even the price. It's the satisfying feeling the client gets opening their curtains every morning and looking out and the laughter of their children playing on it. Their 'grassitude'.

---

33 Quotation often incorrectly attributed to showman PT Barnum, who coined the adage 'There's a sucker born every minute', although that clearly has no relevance here.

Go big or go home:
Getting the maximum bang for your marketing buck

'Do not follow where a path may lead. Go instead where there is no path and leave a trail' is scribbled in the back of my diary.

I've no idea who said it.

My challenge, with zero financial backing and limited resources, was to get maximum bang for my marketing buck. My suggestion to any budding entrepreneurs is to constantly reinvest all profits. The first couple of decades are usually the hardest.

Consider the grim (US but probably fairly universal) statistics.

Four out of five new start-ups fail within the first two years. Some 96 per cent of all businesses are gonzo within ten. Of the 4 percent that do survive, many are barely ticking over. What's more, 95 per cent of *those* companies will never reach USD$1 million in annual sales. Finally, of those rare few, 95 per cent never make it to USD$5 million. Yes, I know, turnover is fairly meaningless without decent net margins. But by the above criteria I think it's fair to say we've done alright.

Before I could even sell I had to tell.

To educate an ambivalent market.

> *'Every battle is won before it is fought'*
> ~ Sun Tzu (and later, Napoleon)

I guess they were referring to having a plan, understanding the market/ battlefield and marshalling sufficient resources/troops. In truth I was more John Wanamaker than Sun Tzu. In the absence of a specific plan, try everything. Then something must surely work. Focusing on 'awareness' and 'branding' (what people say about you when you are not in the room) wouldn't cut any ice. I had to immediately start flogging plastic lawns to once-off customers. Possibly not the best business model in the world as there's not much by way of built-in obsolescence.

You'll recall my first move when home from San Francisco over 20 years ago. I pinned a handwritten note to the local supermarket notice board and a day later I was working in a local schoolteacher's garden. I learned three valuable lessons that day:
- The value of putting yourself out there, regardless of experience.
- The schoolteacher had got three quotes; I was neither the cheapest nor

the most expensive. She said she was nervous about hiring the cheapest guys. Don't be those guys.

- Never bury weeds and roots of weeds. Much better to take them off site.

Word of mouth

In the very earliest days I started simply telling people about it. Anyone who'd listen. Word-of-mouth is a powerful tool. I guess some of my passion shone through. The next logical step was a logo and business cards. Sanctuary Landscapes became Sanctuarysynthetics.ie. I've always insisted on installation teams and sales personnel wearing logoed gear. It adds a touch of professionalism and puts the customers at their ease.

At the Ideal Home Show there's a show home, including a garden, constructed within the venue. We've happily supplied our grass to several designers for it over the years. Thus we have a presence without the expense, pain and grief of always building and staffing a stand of our own.

My friend, the inimitable Michael O'Reilly, runs garden design clinics at numerous shows nationwide. What forms the basis of their stands? You guessed it, our grass. In our first year at GLAS, a horticultural trade fair sponsored by Bord Bia, we unveiled our hairy green caravan and won best in show. It may have helped that we obliged the organisers by putting a synthetic putting green outside for the amusement of attendees.

Branding and livery

I ensure all our vehicles, signage, websites and ads share the same look and feel to give a cohesive feel to our brand. There's a lot of noise out there and we'd have no hope of gaining traction without consistency.

In any market there are always early adopters. An executive commissioned us to landscape around his newly built house including a particularly big artificial lawn, the results of which formed the basis of our first proper **glossy A5 flyer**. I did get a bit of a fright, however, when I went to get paid. The guy was uncontactable. Uh oh! Turns out he had just had a heart attack. Thankfully he survived and the payment came through before I had one myself.

I joined the local Chamber of Commerce. You can't beat **networking** with like minded people who share the same challenges as yourself. I plucked up the courage to enter their annual awards. No joy. Then entered again and failed again. Eventually myself and senior staff enjoyed a black tie dinner in the K Club and were honoured to win **SME of the Year** 2017. This recognition led to more publicity and some bad hangovers.

I deliberately created a **second brand name – Grassland**. It's more Google-friendly. Think Disneyland but green. Sanctuary Synthetics, a mouthful and difficult to spell, is the company and Grassland is the place. At HQ both names feature and are repeated on our vehicles. I've been advised this is a mistake but I'm a bit pigheaded when it comes to these decisions. We'll see.

Website

At over 800 pages – excerpts from this book will likely increase that further – www.sanctuarysynthetics.ie is a long-established and hopefully informative website. Our much-copied template has gone through several iterations. Running a website is an arms race. What was cutting edge even six months ago is now dated and naff, or worse too slow to load. We feature different galleries with copious before and after photos, videos, detailed installation and technical information, testimonials ('wish we had got it years ago' being a frequent post installation comment), a bespoke calculator, our history, FAQs and case studies. Check it out (and subscribe to our e-newsletter for competitions and special offers).

Videos

We jumped on the YouTube band wagon early enough. Our channel has hundreds of videos with, cumulatively, over a million views. Not bad for a niche product in a small country. We deployed drones as soon as they were commercially available (always get permission, folks). **Time-lapse videos** work very well. Notably we set up several cameras at different angles to record the construction and exhibiting of our 2018 Bloom 'Upside Down' show garden. You can watch it here: www. Sanctuarysynthetics.ie/bloom/.

A Dublin GAA sports star asked us to replace his small lawn. Given that he has All-Star awards and, at the time, five All-Ireland medals I suggested we do it for a substantial discount in exchange for an interview. I got Graham, a big Dublin GAA fan from our crew, to interview his hero. Using a prepared script – we had come up with some off-the-wall questions – the chat went very well. We've since laid lawns for other players and some blue grass for the Dubs in exchange for a photo shoot.

We also have a series of **Gift Grass** videos starring famous comedian Mario Rosenstock (see www.giftgrass.ie). If you are not Irish you might not get it. Just take my word for it – he's hilarious. The videos already have about 100,000

The wonderfully gifted Mario Rosenstock came to Grassland for a visit with a few of his well known characters.

Mario as Pádraig Harrington

Michael Flatley meets Father Ted

Mario as Miriam

The formalities of meeting Mario as President of Ireland

Mario as Francis Brennan

Mario as Healy-Rae

Mario as Paschal Donohoe

THE IRISH TIMES

irishtimes.com

Thursday, May 31, 2018
€2.00 (incl. VAT)
£1.50 Northern Ireland.

OECD warns of overheating in Irish economy

Agency points to rapid increase in new mortgages and loans to SMEs

It says lending restrictions may need to be extended to cool credit growth

EOIN BURKE-KENNEDY
and JOE BRENNAN

Signs of overheating have begun to emerge in the Irish economy, the Organisation for Economic Co-operation and Development (OECD) has warned.

In its latest economic outlook report, the Paris-based agency said new mortgage loans and loans to small firms than 90 per cent in the space of four weeks, as investors feared the country was hurtling towards fresh elections and a referendum on its continuation in the euro zone.

However, the yield on Ireland's 10-year bonds have remained within a tight range around the 1 per cent level for the past month.

Employment growth

"Unlike previous periods of euro zone uncertainty, it seems that investors have in effect reclassified Ireland as much closer to the euro zone core than to the periphery," NTMA chief executive Conor O'Kelly said.

In its report on Ireland, the OECD said economic activity here would remain robust in the near term, fuelled by "solid employment growth and consumption", before gradually easing.

It said, however, that the Government needed to keep improving its fiscal position to create a buffer against future economic shocks, most notably Brexit, which posed the biggest downside risk to Ireland's economic outlook.

"Property prices may increase more strongly, which would boost further construction activity in the near term but may induce another property bubble associated with a strong surge in credit growth," it said.

European Commission officials also warned yesterday that "persistent supply shortages" in Ireland's property market was fuelling property price increases.

terday that the steady performance of Irish government bonds in the face of such market turbulence was evidence that investors had "reclassified" the nation's creditworthiness.

The market interest rate, or yield, on Italy's 10-year bonds spiked on Tuesday at 3.44 per cent, their highest level since 2014, having surged by more looking report, their highest level since 2014, having surged by more were extended to cool the current level of credit growth.

Figures published yesterday by the Banking and Payments Federation showed the value of new mortgage lending approved in April jumped by 20 per cent to €842 million compared to the same time last year.

In its report, the OECD also raised the prospect of "another property bubble" if the current rate of annual house-price growth, now running at 13 per cent, continued.

The warning follows a Central Bank study earlier this week which said nearly 4 per cent, or almost 8,000 mortgages taken out before the crash could default in the event of a financial shock. These loans are currently not in default.

The last time the OECD warned about the possibility of a housing bubble in Ireland was on the eve of the financial crash in June 2006, a warning that was ignored by the then government.

Steady performance

The OECD's caution comes amid ongoing political turmoil in Italy that has rocked bond markets in recent days and renewed concern about the sustainability of national debt levels in several EU member states.

The head of the National Treasury Management Agency (NTMA), however, said yes-

■ Debt could damage Ireland's economy, warns OECD: Business

Defying gravity The only way is upside down at Bloom festival in the Phoenix Park

■ Monica Alvarez, a mentor on RTÉ's *Super Garden*, joined a gravity-defying Shane Houlihan in the upside down garden at Bord Bia's Bloom festival which begins in the Phoenix Park, Dublin, today and runs until Monday. PHOTOGRAPH: NICK BRADSHAW

Zappone wants to speed up Adoption Bill

FIACH KELLY
Deputy Political Editor

Legislation that would allow adoptees secure information about their adoptions should pass through the Oireachtas by the end of the year if there is co-operation across the Dáil and Seanad, Minister for Children Katherine Zappone has said.

The Government has denied that the Adoption (Information and Tracing) Bill has been stalled, and Ms Zappone said her department would now engage with TDs and Senators to speed up its passage.

The Minister was speaking during statements in the Seanad last night on incorrect birth registrations.

It came a day after Ms Zap-

pone revealed that up to 126 people whose births were incorrectly registered are to learn that their parents are not their birth parents.

The incorrect registrations were uncovered in an analysis of the records of the St Patrick's Guild adoption society and apply to people who had had their adoptive parents incorrectly registered as their birth parents on their birth certificates between 1946 and 1969.

Tusla, the child and family agency, has allocated a social worker to each of the 126 cases. Its first task is to identify individuals involved and establish their addresses. A helpline established following the disclosure had, as of yesterday afternoon, responded to 85 calls.

On foot of the controversy,

Taoiseach Leo Varadkar and Ms Zappone were questioned about the passage of the Adoption (Information and Tracing) Bill. The Bill aims to provide an adopted person a statutory right to their birth certificate and information about their adoption order, even if this was years ago.

Balance

In the Dáil, Mr Varadkar apologised to those affected and denied the Government was stalling the legislation in question. He said the Government was a minority administration and he appealed to the Opposition to facilitate the Bill's passage through the Oireachtas.

Ms Zappone put forward similar arguments and said the "main thing" was that she wanted to "get this right". The Bill

was published in 2016 and has passed second stage in the Seanad and is awaiting committee stage.

"As we are all well aware, following our second stage debate, the Bill seeks to balance competing rights to identity and privacy, and getting the balance right is proving challenging," Ms Zappone said.

"The Bill is of relevance to persons the subject of incorrect

registrations as well as to adopted persons. My intention is that the Bill will be enacted by the end of the year."

In weighing up competing rights, Ms Zappone said: "We can't enact something that is perceived by the Attorney General to be unconstitutional."

■ Adoption controversy news and analysis: pages 2-3

Journalist turns up at press briefing called to reveal details of his murder

DANIEL McLAUGHLIN

In a scene that could have come straight from a James Bond film, or a gialmi one Ukrainian deputy said was worthy of Sherlock Holmes, dissident Russian journalist Arkady Babchenko appeared alive and well in Kiev yesterday, at a press conference that was called to reveal details of his bloody murder.

Ukraine's SBU security agency said the apparent death of Mr Babchenko – who was reportedly shot at his Kiev apartment on Tuesday night – was part of a sting operation to catch killers allegedly hired by the Russian secret services.

"I'm still alive," an emotional Mr Babchenko told reporters, who gasped and then cheered his reappearance, amid an outpouring of grief from friends and colleagues following the announcement of his murder.

"I'm sorry, but there was no other way of doing it. Separately, I want to apologise to my wife for the hell that she has been through," said the journalist, who moved to Kiev last year after receiving death threats in Russia for criticising its president, Vladimir Putin, and its military operations in Ukraine and Syria.

Mr Babchenko (41) said he had co-operated with the SBU after it told him a month ago that a $40,000 contract had been put out for his murder.

SBU chief Vasyl Hrytsak said his agents had arrested a Ukrainian citizen who had been paid by Russia's security services to arrange the killing of Mr Babchenko.

Russian foreign ministry spokeswoman Maria Zakharova dismissed the affair as a "propaganda" exercise.

■ Journalist 'shot dead' turns up alive: page 11

Weather

Hazy sunshine will give way to cloud and showers, some heavy and thundery in the north and west. Highs of 20-23 degrees.

THE IRISH TIMES
24-28 Tara Street, Dublin 2, D02 CX89
Telephone: 01-6758000
Fax: Newsdesk 6758036 Sport 6758033 Business 6758048 Advertising 6758052
Online: irishtimes.com
The recommended retail price of THE IRISH TIMES in the Republic of Ireland is €2.00
Subscriptions: Tel: 6758659 • Fax: 6758677
Email: subscribe@irishtimes.com

Home News

Abortion: Minister for Health Simon Harris is considering covering the cost of care for all women seeking a termination of pregnancy: page 7

Security: Gardaí in Border stations want the return of machine guns ahead of a possible hard Brexit: Page 8

World News

Turmoil: Italy searched for a last-minute exit from three months of political turmoil, with a renewed attempt to form a coalition government: page 9

Business + Technology

Apple: The State has paid €4.5 million in legal fees relating to its battle with the European Commission over its €13 billion ruling on state aid to Apple.

Scottish football: Concern has been expressed over links between Murdoch MacLennan and Dermot Desmond

Sports Thursday

Rugby: Clarification about where Joey Carbery will play next season is expected today from Ireland coach Joe Schmidt: page 16

Soccer: Roy Keane pays tribute to John O'Shea who is departing the international stage after 17 years: page 17

Vol No 50135, Thursday, May 31 2018

Lotto: 11, 13, 14, 16, 31, 36 (5) – no winner. Plus 1: 2, 5, 12, 14, 18, 19 (9). Plus 2: 4, 10, 19, 22, 25, 42 (29).

ISH TIMES
How to lure the Dragons into coughin
As entrepreneurs are invited to apply for the new series of Dragons' Den, Mark O'Loughlin, whose company Hidbin.ie secured investment on the RTE show, gives them some tips
Mark O'Loughlin: try to anticipate the questions
THE SANCTUARY NURTURE GARDEN
Sponsored by: Sanctuary Synthetics and The Phoenix Park Specialist School
Designer: Dominic O'Donohoe
www.sanctuarysynthetics.ie
This garden showcases the use of artificial grass in a school setting, specifically for children with severe specialist needs by drawing a direct relationship between the nurturing of plants, fruit, flowers and trees and the nurturing of children through their early formative years.
surrounded by multisensory planting allowing children to connect with nature on a safe soft artificial surface. Mature woodland planting surrounds the school comprising mature oak, chestnut and birches, complemented by native planting based on sight, smell, taste, sound and touch on the bottom half of the mound.
sanctuarysynthetics.ie
FANTASTIC SUNDAY WORLD COMPETITION
WIN A GARDEN MAKEOVER
A beautiful new lawn and landscape worth €5,000 could be yours
SUNDAY WORLD
www.sanctuarysynthetics.ie
It's garden time
Michael D finds he has a rabbit fan base on his walk in the Park
vd for flowers and fun
aside – is they ca
hot in warm weath
considering our su
late shouldn't be an
Prices range from €6
depending on quality a
includes installation, re
of existing lawn and all
groundworks.
sanctuarysynthetics.ie
a city in Bloom
Show some real flower power and ban the car
GARDENING
dare winners Bloom with pride
kildarepost 53
Bord Bia Food Village
Bloom 2012
The Growise Garden in association with Kildare Growers designed by Tim Austen, Austen Associates, Wicklow
The Steam Museum Garden designed by Sophie Graefin Von Maltzan, Dublin and Lodge Park Steam Museum Garden, Kildare
The 'Alice in Wonderland' Sanctuary Garden designed by Mark O'Loughlin, Sanctuary Synthetics, Kildare

views and counting on YouTube. They nicely encapsulate our philosophy. Yes, Mario's 'on message' in the videos but first and foremost it's entertaining. It's fun. To break down barriers and hostility you need to make people laugh.

It works for us.

Email marketing

People are sick of spam. I certainly am. But it remains a powerful tool to reach prospects (subject of course to GDPR rules). We regularly send out e-newsletters to more than 5,000 people on our database. We have healthy opening rates and surprisingly few unsubscribes. I guess people are curious to see what others are doing in their gardens. It's another way to remain in the forefront of people's minds. Wasn't Auntie Joan just admiring our lawn. Here, forward her that email. The trick is to be there when they eventually do decide to get the ball rolling. Plus I have a trade blog at www.thefakegrassman.com.

Social media

I only opened a **Facebook** account in 2009. A decade later we've a semi-respectable 8,300 followers, over 1,200 **Twitter** followers and I've a decent LinkedIn presence plus we're growing on **Instagram**, all great visual platforms. We post frequently and get great engagement in terms of feedback, comments, customer pics, recommendations (over 60 five-star reviews) and lots of Grassland check-ins.

What bank can I cash all that in I hear you ask? None. It's just another avenue to reach people. Naturally we are not immune to the ubiquitous trolls and the jealous keyboard warriors.

Giveaways and competitions

I had a spare pair of U2 tickets for a long-sold-out homecoming gig in Dublin's Croke Park which we raffled to coincide with the launch of a short e-book we wrote about rejuvenating childhood games (that could be played on our fake grass of course). Now every time there's a bank holiday we find ourselves giving away some relevant festive door mats or hairy bird houses to lucky winners among our loyal fans.

Sponsorships

We sponsor the annual Garden and Landscape Designers Association (GLDA) seminar and the Association of Landscape Contractors of Ireland (ALCI) awards. These have proven their worth in overcoming hostility and networking. I've even been invited to speak at these events, which was fun.

Because artificial grass is so handy for presentations, shows, expos, decorations, and theatre, festivals and outdoor events we get frequent requests from a variety of charities for donations, many of whom we oblige. I'm always a sucker for getting our grass out in public. We've sponsored sports team jerseys. It's a bonus when they win stuff.

We were once cornered into supporting a fundraising 'Who wants to be a millionaire?' night for a gaelscoil (Irish-speaking school). Couldn't refuse really as we'd covered half their yard months earlier. Later we got the contract to cover the second half of their yard. Our grass is used for pop-up picnic gardens and covering entire streets. There's an urban rooftop gardening charity, to whom we've given copious offcuts, which got TV coverage.

We've twice installed free lawns on behalf of the wonderful Make a Wish Foundation, the second of which was for their televised 1,000th wish granted in Ireland, a new fairy garden in west Dublin. The stories behind the wishes would melt the heart of a stone.

We donate unused offcuts to Recreate Ireland, a recycling depot for artists and schoolchildren. They take all sizes, however small, so it's a win-win with less waste for landfill.

Partnering with Deloitte for a corporate and social responsibility project we revamped a deprived inner city school and have twice donated and installed it in the National Children's Hospice. God love them. Ditto with an adult special needs facility, St John of God's, which struggles to get the same attention.

More locally we support the Tidy Towns. Sometime in the 1950s the weather was so horrendous for the local Saint Patrick's Day parade (yay, no more snakes[34]) that the local council passed a motion to never hold another so we now have an Easter parade instead. We've twice taken part, winning prizes both times. My two kids certainly enjoyed the ride.

---

34 The symbol of Naas, a serpent, is derived from the town's Latin motto: *'Prudens ut serpens'* — wise as a serpent. There is a myth that St Patrick himself drove the serpents out of Ireland and some Naas folk like to believe their town might have been the location of the showdown. Before Emperor Constantine recognised Christianity in the 300s AD, a Christian splinter group, a North African Gnostic sect called the Naassenes, worshipped snakes. According to an amusing apocryphal tale, the Naassenes, facing persecution from the official church, fled all the way to Ireland, settling in, you guessed it, Naas. The Hebrew or Semitic word for snake, *nahash*, is not terribly unlike Naas. So maybe St Patrick didn't get rid of any actual snakes at all but rather, in 432 AD, succeeded instead in banishing snake worshippers!

Press coverage

Before everything went online, I approached a prominent newspaper, the *Sunday World*, about an idea. Over several weeks it ran the Worst Garden in Ireland competition. You had to send in photos of your bad lawn and the winner would receive a €5,000 synthetic lawn makeover. This was a powerful way of getting attention and showing how our product could transform even the worst spaces. All it cost us was the price of giving the winners a new lawn.

Boy, did we get some doozies! There were floods of entries, the worst of which featured on double page spreads week after week. The winners were of course delighted with the results, and the before and after pictures featured prominently.

We repeated this format more than a decade later; this time on the radio.

National press coverage is always nice, but it's easier to start with the **local papers**. Remember, they are gasping for original stuff to cover. You'll recall our Sallins stampede story from earlier. We also got coverage from volunteering to do up the retirement home down the road.

I once did a one-day course in writing press releases. Much more powerful than any advertising.

Leading up to Bloom 2018 and long after my *Dragons' Den* success (see next chapter) I got a call from the *Sunday Independent*. Would I like to be interviewed by well-known businessman, *Dragons' Den* investor, author, speaker and presidential candidate Mr Sean Gallagher?

Does a bear shite in the woods? Absolutely! He had a prominent column in the business section of the *Irish Independent* newspaper (circulation: one million). Soon he was down, staff photographer in tow, and wrote a very flattering article dubbing me the **Lawn Ranger**.[35] I had prepared in advance, with a copy of *his* new book casually strewn on my desk ready to be signed. So even though we were not doing a garden for Bloom that year we featured prominently in the *Irish Independent*, much to the chagrin of some fellow garden designers. 'How the hell do you do it?'

Our gardens have featured in the property section of newspapers and we've been quoted on more than one occasion. In the lead up to Bloom 2016 my long-suffering PR representative Liz came up trumps arranging another business interview, this time in *The Irish Times*.[36]

35 Sean Gallagher, 'The lawn ranger is riding high', *Sunday Independent*, 27 May 2018, Business, p. 10, www.independent.ie/business/small-business/the-lawn-ranger-is-riding-high-36950085.html.
36 Mark Hilliard, 'Sowing the seeds of a new business', *The Irish Times*, 22 May 2013, Agribusiness & Food, https://www.irishtimes.com/business/agribusiness-and-food/sowing-the-seeds-of-a-new-business-1.1401442.

Our 2018 Bloom garden was the world's first upside down garden. The press, TV and public simply loved it. The judges, as we'll see later, not so much. Besides being featured on RTÉ evening news, the garden made the front page of *The Irish Times* on the opening day of the festival and the picture was among the newspaper's photos of the year.[37] Yes, some luck was involved but I had designed it specifically as a photo opportunity.

Having a **professional PR representative** paid serious dividends. Liz got us plenty of coverage we'd otherwise never have garnered, and I owe her my thanks. A positive article or endorsement, which money cannot buy, can be the making of a business.

Famous friends

On the footer of our website lurks a Famous Friends gallery. This is simply a collection of photos of me with miscellaneous celebrities. It's all about sprinkling a bit of stardust. Perhaps a sad reflection on today's shallow culture but I'd be foolish to ignore it.

Radio

I always wanted to try this medium but couldn't quite figure out how to promote such a visual product over the airwaves. In the end I scripted the pain and joy of a bewildered stay-at-home parent – bubbly Irish TV personality Lucy Kennedy. A busy working mother, Lucy well understood the frustrations of having a mucky unkempt lawn and the subsequent relief of getting it sorted. People could really relate to her. While she was our brand ambassador, her hit TV series *Living with Lucy* aired. Lucy would later come down to perform the opening of Grassland. [See photos overleaf]

After this successful Newstalk radio ad campaign we wheeled out our Worst Lawn in Ireland competition, which at first glance might not seem entirely suitable for a non-visual medium. On Today FM's Dermot and Dave show (happily we had done Dave's garden a couple of years previously) we gave away another €5,000 garden makeover where contestants posted entries on the station's website and social media.

I've been interviewed on local radio in connection to Bloom and we approached the researchers from the popular Ray D'Arcy RTÉ radio show in

---

37 Nick Bradshaw, 'Bloom: Super Garden Mentor Monica Alvarez joined a Gravity Defying Shane Houlihan enjoying the Upside Down Garden in the Phoenix Park, Dublin, ahead of the Bloom Festival' [picture], *The Irish Times*, 30 May 2018, p. 1, www.irishtimes.com/news/ireland/irish-news/images-of-the-day-1.3514140.

Grassland Grand Opening

Lucy Kennedy and Mark O'Loughlin

Grassland Grand Opening with Lucy Kennedy

Mark as Sisyphus

Marty Morrissey

Bloom
weather
forecast

Sooo, eh... do
ya come here
often like?...

Photoshoot of Alice heading for Bloom

connection with our 2013 Bloom show garden. The theme was the Wizard of Oz and we said we needed to broadcast an urgent request for 'pre-loved' Wendy houses, which, I knew from experience, littered many gardens, the kids having outgrown them. It was quirky and we invited the many donors on an exclusive tour of the completed garden. We got loads of mentions and airtime culminating in an interview on the opening day of Bloom. 'What exactly is it you guys do anyway?' said Ray predictably.

'Well, Ray, I'm glad you asked ...'

Television infomercial

Hi, I'm Troy McClure ...

Cue the glamorous Kathy Hoffman. She ran a shopping channel and came down to my garden in Naas to shoot an infomercial. We spliced in time-lapse footage of the garden transformation and we ran the ad for quite a while. Later her shopping channel was picked up by RTÉ for morning TV. This time she wanted to shoot us doing a trendy south Dublin garden. Secretly it was her own which had been designed by celebrity garden designer Diarmuid Gavin. Who watches morning TV? Loads of people it turns out and it worked. I saw how being on the telly somehow increases one's credibility. People pay more attention to what you say. This of course excludes immediate family. They never listen.

Besides being on RTÉ's *Room to Improve* we did *At Your Service*. We took part in a Christmas special transforming the residential home and garden for charity Caring and Sharing Association (CASA). The garden was to be made safer, more accessible and attractive. We duly obliged and got our airtime along with that fuzzy Christmassy feeling of having helped to make a difference in the lives of people less fortunate.

We ran **TV ads** on City Channel (a Dublin area cable TV channel) and on the Setanta Sports channel, targeting golf and rugby events to catch our ideal audience.

Of course my colleagues kindly help me to keep my feet on the ground. One Christmas I was presented with a mug for our office Kris Kindle. It features a picture of me with President Michael D. Higgins and a tagline I'd borrowed from 'B' lister Troy McClure from *The Simpsons* – 'You may know me from such things as ...'

Mobile advertising and merchandising

I got a specialist company to attach adhesive strips, featuring Bloom pictures, to our main roller door. I've developed a bit of a fetish for covering things in artificial grass, including vans. Several competitors both at home and internationally have since copied our idea. Our entire fleet is covered. My wife recently drove the hairy green jeep while her car was being serviced. She was amazed at all the smiles, waves and photos being taken as she drove around. My daughter was utterly mortified of course. Logoed up with our phone numbers and a little pointy finger saying 'Ask driver for brochure' this constitutes mobile advertising and it works.

On a whim I bought a second-hand golf buggy and covered it. It's used for occasional charity outings and at shows and parades. Coca-Cola hired it along with our jeep, trailer plus a driver at one point. It's a novelty wherever it goes. I've even had Miss Universe in it alongside yours truly.

By virtue of our involvement in Bloom we were asked by RTÉ if we could cover their giant letters which they display at big events, including our name plaque on each.

QR codes were once 'the next big thing' so we got a giant one lazer cut.

We sell both **hairy green beanbags and furniture** online as well as hiring them out for events. We now have several hairy green couches and armchairs, a coffee table, desks, stools, fold-up seats and a lounger, all ideal for promotions, selfies, product launches and, more importantly, they allow us to sit down at shows by 'demonstrating' how comfortable they are.

Eventually we bought a second-hand caravan (think *Father Ted*) and promptly covered it in grass, inside and out. Hey presto! We've now got a **mobile display unit** fully kitted out with a working cooker, kettle, fridge and even a toilet. It looks the business in grass with hairy green furniture outside. It's an effective and innovative promotional tool and we've had it at lots of shows. It too is available for hire.

I love to recycle, so the lads have a standing order to cut any small offcuts into **hairy green doormats** to leave with customers or for visitors to Grassland to take away. It's cheap goodwill. Of course we also sell them from our online shop at €15 each. We subsequently started making variations such as cutting in red love hearts for Saint Valentine's Day and shamrocks for Saint Patrick's Day. We've done ghost mats for Halloween and doggie paw ones. This way we get to re-sell our offcuts and people put them at their front doors. By virtue of lots of foot traffic the grass gets well tested. Any visitors admiring them will invariably

be told about us so it's a marketing dream really.

Entering Bloom 2013 with the 'Sanctuary Wizard of Oz' garden we accumulated a dozen pre-loved plastic Wendy houses thanks to our radio appeal. We covered one in grass for our display. We rebuilt the stone folly from Bloom as a centre piece of our outdoor display area. It lends an air of permanence to the site. Other features and **props** from our six successful Bloom show gardens have ended up adorning Grassland, giving the place a quirky, child-friendly feel for visitors.

At a German trade show I spotted a guy selling **personalised rubber ducks**. On a whim I ordered 300 with our logo. In green. I then emailed a newsletter along with two supporting short videos, and posted sample-packs and ducks out with a personalised note to our top trade customers. It worked a treat and even led to dormant accounts ordering grass again. It cost just €8 per duck to give a smile to repeat customers.

We continuously give out **logoed merchandise** including pens, notebooks, calculators, measuring tapes, bags, rulers, compasses, torches, bottle openers, diaries, memory sticks, bespoke calendars and retractable knives to name but a few. Basically anything likely to be kept and appreciated. Our Grassland logoed beer as a Christmas gift was especially popular for some reason.

Perpetual motion

It's not always plain sailing with our creations.

Before deploying a **giant golf ball** to win the Paint the Town Red competition (see below) we used it to make a replica of the iconic Naas ball, [see page 166] situated at Exit 9 off the N7; it's a notable piece of motorway art. It was tricky work but we used coloured grasses to match its features and immediately upon completion it was on display at a charity motor racing event nearby at Mondello Park. A week later it was outside the County Kildare Chamber's annual summer exhibition. We loaded it up on a van and for safety reasons I followed behind. On a whim I decided to video it and for a bit of fun I stuck it on Facebook with the title 'Stop thief! Naas ball stolen, last seen heading south on the Newbridge road'. It became a viral hit locally with over 20,000 views on YouTube. Local newspapers also picked up the story.

A few days later we brought it to Bloom where the organisers allowed us to place it near a main entrance, along with our name and logo of course. The crowds recognised and loved it. Once again we were entertaining people and they now knew exactly *where* we are based, the ball being an iconic landmark.

Not everyone was so pleased, however. The very next morning a motorbike courier burst into the office delivering inches of legal documents. The original artists who designed the ball, called *Perpetual Motion*, were suing us.

To be honest copyright infringement had never occurred to me. After all, it was a tiny fraction of the size of the real thing. Many Naas businesses use the image in their marketing. Even the county council has it on it's Christmas cards, for God's sake. Was it not flattery, paying them a compliment?

They wanted payment alright. My genuine written apology was rejected. They wanted it removed from public view immediately if not sooner, with a legal affidavit testifying to its destruction. With my PR hat on I was kinda thinking, bring it on, let's fight this. But the legal advice was to comply. They were demanding thousands in compensation. If we lost in court it would cost multiples of that.

For health and safety reasons we had to wait until the crowds abated that evening before removing it. Meanwhile, unbeknownst to us, RTÉ had been in and shiny TV personality Marty Morrissey had literally been dancing around it on camera. I saw it on telly that evening, just as the ball was being unloaded back in Grassland, and I burst out laughing. Job done. I imagine the original artists were apoplectic.

After a hectic few days in Bloom I was heading off on a well-earned short break. On my way out of the office I wrote a cheque for half of what they demanded. My message was, take it or leave it. They took it. What a shame one can't use a local landmark to promote one's location and business.

Oh, and the ex-giant golf ball is to have a new lease of life. Soon it'll be mostly blue. Representing the oceans. The green patches will represent the continents, all the countries of the world. Well, nearly all. Maybe not the UK, 'cause they are gone from the EU now …

Maybe I do bring some of these controversies on myself.

Horsing around

As mentioned there's a local annual initiative called Paint the Town Red, promoted in conjunction with the nearby Punchestown National Hunt Festival, a horse racing festival sponsored by Bank of Ireland. The idea is to create a festive atmosphere and local businesses from the area are encouraged to decorate their premises with horsey paraphernalia and Punchestown's red corporate colours. As it happens their official logo incorporates a fox to reflect their 200-year history originating in the local hunt. We decided to enter into the spirit of things.

With red grass in stock (usually used in school playgrounds) we did our thing but there was something missing. What about a fox, so prominent in Punchestown's logo? So I turned to social media – would anybody out there happen to have a stuffed fox? Ask and thou shalt receive! Within 24 hours Felix the Fox arrived. He had long languished in an attic having been adopted as an abandoned cub and then raised as a much-loved pet. When he passed away his owner had him stuffed. When, in turn, the owner died, his family relegated poor Felix to the attic and gladly let us have him (we sent them tickets for Punchestown to say thanks).

We mounted him on top of the giant red ball outside the gates of Grassland and promptly won the competition. Besides the publicity, the overall prize was a cheque for €1,500 and a corporate box for the November race meeting. Felix, looking somewhat bleached and bedraggled, now resides in the rafters beside the CCTV camera, a guard fox if you will.

It occurred to me that we could use the prize for our staff Christmas party. Hey, why not sponsor a race since we were there anyway? Given the large prize monies involved I'd never considered it but with subsidies provided by Horse Racing Ireland it was surprisingly affordable. We'd get lots of signage, promo videos on loop throughout the venue, national coverage in the sports pages and TV on the racing channel. I was interviewed live from the parade ring and a photo of me presenting the prize to the winning connections made the local press. Our team had a great day out. I used the €1,500 cheque on appropriate race-going clobber and invested the rest behind the bar for team-building purposes.

The Punchestown Festival is carnival time locally. When I was growing up, all the primary schools in the area closed for the week. Secondary school attendance was patchy too. And that was just the teachers. The festival brings €60 million into the local economy and attracts tens of thousands of mostly English foreign visitors (including their kings, back in the day). The pubs tend to get busy too.

The following year at the festival we created a Bollinger Champagne pop-up garden. The organisers had admired our creativity in winning their previous year's competition and were also aware of our successes at the Bloom garden show (more on that in Chapter 10) so they commissioned us to do something sexy for their champagne drinking guests. How about, instead of payment you sponsor another race at the (big) festival this time? I took their offer. The €15,000 Sanctuary Synthetics two mile maiden hurdle bumper on day one of the festival would ultimately be a good one. Over 120,000 punters attended and

I'm told 5,000 bottles of bubbly, at over €100 each, were drunk in the vicinity of our grass.

It lashed rain all day but the sun came out just in time for our race and I got interviewed on live TV beforehand. The race was a thriller, won by popular Irish billionaire JP McManus. Well, by his horse really.

How effective was all this from a marketing point of view? How do you measure the return on investment, positive association and local goodwill? I was able to give my family, the Sanctuary team and most importantly my 83-year-old race-going dad a good day out. A week later we got a gracious note from JP thanking me for sponsoring the race.

We got approached by a children's charity called Sensational Kids who had partnered with the Irish Injured Jockeys Fund. They had 20 life-sized models of horses painted by well-known artists which were to be auctioned at high-profile events. Our grass (and logos) soon decorated the plinths, and the horses made at least €20,000 *each* for the charities. One of the artists was U2's Edge, which helped with publicity. Over several months the horses toured the county and beyond, appearing in race courses like the Curragh for the Derby and serendipitously at our Bollinger garden in Punchestown, at black tie events and hotels, and they even resided in the main foyer of Kildare County Council.

I have since taken delivery of a life-sized horse of our own, along with two cows, a calf and one sheep. We started by covering Daisy the cow with grass and have since sent her down on hire to the National Ploughing Championships, the largest outdoor event in Europe. Meanwhile the animals earn their keep on our online hire shop. Grassing them keeps us amused on days when we are rained off.

This book

Hopefully it's informative and all, but is it an entertaining read? Does it stand out from the gazillions of other books? It will be the first of its kind. But more than that. First, I get to call my competitors copy cats. Best of luck to them. I welcome competition; it keeps standards high but I do slightly resent the fact that they piggyback on all I've done to promote awareness. Now let's see what books they write.

Rant over.

There's another reason for writing this book.

I once read about an American swimming pool installation guy. Seemingly he refuses, point blank, to talk to prospective customers unless and until they first read his book. At a minimum of $50,000, getting a new pool installed is no small purchase. He prefers his prospects to be educated about all aspects of their decision. To self-select. Besides describing his offering, apparently his book asks 'Is this really the right thing for you to spend your money on? Is it borrowed money? Did you win it? Was it saved? Inherited?' He then frankly lists alternative uses for that kind of money. Why not go on a long cruise instead? Then if, having considered all he had to say in the book, the prospective customer still wants to deal with him, they are now a more knowledgeable and committed customer and consequently a treat to deal with. He's helped them frankly consider all the pros and cons. At the very least he's spared having to repeat the same answers to the same old questions.

Every. Single. Time.

Now *I'm* not going to insist that anyone who wants to buy some grass from us has to wade through this Big Hairy Green Book. But if you *have* gone to the trouble of informing yourself of the ins and outs of artificial grass, imagine how much easier that makes the process? Let's just say we'll be gently encouraging prospects to have a leaf through.

As an added bonus I got to document my own story, calling it work, and will always have the satisfaction of having done so. I don't worry about the horrifically small number of copies that the average new publication sells. This book's mere existence as a tangible marketing tool will suffice. Plus I did it during my career when it can do me, and hopefully you the reader, some good, rather than a memoir in retirement.

Golfing legend Gary Player (echoing fellow pro Jerry Barber) is said to have exclaimed, 'The more I practise, the luckier I get.' People ask me, 'How the hell do you make payroll for 20 plus people week in, week out?' Especially during the recession or during long harsh winters or, say, a global pandemic? Well, the short answer is we don't just sit around hoping the phone rings. We do stuff. Lots of stuff. Some of it sticks and we get business. I become increasingly uncomfortable when not busy planting (plastic) seeds, working on my next marketing wheeze. Seth Godin said 'you will be judged or be ignored'. I choose the former. It's never-ending but, to be absolutely frank, it's the most fun. Putting one's head above the parapet can also be scary. It's like walking into a dragon's den.

Entering The Dragons' Den

'In the future everyone will be famous for fifteen minutes'
~ Attributed to Andy Warhol, 1968

'Hi, I'm Mark O'Loughlin, and I'm here to present my invention called the "HidBin". I'm asking for €50 grand in exchange for 20 percent of the business.

As a landscape gardener, I'm familiar with the concerns of my customers. People are sick of the sight of their wheelie bins, wherever they are stored. They're an eyesore and are increasing in number. Here, at last, is the solution.

It's a modular free-standing frame covered in synthetic hedging that camouflages the ugly and ubiquitous bins, hence our tag line 'from unsightly to unseen'.

The standard unit comes flat packed, fits into car boots, is easily assembled and hides two bins [like so]. Research says that it's not just for terraced houses with bins out front by necessity, but it's also for detached and semi-detached homeowners, allowing them to store their bins where it's most convenient. This design allows for use wherever that spot happens to be.

We estimate a potential market size of 350,000 households in Ireland alone. We aim to sell 4,400 units in 2010 which represents 1.25 percent market penetration. We will sell directly via shows and online but projections are mostly predicated on wholesaling into multiples.

To sum up, the "HidBin" offers a simple screening solution (which isn't only for bins by the way) that is now ready for launch. I'm seeking your investment because I want to roll it out on as big a scale as possible with export markets in mind.

Thank you for your time, and I really hope you do have some questions for me.'

Andy Warhol was wrong. I only got 13.5 minutes, including the mandatory opening pitch above. That was the full extent of my airtime on the Irish *Dragons' Den*, edited down from one and a half hours of intense scrutiny from five Dragon investors. I was there to convince them to buy into my new invention 'the HidBin'.

Gavin, Orla and James

'So, hang on, let me get this straight,' said Nancy, my mother-in-law, beforehand. 'You've got to go into a room with five rich investors that you've never met, to convince one of them to give you a pile of money for an invention they've never seen before, and it's all televised?'

'Yep, that's pretty much it, alright.'

It was recorded late in 2009 and aired in early 2010.

Looking back a decade later I might have been a bit off-script and the HidBin prototype did look a bit homemade (because it was) and clunky. However, there was "a lot of love in the room for the big Kildareman", said series host Richard Curran, and the investors really seemed to like the concept and my pitch.

Gavin Duffy, my eventual investor, later suggested that I came onto the Den to drum up some extra business as, with the Great Recession in full flow, the synthetic grass business was in trouble. Not true. We were ticking over just fine. Rather, with the germ of an idea, using raw materials not dissimilar to our main product, I really just fancied the challenge of the Den, the first series having aired in Ireland the previous year. With the economy in tatters, viewership was huge.

Of course I did have a plan B.

Even if things went horribly wrong – after all I was risking humiliating failure on national TV – I would be standing on a piece of synthetic grass which, assuming I got any airtime, would have to be explained or at least mentioned. I'd have settled for that.

A week before the show I went into famous Dublin tailor Louis Copeland to buy a new suit. As I left the shop Louis stuffed that day's calendar 'thought for the day' into the breast pocket. There it remains.

It read: 'Failure begins when you stop trying to succeed.'

As adventures go this one was a doozy.

I used to be in the scouts. Their motto was 'Be prepared'.

I'd written a comprehensive business plan in tandem with designing the HidBin. It was a lot of work on top of running the company. But necessary. Fortuitously the Local Enterprise Board ran a Write Your Own Business Plan course and I produced a 100 page detailed tome covering all the bases.

Everything was done by the book, built upon comprehensive market research from primary, secondary and qualitative sources along with Google Analytics. Basically I knew lots of people were searching for a solution to how to hide their wheelie bins. We even commissioned an online survey. This was revealing research with encouraging conclusions. One alarm bell that failed to ring

179

was people's price expectations. They were on the low side. Otherwise there were huge positives. 'Brilliant,' said several respondents. 'Why has no one ever thought of that before now?' asked another. Our plan included a path to market, targeting early adopters, and a marketing strategy starting with an effective national product launch thanks to a planned appearance on the *Dragons' Den*. Finally I produced shiny new business cards with explanatory before and after pictures. I believed there was clearly international scalability potential.

None of the above could be brought into the Den with me.

All I could do was suit-up and prepare to slay the Dragons.

The programme's pitch coach warned us to keep it simple, be clear and breathe. That last bit about not forgetting to breathe was vital.

I assembled five friends, whose business acumen I respected, and sat them in my kitchen facing me. Under laboratory conditions I made my pitch and got mercilessly drilled. One of them had a crying baby on her lap which, although quite annoying at the time, probably helped.

Ninety percent of communication is non-verbal. James, one of my mock Dragons, had Toastmasters experience. He asked me why I was holding my hands over my … well, nether regions? It is poor defensive body language of which I was blissfully unaware. Consider what to do with your arms and hands. When the cameras roll it's really not the time to start wondering what to do with them.

Another disconcerting thing I discovered, thankfully in advance, was the strong likelihood that during such a long interview there are likely to be pauses. Sometimes long ones, as information is processed or new film is loaded into the cameras. I had to be patient and cool and not fill the void with blathering. The editing process would eliminate awkward silences and the audience at home would be largely sympathetic.

Facts and stats were my armour, the content of my business plan my shield and my personality my sword. Another mock mentor reassured me about future projections, saying, 'Don't worry, Mark. You can't lie about the future – go slay a Dragon.'

The TV production company gets hundreds of applications. Only a few are chosen for each episode. They called me up for an interview. Opposite their offices was a bank and when, after the small talk, they asked me about the HidBin I said look out that window. Across the street outside the bank there was a row of unsightly wheelie bins, only the last one was now invisible, having been mysteriously covered by a hedge. They quickly got the picture and I was lined up for the next show.

Of all the entrepreneurs who stand before the Dragons only one-third actually get any decent airtime. The rest are quickly dismissed. Of those who actually get featured no more than one or two get an investment. It was crucial to be in that cohort.

I decided to find out where it was being filmed – it turns out it was above a pub of all places and on a wet Tuesday evening a couple of weeks in advance I rocked up to the venue. Ordering a drink, I asked the barman, 'Hey, is this the place ...?' Not having been asked before, he kindly gave me a tour of the studio upstairs and showed me where I'd be standing and where the famous five chairs and cameras would be positioned. Then he left me for a few invaluable minutes so I could visualise the whole thing.

Regular viewers will know that many *Dragons' Den* visitors are like rabbits caught in the headlights.

Not me.

It worked and I got my airtime. And investment.

I got a real buzz out of the whole experience. The person who was on before me came away crying. The person after me cried during it. The editors kindly cut out their tears. My 90 long minutes were heavily edited but more or less captured what went down. Eminent media guru and investor Mr Gavin Duffy bought into my idea, came on board and the future for the HidBin was bright.

But now the clock was ticking.

It was only a couple of months to the broadcast date and to capitalise on the publicity both the product and website had to be ready. I'd only shown them a prototype, just about getting away with it on the show. I employed product engineers and worked to come up with an improved version. After much frustration we settled on a workable design and off I went to China with a production manual under my arm. Eventually pushing the button on production I went home to finalise the packaging. Thanks to preliminary finance from Gavin, now a shareholder, we were able to make things happen.

Gavin also kindly gave myself and two other investees some valuable media training to prep for all the inevitable media interviews. I organised a party back in Lawlor's Hotel in Naas for the night it aired. Most people are a bag of nerves given that the programme's editors can either flatter or damn you, depending on what way they cut the material. Thankfully Gavin got me a DVD copy in advance. The public's reaction to the TV show was very positive and we took over 100 orders online in advance of its official launch. I even got some online hate mail which I took as a sign that we were on the right track.

At the Ideal Home Show in Dublin's RDS soon afterwards I managed to organise a free exhibition stand, along with two fellow Dragon slayers in whom Gavin had also invested. He in turn was able to plug our appearance in advance on *The Late Late Show*. Gavin was able to demonstrate his crowd-pulling powers of persuasion, standing on a stool and giving it the whole 'roll up, roll up' thing. Hurray!

Then he made me stand up on the stool. Oh shit!

Luckily other vendors from nearby stands complained about us hogging the limelight and we toned things down a bit.

Our first container arrived from China soon afterwards. It took us two full days to deliver all the pre-ordered HidBins. We had offered to assemble the initial batch free of charge in order to get more on-site before and after pictures.

The rest sold out over the following months, although not as quickly as we'd hoped. We were mainly selling via the website as the margins were simply not there to retail them at our chosen price point. Half our sales were exported, mainly to the UK. I knew there was an international market for us.

To save us explaining the same stuff over the phone again and again I did a short demonstration video. It quickly garnered 9,000 views on YouTube. Perhaps bitten by the limelight bug, we went on to produce three fun promotional videos.

The first one opened with me explaining 'In life there are some things one just shouldn't see' and climaxed with me shoving a 'flasher' into a wheelie bin. The follow-ups used a fake cat and a fake crow. All were great craic to make but fully on message, demonstrating the benefits and including the tag line 'From unsightly to unseen'. Between them they garnered almost 90,000 views. Have a look on YouTube.

After our *Dragons' Den* episode aired I engineered an interview on a TV talk show with the then popular City Channel. Soon afterwards they persuaded me to take out an ad with them. We already had our flasher video footage and it seemed like a good deal so we agreed a three-month run with payment in installments. Days after my first payment the station folded, yet another victim of the demise of the Celtic Tiger.

Funnily enough, that turned out to be great news in the end. For some unknown technical, probably contractual, reason the station's last day of broadcasting was repeated every single day for the rest of that year. This continuous broadcast included my ad several times during their breaks. Because City Channel was pre-programmed onto number one for many cable subscribers throughout the city, it popped up first when the TV got switched on. Thus images of me chasing a flashing pervert around a park were on at random times of the day and night, month after month. Over time I got a lot of calls from friends and acquaintances – 'Mark, WTF'? – I think it's fair to say awareness was not a problem.

Unfortunately by the time we were ready to reorder, our Chinese suppliers were no longer operating. It was back to the drawing board. I spent months trying to source a new improved version preferably at a better price. Ultimately it proved impossible. After all the work, the fanfare and the obvious demand, the whole project slowly petered out.

My investor Gavin was a great mentor, adviser and marketeer. He didn't get back his initial investment for ages and I was personally seriously out of pocket. On the plus side we've since imported containers of synthetic box hedging – the raw material for the HidBin – and we continue to sell it at a half decent margin. Ultimately its cost was too high in a depressed market and without a margin for distributors and retailers there was insufficient volume to make it a success.

Over the intervening years I have continued to experiment, on and off, with alternative materials for the HidBin Mark II but have not quite hit upon the right formula.

Yet.

The concept is sound. The market is there. Watch this space.

Yes, the HidBin, like many businesses and quite a few *Dragons' Den* prospects, ultimately failed. While this is the end of this chapter, I'd like to think there's still more to go in the HidBin story. Meanwhile I guess the media exposure and my increased profile did no harm whatsoever to both my confidence and the artificial grass business.

Do I regret having tried it? Not for a second. The real failure would be in not using what I learned and applying it to other things. Things like mustering up the courage to enter a show garden in Ireland's version of the Chelsea Garden Show – Bloom. Besides, now I'm no longer a hurler on the ditch. I can now watch others face the Dragons and pass all the smart comments I like. No one can take that from me.

Chapter 10

Bloom – behind the curtain

'What you can do, or dream you can, begin it.
Boldness has genius, power, and magic in it'
~ John Anster's English translation of Johann Wolfgang von Goethe's German play *Faust*

Being in business has allowed me to indulge in many delightful pursuits. None more so than our forays into show gardens at Bloom, Ireland's answer to the Chelsea Flower Show. Having survived the *Dragons' Den* I was emboldened to see what else I might be capable of. My office cleaning lady once told me "don't give power to doubt".

Bloom was launched in 2007. Under the auspices of Bord Bia (Irish Food Board) the garden festival was to be a showcase for amenity horticulture. It has since broadened its remit to encompass food and drink, fashion and lots more. Unlike Chelsea, it even lets children in. Each June bank holiday weekend Dublin's Phoenix Park hosts over 120,000 paying visitors.

I decided it might be a good place to exhibit our wares despite the economic crash. We made a bit of an effort with our stand and got a great reaction from an encouragingly high percentage of the public. So we went back. Again and again. Over time we've observed a progressive acceptance of our synthetic grass. All the while I became increasingly interested in the main attraction, the actual show gardens.

Eventually I thought, hang on a sec, *we* could do that.

What better way to present our grass than incorporating it into a show garden? We could entertain and educate the public from the garden and then sell to them from our exhibition stand nearby.

How hard could it be, I thought to myself, somewhat naively.

A note on garden design

Rather like the lawn itself, garden design has historically been about privilege and snobbishness, both being symbolic of landownership and leisure. Having land *not* reserved for food production was long seen as the ultimate extravagance and a public demonstration of wealth. It was said to be a fitting occupation for a princess. A well-designed garden demonstrates sophistication. Subject to ever changing fashion, gardens define how we see ourselves. Nowadays the garden is almost another part of the house.

Yet most gardens, particularly in suburbia, simply evolve.

New owners are initially more worried about paying the mortgage and saving up for a couch and curtains than how the garden looks.

The obligatory shed has to go somewhere – stick it in the back corner. What junk fills them anyway (besides the lawnmower)? Is it all really that indispensable? When's the last time you needed any of that painstakingly accumulated collection of half full paint tins and unused home fitness paraphernalia?

Next, a path is made to its door, often doubling as a route alongside the washing line. The bins need a home, preferably near the back door. You've no choice about where the oil tank/gas tank/heat exchanger gets plonked. That back wall is a bit bland. Let's plant a few random things along it. Some grow huge; some get smothered and die.

Ever the optimists many invest in a barbecue, then realise they need garden furniture. Oh, and a patio to plonk them on, ideally with a couple of potted plants. In laying out housing estates developers certainly take no cognisance of where the sun rises or sets. Do the householders?

Of course all this is naturally and unthinkingly arranged around – yes, you guessed it – the obligatory lawn. The canvas onto which all else is smeared. Unless of course you call in a garden designer or landscaper. Applying their vision and using a handful of proven principles can transform a garden. One lady I know says to prospective clients, 'Don't tell me what you want it to look like, tell me how you want it to feel.'

Because the living garden is dynamic thanks to the seasons, one has to think in several dimensions, including time.

Consider the practicalities first, bins, storage, clothesline etc. Then the threshold – is it inviting? How will it be used? Is there contrast? Balance? Unity? What's the topography like? Do the levels create interest and depth? Can a microclimate be created? Can ugly sight lines be disguised or hidden? Is the aspect used to maximum effect? What's the genus loci (sense of space and feel)? What's the soil type? Where's the prevailing wind coming from? Are there edibles? Is the space clustered or serene? Is it open or enclosed? What emotions does it evoke? Could it be a sanctuary? Any rainwater harvesting? What about the sound of water? Does it have a focal point? Is there intrigue – what draws the eye, such as a glimpse of a statue or feature?

What is the garden's style? Is it traditional? Has it a modern twist? Formal or informal? Curvaceous or rectilinear (wavy or boxy)? What of scale and proportions? What's the balance between hardscaping and soft planting? What role has nature and wildlife? Is it fun? Is it practical? Is it high or low maintenance? Is it delicate or robust? What of the form and fabric? Does the edge complement the space? I've got my own garden design theories, incorporating sacred geometry, but that's for an entirely different book … watch this space.

Just as I've managed to infiltrate the thinking of leading garden designers when it comes to synthetic grass, so have their philosophies affected mine. I've long appreciated the rejuvenating and transformative powers of gardens but I'm more cognisant than ever of the power of good garden design.

Every design is bespoke as there's only so much 'off the shelf' stuff that can be applied. Potential clients must be interviewed, sites properly surveyed, requirements painstakingly recorded before the thinking hat is put on. Next, plans must be produced: simple enough to be understood, attractive enough to sell the concept, robust enough to be interpreted by a third-party contractor and, finally, detailed enough to provide an accurate costing.

I think garden design is a seriously underrated and financially under-rewarded profession, notwithstanding the pleasures of seeing one's ideas physically manifest.

Our first show garden foray

Show gardens are to regular gardens as Versace is to Primark. You are given a barren piece of land, a completely blank canvas, and are expected to produce catwalk magic.

In our first year, I clearly recall the snide comments of one snooty fellow designer working on a show garden beside us. After days of ignoring us she eventually deigned to address me. Looking around with disdain she exclaimed, 'I understand you are entirely untrained …' and before I could answer, off she flounced. I thought her garden was appalling by the way. The judges loved it … Hmmm.

Mostly, though, we got huge encouragement and support from everyone on-site. We were the newbies but we were all in the same boat. One decorated designer frankly told me, on judging day, that he had been deeply worried watching the progress of our garden. He had absolutely no idea what we were trying to do and was most relieved that it somehow made sense in the end.

Personally I wasn't worried. OK, admittedly we were complete show garden novices, but we did have form. After all, we did (and do) several gardens a week, throughout Ireland, throughout the year. No other outfit in the country comes anywhere close. I conservatively estimate we've done over 14,000 gardens over the last 20 years. Sure, we're mostly installing new artificial lawn but there's often a bit more to it than that.

We have a responsibility to our customers. We endeavour to guide them towards best practice, best layout, best design. I guess we've picked up a thing or two over time. Largely self-taught, I credit hands-on trial and error, reading relevant publications and books, the Garden and Landscape Designers Association – with particular thanks to mentorship from Jane McCorkell – and the combined skills of our team for our success.

Being an outsider meant independence of thought, allowing me to produce something different and new. In my ignorance, my ambition and imagination knew few bounds and, after a few years watching others do their thing, I dived right in at the deep end.

Alice in Wonderland (2011)

Oblivious to the magnitude of the challenge I chose the Large Garden category for our first foray: 200 square metres of ground (20m × 10 m). I blithely eschewed the easier small or medium options. Now it was sink or swim.

Inspired by my own young children, I hit upon the idea of doing an Alice in Wonderland garden. The Johnny Depp film had come out the previous year. I worked hard on the design application and we were successful in persuading the show garden manager and overall boss Gary Graham to accept our submission. In the absence of corporate sponsors (we did try), Bloom would pay about 25 percent of the cost. I was determined to repay their faith.

We were not only the conceivers of the project, but also the designers, de facto sponsors, builders, exhibitors and promoters. We would also be, after the show closed, its demolishers. Looking back through all my notes, doodles, drawings and things-to-do lists, and with a decade's perspective, I marvel at the innocence and ambition of it all.

I treated the space more as a stage than a garden and had 44 different outsiders including actors, volunteers, collaborators, suppliers, artists and craftspeople on board. I could never have managed without the faithful support of Mary, Dominic, Krzystof and of course my wife.

In Wonderland nothing is as real as it seems. Against advice and perceived wisdom we had elected to invite the public to walk through the garden, all the better to appreciate the features and detail. I removed a huge old tree stump, complete with moss and mushrooms, from Dad's farm and affixed a Lewis Carroll quote in 3D wooden lettering to be read as one exited the garden. It read: 'And home we steer, a merry crew, beneath the setting sun'.

A blazing row

The design plan was painstakingly laid out on sacred geometrical principles, using the 1 to 1.681 golden ratio carefully set into the 20m × 10m plot. After all, Mr Carroll, the author of the story, was a mathematician and this was our nod to his genius. My contention being that sacred geometry and the golden mean are almost entirely absent from modern gardens and it's high time they were reintroduced. With less than a week to go before the build the organisers announced they were reducing the plot to an 18m × 10m plot. This seemingly modest reduction threw off my calculations entirely and threatened to destroy the cohesion of the garden plot. I lost the plot and complained bitterly.

From their point of view I was only one of four or five large gardens and one of approximately 30 gardens overall. They had their own logistical challenges in a restricted show garden area – ironic as it's in the centre of the biggest public park in Europe, with vast acreage – plus they had to contend with lots of other cranky artistic types.

So we came to an arrangement. They stuck to their guns and I ignored their plot size specifications. I'm not sure they ever noticed. The task was made easier by blurring the boundary line somewhat at the entrance. Visitors were invited to enter via a fake internal house facade. They then went through the patio doors of a regular suburban kitchen complete with sink (yes, I threw everything at that garden), presses, plates, cutlery and even a washing machine. And then out onto a distinctive chequered patio which led, well, further down the rabbit hole.

I had studied Carroll's writings and the walk through the garden was to reflect Alice's journey in Wonderland. It was a big ask for a novice with limited resources, time and money. But I had no shortage of ideas and was wise enough to recruit others more gifted than myself.

Don't forget it had to somehow incorporate a large swathe of artificial grass.

My overriding aim was to please the public. I felt a duty to put on a show. As for what the judges would think, I had no idea. There was the predictable hostility from certain quarters towards artificial grass for starters. Who does this

Bloom 2011

Sanctuary 'Alice
In Wonderland'
garden

Silver Medal
Winner

189

Bloom 2011

Sanctuary 'Alice In Wonderland' garden

Silver Medal Winner

upstart think he is? A trip to Bristol and Bath in the UK yielded my 'lawn spawn' and fake folly (see pics) respectively. The former made it onto a post office stamp collection and the latter later featured in a book of Bloom highlights.

We had a disappearing Cheshire Cat (clear Perspex and a tail), a hookah, giant slugs and toadstools, playing cards, several '10/6' top hats, 3D wood and stone lettering ('You're all late for tea!'), a giant cup and saucer, a black and white chequerboard, a knight and his sword, a treehouse, a road disappearing into the distance (a hand-painted mural scene on canvas), butterflies, up-lit paths, an actual gothic ruin, a pergola, red and white roses, a toilet, a rabbit hole (really a grass-covered concrete pipe), chestnut fencing and plenty of stunning planting. Somehow, thanks to the golden mean pathway, all these elements tied together and worked beautifully.

What no one knew about was my secret weapon: actor Seána Kerslake, aka Alice. What a gem she turned out to be! She has, predictably, gone on to much greater fame, starring in TV and film. Dressed up in the iconic costume, 'Alice' totally charmed the public for us, bringing the garden to life with droves of excited kids lining up to meet her daily. Liz Kent from Pivotal PR got us up horribly early one morning for a photo shoot. Leaving no stone unturned our star duly grabbed a bit of welcome pre-show publicity.

Certainly the public thought so. They loved it.

Lights, camera, action!
From the first minute to the last, over five long days, there was a constant queue of people trailing through the garden, oohing and aahing as they noticed hidden details throughout their slow journey, all the while interacting with a real life Alice and her faithful (giant) white rabbit – when he wasn't late. We estimate at least 40,000 visitors walked through our wonderland over the five days, all with smiles on their faces. The reaction was fantastic. Despite all that traffic, including large numbers of children of course, there was hardly a twig out of place or a flower petal plucked. I learned that you could trust the public if they liked what they saw. Crowd control was a challenge though and the organisers gave us plenty of grief even as their patrons clamoured to get in.

Media and judging day comes before opening to the public. I became disgruntled watching celebrity guests and VIPs being ushered straight past us. They can only see and visit so many gardens, I get that. But when Senator David Norris, a Joycean scholar, stopped to read our quotation on the tree stump only to be literally pulled away I started to get a bit paranoid.

One government TD did wander in on his own and I had a great chat with him, discussing all the literary references scattered throughout. At the time he was running for president and a picture of him standing with our white rabbit (Alice was on a break) made the Sunday papers.[38] Said TD, Michael D. Higgins, is now well into his second term as President of Ireland.

Towards the end of that day, with almost everyone gone, I was languishing around, watering some flowers and smoking a thoughtful cigar when a cameraman passed. A moment later he backtracked and asked me for a light.

'Certainly.'

'What's the story with this garden anyway?' he nonchalantly asked.

Although exhausted after three nonstop weeks of a build and a long and frankly disappointing media day I talked him through it.

'Hey, would you mind repeating all that to the camera?' he asked. 'And maybe lose the cigar.'

So we did a full walkthrough with me yapping away about all the different elements. Lo and behold it made the main evening news, to the exclusion of almost all other gardens. I delighted in the consternation the next morning. 'How the hell ...?' The big sponsors have certain expectations and favourites must get their pound of flesh. Who was yer man getting all that exposure? Why, he only got a silver. Well, I never.

The second morning we had the minister responsible for the Office of Public Works (OPW) – basically Bloom's boss – swing by to cut a ribbon declaring our garden officially open. That made a few people sit up and take notice, alright. Basically, he's married to my first cousin so that helped.

I had also invited the Queen of England to open our garden but she politely declined. Visitors to the toilets in Grassland will see a laminated letter from Her Majesty hanging on the wall. Although dated 1 April 2011 it was not an April Fool's joke. The queen's first ever and long overdue historic visit to Ireland coincided with Bloom in 2011. The Bloom show gardens are situated immediately adjacent to Áras an Uachtaráin, our President's official residence, where protocol dictated the Queen visit. Given her enduring love of the Chelsea Flower Show, the fact that she was to be in the vicinity of the Bloom festival and the prominence of a queen in the Alice story that inspired our garden, I thought it appropriate to formally invite her to open our garden. Unfortunately, as her itinerary was at an advanced stage, she politely explained via her private

38 Damien Eagers, 'Michael D. Higgins in discussion with the White Rabbit at The Alice in Wonderland Sanctuary garden at Bloom 2011 yesterday' [picture], *Irish Independent*, 4 June 2011, News, p. 11.

BUCKINGHAM PALACE

1st April, 2011.

Dear Mr. Loughlin,

Thank you for your letter of 28th March to The Queen regarding Her Majesty's visit to Ireland this year.

It was most thoughtful of you to have written, and your kind invitation to The Queen to open your show garden at the annual Bloom garden festival has been carefully noted. However, I should let you know that planning for Her Majesty's visit is at quite an advanced stage and The Queen has already received a considerable number of invitations. Therefore I would not wish to raise your expectations too high.

I would, nonetheless, like to thank you again for taking the time to write to Her Majesty.

Yours sincerely,

Edward Young

Edward Young
The Deputy Private Secretary to The Queen

Mr. Mark O'Louhglin.

Planning The Wizard of Oz garden

The Wizard of Oz scarecrow

secretary that it was unlikely she could accept and that I was not to get my hopes up. As RSVPs go it was as gracious as one could expect.

I sometimes wonder if the palace ever did contemplate a surprise visit to Bloom. I guess that for a delicate first visit to the country it was a bridge too far security-wise. That said, I'll never forget being escorted by two motorbike cop outriders into the officially closed Phoenix Park (to continue the work on our almost-finished garden) the day the queen did pop in to see the president. We could see her passing motorcade from our garden as we worked. I could swear she waved over at us.

All agreed that the queen's first visit to Ireland was a great success. She even spoke some Irish at a gala dinner in Dublin Castle. Anglo-Irish relations had never been so good. Boris and the Brexiteers — they sound like a bad punk tribute band— have since managed to reverse much of her good work.[39]

In 2011, I also took the liberty of inviting the then US President Barack Obama to Bloom as he, too, was to be in town at the time. As it happens, the US ambassador's residence is literally just across the road from Bloom. He never replied. The rotter.

The people's vote – stealing the show
After all the team's hard work in putting together such a complicated 'production' as the Alice in Wonderland garden, we thoroughly enjoyed the reaction from the public.

At 3 p.m. on day five the People's Choice garden was to be announced. Photographers and press, including the official Bloom guy, all gathered in our garden. A wink said it all. Happy days!

Suddenly a couple of phones rang. 'What? No, we're here … huh?'

They started to disappear. The winker looked sheepish and muttered an unedifying apology. A small garden over the other side had won. Now, perhaps the assembled media had merely assumed we'd won. Suddenly left standing alone, I smelled a rat but was powerless to do anything about it.

The Alice in Wonderland garden had cost our little company approximately €30,000 and had taken weeks to complete, along with the untold hours and sleepless nights as I built and rebuilt it in my head in the months leading up to Bloom. As a percentage of our turnover it was no small change, especially

---

39 Ireland is often said to have suffered for centuries at the hands of our bigger, imperial neighbour but we have pretty much agreed to let bygones be bygones. A couple of years ago I was privileged to be in Croke Park for the epic Ireland vs. England rugby encounter at which 'God Save the Queen' was sung with gusto by the visitors and respected and applauded by the home fans. We kicked the visitors' asses. Long live the Queen!

considering the opportunity cost of being out of action during peak season. But we had pulled it off. We might not have officially won the People's Choice Award but we certainly stole the show. Tens of thousands of visitors had been simultaneously entertained and introduced to the concept of artificial grass in a subtle but attractive way.

Plus we somehow managed to get the desired press and TV coverage.

To this day, people still talk to us about that garden.

So no regrets.

But I swore never again.

We were awarded a Silver Medal.

The Wizard of Oz (2013)

The following year I still had no intention of doing it all again.

To make up for my prolonged absences the previous May I'd promised my wife a trip to London to take in the Chelsea Flower Show instead. Here we marvelled at Diarmuid Gavin's magnificent seven-storey-high hanging gardens pyramid. His boldness was certainly an inspiration to me.

I've often compared doing a Bloom show garden to having a baby – not that I'd know first-hand – getting pregnant, i.e. conceiving of the idea, is the fun part. Then there's gestation and labour involved, climaxing with the birth. The new baby, or garden, is very vulnerable initially and needs nurturing. But over time the parent, or designer, gradually forgets the pain and is left with only love for their (brain)child. Having skipped a year, I went back in 2013 like an addict looking for another fix.

To be part of the magic, the creativity and the beauty that is Bloom is an honour and privilege, especially working alongside so many talented designers. When it comes to garnering publicity – something the aforesaid Mr Gavin knows all about – it's every person for themselves. But during the build-up, once the judges and media are gone, we're all best buddies. Comrades in arms.

It's easy to spot a veteran. It's that look in the eye. The sunburn or tan can also be a giveaway. I was already a veteran, battle-hardened and steely eyed. But soft enough to conceive of another fantasy family-friendly show garden.

This time I decided to do the Sanctuary Wizard of Oz garden, recreating Dorothy and friends' epic journey to the Emerald City. Here's the backstory of how I believe we somehow managed to capture the zeitgeist in the summer of 2013.

'We're not in Kansas anymore' – a look behind the curtain

As Glinda the Good Witch declared, 'It's always best to start at the beginning.'[40]
Step one: come up with the idea. Step two: read the book(s). Step three: watch
the film a few times. Get mesmerised. Learn about the author. Visualise. Draw
with no filters, no constraints.

Then start to figure out how the hell to pull it off.

My late mother took ill around the same time this garden was conceived. She
was given three months to live. She lasted 14 weeks. I dedicated the garden to
her memory and in my heart I know she helped me along.

The Wonderful Wizard of Oz was written by Frank L. Baum and published
in 1899, and immortalised by the 1939 Metro-Goldwyn-Mayer film starring a
young Judy Garland. Thus it's in the public domain and long out of copyright so
ripe for reinterpretation as an Irish show garden during another Great Recession.
Like Diarmuid Gavin, who was not afraid to rock the Royal Horticultural Society
establishment in London, I wanted to do something bold, new and novel back
in Dublin.

I knew the Irish public, battered by a relentlessly depressing media, widespread
negative equity, the stock market collapse and massive emigration, badly needed
a lift. Bloom would help but I wanted to ramp up the eccentricity.

Having learned lessons from the last time out I sought sponsorship. I targeted
some companies and explained our vision to them. Unfortunately they lacked
any. After our previous success I had been confident of support. None was
forthcoming. Again with limited assistance from the organisers I pressed on
regardless.

I can safely say that the second time around was no easier.

I'd lie awake every night running through long lists of possibilities. My
motivation? Not medals, although that would be a nice bonus. No, we'd set our
own standards. Was it ego? Sure, partly I guess, but it was also about the message.
It felt almost like a civic duty. I saw my job as having to add to the gaiety of the
nation, all the while having an eye to the garden's commercial function: to show
off and sell artificial grass. To do all this I needed media exposure. But it was
about more than that. The aim, once again, was to simply steal the show.

So I took out my little black book and recruited some of the artists who had
helped make the Alice in Wonderland garden happen. Lucy, my lawn spawn
lady, made my 'twister' from blue artificial grass. Craig, my model maker, made

---

40 *The Wizard of Oz*, Directors Vidor, King, Victor Fleming, George Cukor, Richard Thorpe,
Norman Taurog and Mervyn LeRoy, Metro-Goldwyn-Mayer, 1939.

The Tin Man and Joe, my movie effects man, made an exact replica of The Scarecrow. Michael, my canvas artist, immediately grasped what I had in mind and his backdrop art seamlessly integrated into the garden. If I say so myself this was the money shot. Possibly the most photographed vista in the history of Bloom. Slowly it started coming together.

I can let you in on a little secret.

It's long been my own little private joke but, in collaboration with bio-architect Michael Rice, I used the *identical* layout as the previous garden. The golden ratio spiral formed the same central pathway, becoming the yellow brick road. No one ever noticed. I'm convinced the pure mathematical simplicity of its geometric shape once again helped tie the garden together.

In fairness how could I have expected the judges to ever grasp the multiple layers of meaning in the Oz garden? Let me elaborate.

Old Frankie, the Wizard's author, certainly knew what he was at, just like Lewis Carroll with his children's stories, satirist Jonathan Swift and the other greats who stand the test of time.

Frank wrote his series of books after turbulent economic times in the US. Ironically the subsequent classic film was made during the Great Depression. So my timing was good. Research it yourself, but the yellow brick road represented gold ingots, Dorothy's ruby slippers were originally silver. This was changed for dramatic purposes as the film exploded from black and white sepia into the newly available magic of technicolour. The old slippers had represented silver-backed currency, while the illusion of Emerald City, all huff and puff but no substance, represented the Federal Reserve's greenback, aka the dollar.

Who was the great Wizard pulling the strings? If he was a banker he certainly didn't have all the answers. As we built the garden in the Phoenix Park, teams from the International Monetary Fund (IMF) were in town, about three kilometres away as the crow flies. They were now calling the shots and inflicting more pain on the struggling Irish public.

Serendipity

Newbridge Silverware is a long-established local company with a famous museum of style icons. Coincidentally they had Judy Garland's original pinafore from the film as part of an exhibition and were advertising it on the front pages of the weekend newspapers in the lead up to Bloom. I couldn't have done more if I tried. I tried and failed to persuade them to do a tie-up with our garden but ultimately that was their loss.

Bloom 2013
Sanctuary 'Wizard of Oz' garden
Silver Medal Winner

Bloom 2013
'Emerald City'
Silver Medal Winner

One of my first calls was to Seána Kerslake, formerly 'Alice'. Would she be our Dorothy? Happily, she said yes and it was virtually the same dress as Alice had worn two years earlier. Next, I found an old bike and a broom, cast a witch and we were in business.

We even got permission to do some pre-show publicity shots within the Phoenix Park. In a forested valley nearby, called the Furry Glen, we rolled out our yellow (schools grass) brick road and took some shots. Once again we made the papers even before Bloom started.

'How the hell do you do that?' I kept getting asked. Simple. By trying. Little did I know that the Furry Glen is a well-known spot for gay encounters. I will also admit to being initially oblivious to the fact that Dorothy was a gay icon. I was not, however, ignorant of the promotional potential. The LGBT community was very supportive of the garden. Great. Welcome aboard.

The design was to reflect the sequence and story arc of the film. I wanted to start in sepia before exploding into colour. We got a second-hand battered old wooden shed and set it askew as if it had just crash-landed. This was Uncle Henry and Auntie Em's wooden farmhouse – another victim of the *falling* property market. A pair of dead witch legs, her mortal remains, protruded from underneath. We put on some old roof tiles, scattered some on the ground, added 1930s farmyard paraphernalia, painted everything grey and put up the first of three canvas backdrops. Then we popped in the bespoke (grassed-up) twister and hey presto, Chapter one, Scene I in the can!

Over the stone bridge was Scene II, Munchkin Land. This multilayered multi colored reimagining was to appeal to adults' sense of nostalgia, to be fun for the kids and yet be a satire on modern Irish society; Munchkin Land had a sign outside ('This ghost estate belongs to NAMA'), which the visiting President Michael D. Higgins later found most amusing. Indeed I was worried, given his diminutive stature, that his handlers might not let him anywhere near Munchkin Land, lest unedifying comparisons be made. In fact it was hugely gratifying that he noticed and understood many of the nuances in the garden. If only he was a judge. Needless to say, having been a virtual VIP-free zone last time around, I was leaving nothing to chance. I had written to him well in advance, encouraging him and his wife to stop by. I reminded him of his visit to our last garden and emphasised its inspiration and message. It worked. There was no way he was going to let himself be marched past us.

The dozen pre-loved plastic Wendy houses I mentioned earlier, which were donated by the public following the national radio appeal on RTÉ's Ray Darcy Show, surrounded a floral spiral start of the yellow brick road. Further along we meet The Scarecrow and Dorothy at a crossroads before a dark forest. One road leads through cornfields and over a rainbow in the distance – is *that* where the LGBT community got their emblem from? – and the other path goes through the forest where The Tin Man and Cowardly Lion lurked, past drowsy poppy fields – what was the author warning us about there, do you think? – and on to the imposing facade of Emerald City, fully clad with, you guessed it, artificial grass. I'd enlisted my brother-in-law Tom to build the wooden framework. Then the health and safety people got involved. Fair enough, it was a huge undertaking so had to be properly designed and constructed. We used elaborate scaffolding and weights. That cost me plenty but a bonus was that we ended up with a secret back staircase leading to a gallery at the top, complete with turrets and battlements, from where we could survey the entire show. We repurposed the folly from the Alice garden as part of the emerald castle's structure. The majestic Emerald City's environs featured a synthetic grass lawn (of course), gargoyles and another canvas continuing the vista.

We invited family, friends and customers up to the viewing gallery, and graciously allowed the media, including RTÉ, to use it. A lot of footage was shot from there. I note that every year since there has been a two-storey viewing platform constructed by the organisers.

The public understood it.

In their droves.

Gratifyingly, once again, tens of thousands queued to walk in Dorothy's footsteps. Seána's face was sore from smiling for photos non-stop all day long for five days. Touchingly, lots of little girls showed up dressed as Dorothy. On the morning of day two, while driving along the city quays on my way to the show, I spotted a little girl who happened to have Down's syndrome, resplendent in her 'Dorothy' pinafore, pulling her mother's hand as they rushed along the path to the park's entrance.

What a responsibility. What a privilege. This went beyond a testament to the garden's popularity. Maybe it was exhaustion catching up with me or relief from the pressures of the build, but I was glad I was wearing sunglasses. I cried.

No gold

The judges awarded us a Silver Gilt, a notch up from a Silver Medal, a notch down from a Gold Medal, however fitting that might have been. Maybe all the sombre, well-financed and worthy charity gardens had used up the Gold Medal quota already. Besides, the public like what they like and largely don't give two hoots what medal a garden gets.

On media day Seána was unfortunately unavailable.

'So what, she'll be there for the public over the next five days,' I said.

'No! You must have a Dorothy,' insisted Liz.

Having just about managed to finish the garden on time I was floored and at my wits' end.

'Nobody could replace her.'

True, but Liz stepped up and produced another 'Dorothy' (and Witch) and they duly appeared in all the newspapers the next day. The moral of that story? Listen to the professionals. My friend Brian Cregan, a professional photographer, once again captured the soul of the garden. It has long since ceased to exist but elements and photos of it adorn the walls of Grassland … after all, 'there's no place like home.'

Creating and then destroying a show garden is such a surreal experience.

That was that. Box ticked, ambition achieved. I even got to shake hands with the then taoiseach Enda Kenny. Time to move on. To 'somewhere over the rainbow…'

Back with my feet firmly on the ground it was time to knuckle down, capitalise on our raised profile and simply sell more grass. No more mischief.

More mischief – The Secret Life of Pets (2016)

After the Oz garden we got busy, growing the business and establishing our own Emerald City – Grassland. We had eventually got the keys to the derelict old paint factory in January 2016. There was, as described, a mountain of work to do. What kind of idiots would contemplate doing yet another Bloom garden just five months later? Answer: Us guys.

'Please tell me you are joking?' and 'Are you mad?' were just some of the reactions from colleagues. In sport you are only as good as your last game. Old glories fade. Maybe one last fix.

I'd been playing around with a concept I'd seen on YouTube. How cool would it be to have a retractable synthetic lawn covering a secret swimming pool? A garden with moving parts. As it happens, that same year Diarmuid Gavin had his mechanical twirling Harrods Garden at Chelsea.

So I put together some 3D plans, lashed an application into Bloom's Garden Advisory Group and thought no more about it. It was more to keep my hand in than a serious proposal. Besides, we were far too distracted making Grassland a reality.

Then I got a belated call from newly appointed Show Garden Manager Kerrie Gardiner, whom I'd never met, saying she had a high-profile last minute sponsor who'd like to meet us. Some outfit called Universal Studios. They had a new family fun film coming out and were willing to finance a promotional garden. It was *The Secret Life of Pets*.

Kerrie figured our submission might fit the bill. Their budget was €10,000. I said sure, let's meet them. They were cool, trusting and, unlike some nightmare sponsors I'd heard about, a pleasure to work with. Hey, it's only a small garden –we'd previously only done large – how hard could it be, despite the tight timelines? After all, kids, families and their dogs were our target market. My fun design would need minimal tweaking. Having failed to find sponsorship in the past it was gratifying that this time they found me. I added the idea of having the garden fence as well as the lawn disappear; that way I could incorporate a backdrop from the film.

Ever hear the expression 'When the cat's away the mice will play'?

Well the idea of both the film and our garden was to answer that question – when the humans leave, what on earth do the pets get up to? In the case of our garden the answer was, you guessed it, they have a pool party.

Third time on the merry-go-round

How could we have refused? Yes, we were already swamped with both regular installations and HQ renovations but this project really appealed and, in theory, would be relatively painless financially. The film was being heavily advertised. It came out a few weeks after Bloom and became a big hit, genuinely hilarious with a great soundtrack. I just loved the fat cat. To their credit Universal just let us get on with it.

Perhaps third time lucky. Krzystof, my foreman, was willing as always.

'Nice idea,' he said, 'but how we gonna build a disappearing swimming pool, exactly?'

I'll admit to a flicker of self-doubt but knew it could be done. I'd consult the experts. Once again I sat down with my in-house consultants, Orla (then aged 13) and James (12), to brainstorm and soon had lots of new ideas and detail.

Then I drove up to Wicklow to see set design gurus Joe Fallover and his da. Like Yoda, 'Impossible is nothing' is their attitude and together we engineered a sliding rig that worked a treat. It blew half the budget but was worth it. Using

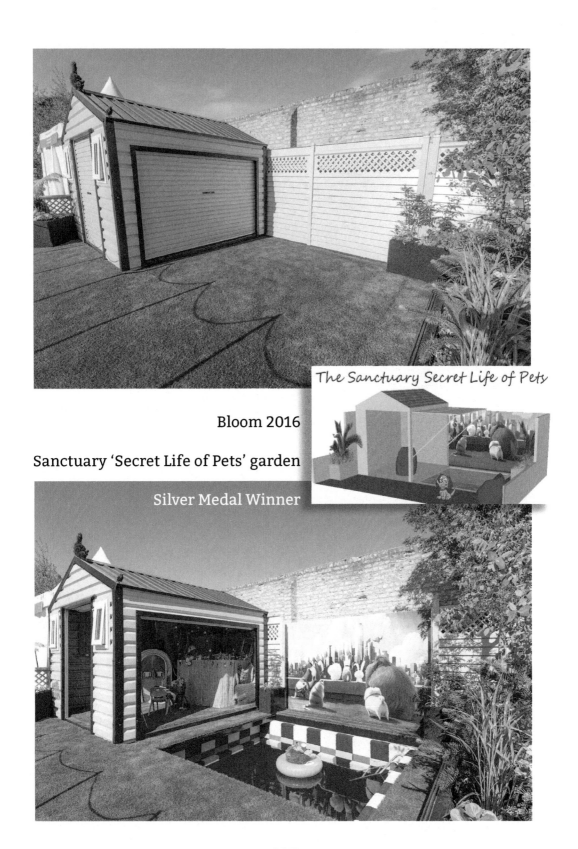

Bloom 2016

Sanctuary 'Secret Life of Pets' garden

Silver Medal Winner

The Sanctuary Secret Life of Pets

Bloom 2016

Sanctuary 'Secret Life of Pets' garden

Silver Medal Winner

a simple pulley system anyone could pull a string and ta-da! The garden was transformed.

Clane Steel Garden Sheds kindly built me a bespoke cabana. The lawn was to disappear beneath it and the fence behind it, all within the confines of a small space. Yikes! There was limited room for plants but we made every effort, only planting species with common animal names (dog daisies, elephant ears, etc). Mary Ryan from the Dublin School of Horticulture was once again a font of wisdom in this department.

This time, with a much smaller crew, the build went relatively smoothly. Note to self: smaller ain't necessarily easier. First we dug a big hole. Anxious to use as much of our product as possible I stuck on blue and white panels of our schools grass to line the 'pool'. Of course I was very careful with the dig, putting in block walls and using proper pond liner, protecting the edges with our shockpad. Then I robbed a small ladder from my kid's trampoline and, when filled, the hole suddenly looked like a mini swimming pool. Water features in any garden can be tricky. I'll let you in on another secret. It leaked. We had to keep topping it up periodically during the show on the sly. I hope no one noticed. Keep that under your hat too, will you?

The picture tells the story far better than I can. We got it done.

I wanted and got a 'before' scene of boring suburban banality. Many observers looked on with pity or contempt, some even moving on before the 'after' party-time scene was revealed.

Then media day came around.

Universal studios had organised for top model Roz Purcell to come along with her pet dog. Liz also insisted on volunteering her own daughter, a friend and their pet dog to be photographed in the garden. Guess what? The little girls got all the attention and Ros hardly featured by comparison. Go figure. The studio had hired marketing company Verve to staff the adjacent stand, allowing us to hang out in the garden instead. They handed out about 20,000 of our flyers along with stickers, badges, wristbands and such, all featuring characters from the film.

Once again we got a massive positive reaction from the public.

Virtually every time we opened up the lawn revealing the pool – which was every couple of minutes – we got spontaneous rounds of applause. Once again the judges were on an entirely different wavelength. They didn't get the joke. We got a Silver Medal.

Small gardens naturally don't get anything like the same media attention as the large ones but we certainly got our fair share of press. Entertaining the public was our priority as always. Word quickly spread.

'Watch what happens in The Secret Life of Pets garden.'

I had initially planned to open and close the lawn covering the pool only every 10 minutes or so. We ended up doing it many, many hundreds of times. Non-stop. Everyday. Just as well we over-engineered the moving platform. It was much photographed and videoed and brought a big smile to anyone who lingered long enough to witness the transformation. By having such a mundane 'before' vista, I was toying with people, and possibly annoying the judges, before the big reveal.

This time I boycotted the People's Choice Award.

All the while we were also staffing our outside retail exhibition stand nearby but it remained a challenge to get people to make the connection. After three show gardens and many years exhibiting, some people finally twigged. 'Ooh, you are the guys who did the Alice/Dorothy/Pets garden. I think ye did my aunt's/ cousin's … Tell me more about your fake grass.'

Bingo!

At last. Now I could retire with a hat trick of gardens under the belt. Maybe knock the cobwebs off the old golf clubs.

It was fun, but never again …

Turning things Upside Down (2018)

After the Pets garden our new Grassland HQ rightfully took priority. And all our money. Investing time, energy and funds into a place that, unlike show gardens, did not have to be disassembled almost immediately was a rather nice experience. We had to capitalise on the exposure, to keep on keepin' on, selling and installing synthetic grass nationwide every day.

Another year passed. Both myself and Dominic independently toyed around with a couple of show garden ideas during the winter of 2017, not thinking for a moment that either would ever come to fruition.

Ha, or God forbid, that both might happen.

This might be a good time to discuss failure. On the flip side of our Bloom triumphs are the failures. The show gardens that never got beyond the drawing board. I've a collection of 'never happened' concepts. Some are a long time in gestation. One can blame nervous sponsors, political machinations or just my own lack of faith. A couple could have been epic but that's the way the cookie crumbles in the dog-eat-dog world of show gardens.

In Chapter 9 I mentioned having created a replica of the Naas ball sculpture *Perpetual Motion*. In 2017 just for the craic we brought the replica to the Phoenix Park to do a photo shoot just before Bloom started. Although we had no show garden that year we thought we'd chance piggybacking on the media interest. Although the ball pictures were great, none were picked up by the press.

However, as an afterthought, we had also brought along our giant hairy green bunny. Once again Liz's daughter and friend posed for us and once again we made the papers for the opening day of the show, even getting a bit of a write-up on previous gardens we had done. 'Damn it, Mark! How the hell do you manage it?'

The hell of Bloom

So, after the 'Pets' garden I was sure I was done, even writing in my blog about 'the hell of Bloom'. I thought I was cured of my Bloom obsession. Dominic was now talking about taking the plunge and doing something – great – go for it, I'm right behind you (hopefully at a safe distance).

While I'm genuinely in awe of the achievements of the majority of fellow Bloom garden designers, part of me looks at some of the more conservative efforts and thinks how much easier it would be to be safe, normal and pretty. The ones picking up the Gold Medals.

Why do I even bother? Then another part of me (the obstinate, rebellious part) pipes up – screw them, I'll do my own thing, and the naysayers be damned.

I can't for the life of me remember what made me, once again, submit drawings of the Upside Down garden. Wisely, due to the engineering challenges, it was entered into the Small Concept Garden category. Not that anyone can define what the 'Concept' category actually means. It seems to continue to confound the judges too. At this stage I was plenty familiar with their criteria, meet the brief, blah, blah, blah …

I'll admit to an element of self-sabotage, or boldness as I like to call it, by declining to include any plants. Whatsoever. No trees, no flowers. Nothing that grows. Nada. That would put it up to the judges alright.

Hey, it's an upside down garden FFS! What better way to demonstrate our artificial grass, and artificial hedging and synthetic plants? The tag line being 'Look at your garden in a different way'.

I've a cousin Bosley, a bog oak artist, who came up to me in the Upside Down garden during the show. He said, 'Hey, you did it at last, fair play to you.'

'How do you mean, Boz?' I answered.

'I remember standing with you in your first Alice in Wonderland garden [seven years previously] just over there – pointing – and you were talking back then about doing an upside down garden someday.'

I have no recollection of that conversation whatsoever but it just goes to show that ideas for gardens percolate away, sometimes subconsciously, for a long time before becoming a reality.

As it happens, repeat Bloom corporate sponsors Savills property agents had just undergone a corporate image makeover with a 'Look at property another way' tag line, along with, interestingly, an upside down map of the world as a backdrop to their corporate ads. Perrrfect.

Just like the Universal Studios Pets garden, this would suit both parties nicely. So I said to Bloom, hey, put me in touch with these guys. No answer. I pressed … yeah, no thanks. But before I knew it and in defiance I was back into the madness.

In for a penny in for a pound

Wouldn't it be a great advertisement for the grass, I convinced (mostly) myself, to show it off in an amusing, intriguing and novel way? The entire Sanctuary team was fully supportive.

Indulgent is another word I could use.

We must be mad.

I'm pretty sure mine was a world first. I'd seen the upside down house on International Drive in downtown Orlando, Florida, but never an upside down garden. Images of visitors in upside down kitchens and living rooms are freaky but cool.

Paper never refused ink and while it looked feasible on the drawing board the health and safety police had their own opinions. When I got the green light it became high time to actually figure out how it could be done. Wood, nails and gaffer tape would not suffice. In the end I got a local engineering metal workshop to draw me up the required plans. Once accepted they would fabricate the framework for me for another few thousand euro. Turns out they were the same firm that had made Diarmuid Gavin's hanging Sky Garden at the Chelsea Show. With our expensive steel and aluminium Meccano set we arrived on-site. A lot of it had to be figured out as we went along. Luckily I had Tommy's and Grahamo's skills to count on. We set up time-lapse cameras for posterity which is great footage to have. You can't see all the head scratching as it's speeded up so much.

It was Show Manager Kerrie who suggested – in jest – where I'd go to find an acrobat capable of hanging upside down thus bringing the garden to life. After simply recalculating all the weight-bearing ratios of our steelwork from scratch, including independent certification and an insurance inspection, we figured out how to hang a man from the ceiling. Upside down. Standing on the lawn. In a safe but unobtrusive way. I was very lucky to find a man with his own trapeze school who to this day is in my phone contacts as 'Upsidedown Shane'.

Bloom had had a bit of a corporate makeover that year. Along with new logo they incorporated a cartoon gardener figure. In a totally unrewarded (possibly unnoticed, certainly unappreciated) stroke of genius we dressed Shane up just like the cartoon figure, complete with bright yellow wellies, dungarees, a digging fork and straw hat.

It's the little details that count.

Or not.

Although the entire garden was designed first and foremost as a photo op, we now had a great focal point for selfies. Shane, a former school principal, was brilliant with the public, especially the children who loved his antics. How he managed to flip upside down and stay in position so often and for so long I'll never know.

Once again we had a big hit on our hands.

Although a few people just didn't get it. At all. At one stage I was sitting having a break in the adjacent pergola tent, the door flap ajar, when I overheard a couple of women as they looked in.

'Is this the so-called upside down garden that Bernie was talkin' about?'
'Looks a bit untidy to me, Nora.'

'Well, I don't think much of it at all, Betty.' (Not their real names.)

And off they toddled, past the actual garden, no more than two metres away from the tent. Some walked past seeing only the blue and white grass on the ground – representing the clouds and sky – and failed to look up, or even notice that the house facade was in fact, the wrong way up. 'Oh look, that's a treehouse down there … c'mon'.

On the other hand the vast majority did get it. And laughed.

In my brief I declared I would challenge, engage and amuse visitors.

Just like our Pets garden, the frowns of visitors soon turned to broad smiles. Entire classes of school kids piled in, lying on the sky, looking up at the ground. Once again we'd taken an unremarkable everyday city garden and turned it on its head.

OMG, that's my door!

The 2018 upside down garden featured an upside down house facade. It was modelled on a Victorian Dublin terraced house and had genuine sash windows and roof slates. Admittedly the brickwork and quoins were fake.

Dom and I had visited salvage yards to pick up bits and pieces for our respective gardens. Top of my list had been the perfect door. I knew what I wanted. It had to have a polished brass knocker and fittings, glass panels and a traditional Georgian fanlight. In the end I found a red one fitting the bill in a place just outside the walls of the Phoenix Park.

While at least two TV crews filmed their reporters emerging from the door, as planned, imagine my surprise when, a couple of days later, during the show, I overheard someone say, 'Hey, that's my door'.

'Excuse me?' I had paid €250 for it.

'Do you mind letting me have a closer look?'.

With Shane constantly hanging upside down the garden was roped off for his safety. There was a strange look in the man's eyes.

'Sure, come on in,' I said, lifting the rope.

'This is it. It's 751' said the man, accompanied by this wife, reading the upside down numerals. Number 751. 'That's from my mother's house, where I grew up. That's my front door.' Tears and selfies followed.

The couple were in their 60s. The house had been long since demolished and the man's mother, then well into her 90s, was still alive and in a nursing home not far away. Well, the couple certainly had a tale to tell her on their next visit. The entire facade is now the right way up in Grassland. That door has history. No way was it going into a skip.

The money shot

Inside that rather special front door I'd placed a 4ft × 8ft sheet of plexiglass mirror. By virtue of being bendable at a certain angle it inverted the image so that when the door is opened, the observer sees themselves, like the rest of the garden, upside down. Ta-da!

But I had bigger plans.

We'd left just enough space inside the front door so that a person, say a journalist maybe, could stand inside with the door closed. Then they could open it from the inside and step out onto the sky with the garden path, lawn and hedges over their head.

As envisaged, both RTÉ and TV3 did just that.

Bloom 2016

Sanctuary 'The Upside Down Garden'

Silver Medal Winner

Bloom 2016

Sanctuary 'The
Upside Down
Garden'

Silver Medal Winner

214

On media day Liz once again did her thing. By the end of the day, with five full days of exhibiting ahead and a gruelling build behind, I badly wanted to exit stage left. I'd come down from all the excitement and was feeling a little deflated about our medal – we were awarded a Bronze Medal, the lowest level award.

'Mark, don't bloody move,' said Liz.

'Ah George, it's yourself. C'mere till I show you this. Have you met Mark, he'll talk you through it.'

It was RTÉ's environment and science correspondent, George Lee. He already had plenty in the can by that time as we were the last garden on the way out. But intrigued he waved over his camera crew and … action!

That evening we were once again featured prominently on RTÉ's *Nine O'Clock News* with me breezily explaining the concept and the fact that, by the way, we sell artificial grass. Our medal could be seen hung upside down (my petulant but rather fitting protest) in the window of the house. From a distance it could have been gold. God bless the RTÉ news editors.

That's the trick. If the money shot is the money shot, you can say whatever you like. Thanks Liz, thanks George.

But it was to get even sweeter.

The next morning, day one of being open to the public, I popped into the newsagents on my way up to the park. Holy cow.

My garden had made the front page of *The Irish Times*. The photographer had captured a moment in time with Shane hanging upside down and Monica, a super garden judge, bending over to grab her hat that had just fallen off.

The caption named the photographer, Shane, Monica and of course Bloom but failed to name either me or the company – the people who conceived, financed and built the damn thing. Still, no time to be churlish. Rocking up to Bloom that morning was a pleasure.

Incidentally that front page is now framed and on our office wall, just beside an upside down bronze medal. To my mind at least the judges failed to rise to the challenge of judging it on its merits. They had no boxes on their clipboard notes to cover anything like our 'concept'. Designers have a quick two minute chat with the judges in the garden and then must bugger off to let them deliberate. Observing from a safe distance I became quite optimistic. After all they were passing their phones around, taking turns photographing themselves in the topsy-turvy garden. I didn't see them do that in other gardens. What does that tell you?

I reckon that Bronze Medal, that one last perceived slight (one gets emotionally invested) is what eventually cured me of my addiction to Bloom.

Waste not, want not. The expensive metal framework for the garden was recycled and now houses machinery in the corner of the yard at Grassland. The house facade was rebuilt bordering our display area, the right way up this time. The hedging has since been reused in our pop-up Champagne Garden in Punchestown.

The Sanctuary Nurture Garden (2018)

That same year, wouldn't you know it, things fell into place for Dominic at Bloom.

Developing our primary schools market, he was seeking a way to promote the concept of our safe, soft play surface. He partnered up with Matthew Swaine, an enlightened principal of a special needs school just around the corner, and an idea evolved to highlight their work with an outdoor classroom and nurture garden. With help from the Office of Public Works and drawing from our collective expertise, despite stretched resources, Dominic produced a fabulous medium-sized garden that went down a storm.

He was disappointed to only get a Silver Gilt and I personally think he was robbed. We suspect residual hostility to artificial grass among the conservative judging panel, even when shown to combine beautifully and practically with great planting.

This garden deserves much more space but really it's Dominic's story to tell. Between himself and Matt they garnered serious media attention and were prominently featured on the *Bloom Live* TV programme, Dominic being interviewed at length within the garden. The school and the public contributed financially and we were happy to make up the difference.

Better still, the garden was to be transferred over to the school afterwards. The then taoiseach, Leo Varadkar, even recorded his vlog in the garden the evening the show opened.

So that's how Sanctuary Synthetics ended up doing not one but two gardens in Bloom 2018. It was a huge ask but working as a team we had pulled it off. Dominic's garden was eventually rebuilt in its entirety back in the Phoenix Park school along with their entire yard being covered with, yes, you guessed it, artificial grass. Happy days! It's fair to say Sanctuary kinda dominated the show that year.

Bloom Live's TV presenter and producer were so taken with the story of the Nurture garden and the special needs kids that they insisted on visiting the

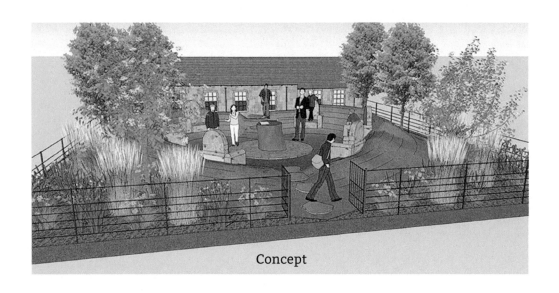

Concept

Bloom 2018

Sanctuary 'Nature Garden'

Silver Gilt Medal Winner

Rebuilt in Phoenix Park
special school, 2019

nearby school and highlighting its lasting legacy on their opening Bloom special the following year, 2019. Which was nice.

The ones that got away

A few concepts never got off the drawing board, for one reason or another. C'est la vie. Before Covid I got an unexpected call from Bloom. Universal Studios had another Gru and Minions film coming out. Would I be interested? I reluctantly declined on account of late notice and being so busy. That night I accidentally designed an entire garden in my sleep, complete with cannons and a giant crater. The next morning I committed nothing to paper. Five show gardens (no, six – a mini pop-up recycled grass-themed one that Dominic subsequently designed) in a decade is quite enough. Unfortunately, I have one or two more ideas in my head so never say never.

Following almost two decades in the grass business, having invested significant capital promoting it (in Bloom and elsewhere) and making artificial lawns a reality for thousands of people, I can only imagine what the future might hold for the industry and for the Fake Grass Man. Let's examine that in the next chapter.

Chapter 11

The future is green

'The trouble is, you think you have time'
~ commonly attributed to Buddha

In this book I wanted to cut through all the blather and propaganda one reads on industry websites and give you the unvarnished truth about the growing phenomenon and untold story of artificial grass.

We've looked at the genesis and flawed logic of real lawns, hopefully establishing that they are not necessarily the answer and that faux grass is no passing fad. We've traced its development and you now understand the distinction between sports grass (Astro) and artificial grass for lawns.

I've outlined, to the best of my ability, the pros and cons and I will soon describe how it should be laid in Part 2, the Buyer's Guide. Also coming are answers to frequently asked questions, advice on how to pick the right professional as well as how to measure and price it up.

We've examined the diverse applications of our grass and indulged in reminiscing about our marketing wins, my *Dragons' Den* foray, the genesis of Sanctuary and Grassland, and our Bloom show garden highlights. Cumulatively this should give you a good grasp of our little niche industry and our role in normalising the product.

Sustainability?

I'm aware that the RHS have banned artificial grass from Chelsea.

At the most recent Bloom show a lady approached me 'Hi Mark, do you remember me?'. I didn't.

'Course I do, how are you keeping?'

'You did my small lawn 10 years ago. The grandchildren love playing on it while I get to concentrate on working on my beds'

She was and remains a leading member of the Royal Horticultural society of Ireland.

'Ha, pity you were not here 10 minutes ago' I said. We'd just been attacked by a ranting eco warrior who stormed off before we could even begin to defend ourselves. Later that day there followed a rather vicious and personal attack via Twitter, mostly from UK keyboard activists. These I ignored.

I know I've invited the ire of many in publishing this book. It's really not my job to save the world but I have not shied away from the important ecological debate. Yes, I've attacked the very concept of real lawns yet I'm a firm advocate of rewilding – only not necessarily in tiny suburban gardens – and I am an active supporter of native woodlands. Without rehashing all the arguments from Chapter 6, my answer to the accusation that it's killing pollinators by depriving them of habitat and food is that they are attacking the wrong product. Monty Don recently attacked the "obsession" with a tidy lawn, arguing that fossil-fuel-powered mowing was noisy and "about the most injurious thing you can do to wildlife".' (*The Guardian*, 13 March 2021). Interestingly, the state of California has just banned all gas (petrol) powered lawn mowers. 'No mow May' is a current campaign by Plantlife promoting the ecological benefits of letting the grass grow unmolested for longer.

Synthetic lawns are an easy target for naysayers, but they can coexist with a well-planted garden and still have plenty of butterflies. Having a carefree lawn gets you outside and increases the likelihood of actually doing some gardening. I sometimes wonder if the objections are driven by snobbery rather than genuine ecological concerns. I confidently predict that in 10 years' time people will see a neatly mown real lawn and tut. The 'weed and feed' obsessed men – it's mostly men – will mostly disappear in a generation.

I've addressed conflicting consumer trends: the unheralded (until now) explosion in popularity of artificial grass versus increased awareness of the environment, in particular the damage being caused by plastic waste. I want to lay down my challenge both to the industry and the public. EU directives and tighter government legislation are required, both of which need public pressure first. SYNlawns in the US use renewable sources like oil from soy and sugarcane to create (at least partially) 'biobased' grass. SYNlawn in the US claim this has replaced 70% of the petroleum used to make the backing of their grasses whilst making it more durable. In Sanctuary we stocked 80 per cent recycled grass immediately upon its availability yet it has been disappointingly slow to sell. More recently we have 80 per cent recycled grass that is 100 percent recyclable, with no latex backing so any industrial recycling plant can easily handle it.

My argument with our Dutch suppliers goes something like this: 'Hey, you are the guys with all the dykes and sea walls so will be among the first to be flooded when sea levels rise.' I want to see a proper cradle-to-grave cycle. One token sports grass recycling plant in Holland is not enough. White-goods retailers charge a recycling premium to cover end-of-life disposal cost – why can't that be the case for artificial lawns too? If that adds a bit to the initial cost, so what, given its longevity? If every synthetic lawn remains destined for landfill, then the critics will have been proven right all along. We are currently in advanced talks with Limegreen® whose new grass is made from a single polymer, with a lower carbon footprint in production and maximum recyclability – a 100% circular solution. Thus I hereby call for public pressure to hasten the switch to a recycled and recyclable product. Only then can it truly be considered to have come of age. Let it be part of economist Joe Stiglitz's 'Green Recovery'. Both the EU and US are talking about a Green New Deal. I sure hope it happens. Capitalism's mindless consumption has run its course. The trouble with the rat race is that even if you win, you're still a rat. Modern society has given us the digital watch, a wide assortment of breakfast cereals and near-term human extinction. We're on a slow-moving collision course with reality. Time for conscious capitalism instead.

Although it's *not* my field, my prediction is that 4G rubber infill 'Astro' grass will eventually be forced to abandon combining quartz sand (harmless) and granular rubber infill (not necessarily harmless) on health and safety grounds. Future sports grasses will have alternative, perhaps organic, infill or more likely, none at all. I suspect future sports fields will be made from denser artificial grass laid over improved shockpad systems using no infill material. This has worked a treat for us.

Or indeed both may be abandoned in favour of hybrid. Given continued advancements in both biological turf systems (real grass, to you and me) and artificial grass, the arrival of a hybrid was, in retrospect, an inevitability. Irish sports grass company SIS are leading this development. Essentially it uses relatively sparse synthetic grass, which is then filled, not with sand or rubber granules, but with soil. This is then seeded, nurtured and grown to a height above that of the artificial fibres. Thus the grass gets the look and comfort of biological turf with the resilience and resistance to tearing up of artificial grass. Both systems require specialist maintenance but fields like the GAA's Croke Park in Dublin have proven very successful and this looks like the way forward for sports.

I would like to see such a hybrid system used for parks and playgrounds and as a feasible alternative for the domestic market someday.

It's not as if we've been responsible for covering massive swathes of this country. I estimate that we've done north of 14,000 gardens in Ireland to date. As housing density rises, garden size is unfortunately shrinking. Many house buyers have no objection to this. Assuming gardens average 50m² each, that amounts to about 150 acres (about 60 hectares) which would be about one modestly sized farm or about 80 football fields.

An outdoor room

John Brookes's 1969 classic *Room Outside* first sold the concept of gardens being another family room for dining and leisure. Such green spaces certainly offer a welcome respite and succour in these challenging times. There are definite changes afoot in how we use 'yardens' – our outside garden/yard space. This is down to five reasons:

- The majority of the workforce now live in cities and work indoors. Most yearn to get outside a bit more and will pay to enhance their home space (and enjoy a lockdown haven).
- Large patio doors and big windows are standard these days. So it's all the more important to have something nice to look out onto.
- With foreign holidays now being the norm (pandemics aside) rather than the exception, people have discovered the charm of eating al fresco.
- There continue to be lots of garden makeover programmes on TV. Thanks, Alan Titchmarsh.
- The fact that our lifestyles are busier than ever (except when in lockdown). There now appears to be a profound post Covid shift in work/life balance.

I could add the availability of decent-looking synthetic grass to that list. The reality is that it can form the transition from the entertainment area at the back of the house and the office at the back of the garden.

My wife, like many, has suddenly discovered the pleasure of GIY – grow it yourself. Once, having exotic plants and an immaculate lawn was the goal. Now gardens are being paved over allowing for outdoor living and open air seating. Sales figures for garden centres and DIY chains reflect this increased desire for Continental living, regardless of the weather. So it seems lawns are disappearing in any case, falling victim to larger patios, timber/composite decks and concrete.

223

At least with fake grass the green and pleasant land, as immortalised by William Blake, remains green. A recent UK survey states that of the 86 percent of all houses that have a garden, a staggering 75 per cent report having removed at least part of their lawn in recent years. Eight out of ten homeowners claim to have revamped their gardens to some extent in the previous five years. Even if exaggerated, the trend is clearly towards making more and better use of our open-air environment. Surely that's a good thing?

The same survey said that nine out of ten adults reportedly prefer entertaining guests outdoors than having a formal sit-down at the dinner table. Some 57 per cent own a barbecue, 46 per cent claim they use the barbecue once per week during the summer and 21 per cent say they regularly eat outside. Even if that survey was taken at the seaside in southern England during a heatwave, the picture is pretty clear.

Artificial grass fits nicely with these aspirations.

The lockdown effect

Post-Covid-19 many habits will have changed. Gardens are now seen as a place of solace and consequently deserving of investment. Indeed the popularity of the term 'artificial grass' tripled according to Google trends for the UK and Ireland with a 185 per cent jump in May 2020 compared to the same period 12 months earlier. Here the spring 2020 heatwave led to patchy grass and a much earlier need to water. With people suddenly spending much more time at home, both online shopping and gardening projects proliferated. A just-published market forecast predicts, despite the economic impact of Covid-19, the global artificial grass market will reach USD$4.44 billion by 2025.

The cutting edge

What does the future hold for the Fake Grass Man?

Upton Sinclair said, 'It is difficult to get a man to understand something when his salary depends on not understanding it.'[41] Yes, this book has sought to validate what I do. But I've sought to understand the ramifications and share as much as possible.

Sanctuary has grown between 10 and 20 per cent per annum over the last decade and a half. I see only one direction in the future. We've embarked on a 'Lean' programme of continuous improvement and have added synthetic hedging and a range of artificial plants for hire and sale to our range.

41 Upton Sinclair, *I, Candidate for Governor: And how I got Licked*, Introduction by JN Gregory, First Edition, California, University of California Press, 1994, p. 109.

On a recent visit to our manufacturers in the Netherlands I saw experiments with luminous grass, perfect for walkways or their many cycle paths at night. There are exciting possibilities for incorporating fibre optic lighting that we've already played around with. There's a promising new drain base system on the market. It's a plastic grid made from 100 percent recycled HDEP (high density polyethylene) and is also fully recyclable.

A new 'Pureti' technology has recently come on the market with the bold claim that $1m^2$ of Pureti treated grass is equal to the air purifying efficiency of one fully grown tree. This nanotechnology, activated by sunlight, reduces NOx gases, Formaldehyde and Methane. Furthermore it breaks down the odor and urine of pets, no longer requires the use of biocides and it prevents the growth of mould, moss and algae.

Disruptor technologies can replace old industries overnight. Robotic and battery-powered lawnmowers will soon replace petrol models. As for real lawns, they have their charm of course, but I contend the only natural grass with a really bright future (in several US states so far at least) is now sold in licensed cannabis dispensaries! I'm aware hemp is beginning to be used as a raw material in the backing of some artificial grasses. I hope research and development in that direction continues.

The industry is still relatively young but growing fast. Could artificial grass ever be banned or boycotted? Possibly, but I doubt it somehow. A wise woman once told me to avoid clichés like the plague but the one certain thing in life (besides death and taxes) is change. In our market we are big enough to handle the opportunities that come our way but hopefully remain nimble enough to adapt to any and all changes. Small enough to care.

I count myself a lucky man to have stumbled across such a cool product in the first place. I certainly don't envisage hanging up my cape and moving on to greener pastures any time soon. I was recently asked would I ever sell up – My immediate and automatic answer was 'no way, José'. We've worked way too hard to get this far and I'm still enjoying my job way too much. Leadership of the industry in the Emerald Isle will have to be prised from my cold dead hands.

I won't lie – sometimes it's been tough. Being in business requires guts and it can be a lonely place. I've been flat broke more than once. I've had to fire people (hardly ever fun to do). I've been sued, twice – happily on Mickey Mouse grounds – we've had to deal with our fair share of rogues. I've been kicked when down and made plenty of mistakes but I can tell you one thing for sure, I've rarely been bored. We've travelled the length and breadth of the country on grass business, grassed atop a sacred mountain, given our President of Ireland a tour of MunchkinLand. I've been advised by the Queen of England 'not to get my hopes up', Monty Don admonished me on Twitter, we've sponsored horse races, designed far-out show gardens, won a hatful of Bloom medals and been SME of the Year. I've buried a business partner, helped pay a good few mortgages, invented the HidBin and fought Dragons, shared a hairy green buggy with Miss Universe and made the front page of *The Irish Times*. I've spoken in public, been interviewed on the main evening TV news twice and pioneered an entire industry.

Not bad for the big clueless farmer's son from Kildare. Artificial grass has allowed me to be creative *and* build a business, raise a family and touch the lives of thousands. The debate will continue but I guess what I'm asking for is just some respect.

For me 'heartificial' grass has been a blessing. You've seen the many weird and versatile uses of artificial grass, another reason I remain so enthusiastic. My message to the traditional garden world is that it's high time to embrace artificial grass. It seems to be recession-proof as well as weather-proof. To the people who laughed at us when starting out – who is laughing now?

Each weekday afternoon I get WhatsApp pictures and videos of installations from our crews. I love seeing the transformations we perform and hearing the testimonials of our customers. Remember, faraway grass may seem greener but someone still has to mow it. As always, I look forward to Monday mornings.

That surely is the test.

Thank you for sharing my journey. I sure hope I am granted time to add more adventures and new chapters in the future. As I write these concluding words I'm looking out the window of a charming guesthouse in the middle of the Burren in County Clare. It's where my ancestors, once Vikings, settled.[42] There's a castle in the distance and further still, miles of grey limestone slate hills. There's pure silence save for the occasional cow lowing and bird chirping.

'No-one is finally dead until the ripples they cause in the world die away'
~ Terry Pratchett, *Reaper Man*

I do take pride in our legacy of work to date. I'm not too worried about any artificial grass epitaph, but there's one thing that will now always be true – I wrote the book.

42 The surname O'Loughlin is that of an ancient Gaelic sept from Thomond in the southwest of Ireland. The name stems directly from words meaning 'Norse vikinger'.

THE END ...

... except for one last four-chapter-long technical and informative section: your Buyer's Guide. It includes a few more yarns, but starts with answers to some questions you might still have.

PART 2

YOUR BUYER'S GUIDE TO ARTIFICIAL GRASS

Before & After

Chapter 12

Buyer's Guide: FAQs and SAQs

Having soldiered this far you'll already know some of the answers to the frequently asked questions (FAQs) and should be asked questions (SAQs). First up is our top 50 FAQs. After that, we'll look at the pivotal questions you *should* be asking.

FAQs
(frequently asked questions)

1. How often do I have to cut it?
Ha, ha. Please don't. We've been asked a million times and it's really just not funny anymore.

2. My garden is in an awful state, would you come and see it (despite my embarrassment)?
Of course, within reason most suppliers will gladly carry out a site survey free of obligation. Don't worry, they'll have seen worse. No garden is beyond redemption. A good installer should relish the challenge, as the before and after pictures will be all the more impressive.

3. What does it cost?
It depends. In Ireland it's priced per square metre. See Chapter 14.

4. Do all grasses need a sand infill?
Some do but many landscape grasses don't. If it's for heavy use, sand can be added for extra protection even when not required for structural integrity.

5. How do I measure?
Not necessarily as straightforward as you'd think. Do it carefully. Also covered in detail in Chapter 14.

6. What is the expected lifetime of artificial grass?

A well-maintained decent quality surface should last over 20 years. It's largely unaffected by the elements. It's UV-stabilised and waterproof (although porous). Installed worldwide, it's exposed to freezing temperatures and hot desert sun.

7. Which is the best grass?

Impossible to answer really. Everyone has their own preferences. Different types cater for different budgets and applications. See Chapter 13 for more insight.

8. How do I install?

What preparation, base, fixings, etc. are involved? All this is explained in Chapter 15, folks.

9. Can't you just throw it down over a hard surface?

No, not really. I've seen examples of where people have got away with it, possibly weighed down with sand, but it ought to be fixed into position with a specialist glue and spot-glued so as not to interfere with rainwater escaping. If it's going onto timber, then screw or nail it around the perimeter. Even if it's only a temporary installation, to avoid it becoming a trip hazard use gaffer tape on the edges or double-sided tape underneath it to hold it in position.

10. Won't it feel quite hard straight on top of my yard/patio/deck?

It'll certainly be softer than what's underneath. How soft will depend on the length of the blades (pile height) and its density. So buy accordingly. Or add a shockpad.

11. Do I need shockpad?

Really it's an optional extra, certainly not necessary in most cases. If play equipment has a specific critical fall height (or HIA) requirement, then add a layer of certified shockpad under the grass. It feels softer underfoot but won't interfere with the bounce of a ball too much. It also extends the life of the grass, cushioning it from wear and tear. I used it in my garden.

12. How well does it drain?

The grass is perforated with small but unseen drainage holes that allow for a certified rate of 60 litres per square metre per minute (or 30 inches of rain per hour per square yard if you prefer) to soak through the build-up. Thereafter, it seeps into the water table underneath.

13. How real does it look?

These days it can be hard to tell the difference. It wasn't always, so get samples and judge for yourself – the bigger the samples the better.

14. Is it guaranteed?

See Chapter 13 for the lowdown on warranties. Expect a written warranty covering the grass, 5–12 years would be standard, *and* the workmanship for at least 12–24 months.

15. What if my garden is a swamp?

I've yet to come across an area where it's just not feasible to install. You might need a deeper than usual dig-out and build-up, perhaps with some additional drainage work, so it may be a little more expensive due to the additional labour and materials.

16. Can it be laid directly onto topsoil?

Nooo! Haven't you been paying any attention? Please don't lay it directly onto topsoil. Again, I've seen it done and if the base is rock solid, level and compact, you could get away with it, but we would strongly recommend a proper dig-out and build-up for longevity.

17. Can it be fitted into irregular shapes or as a circular lawn?

Yep, sure thing. Just like a carpet it can be cut and joined to fit any shape but be aware that this is likely to involve more waste and additional joins.

18. Is it dog proof?

Frankly, no. When my dog Darcy was a pup he chewed the legs off the wooden kitchen table and chairs. We had to replace the lot. (Secretly I suspect my wife encouraged him! She'd wanted new dining furniture for years.) Thankfully he never did anything to the lawn. But of the many 'dog gardens' we've done, a small handful do get damaged. Lonely, frustrated (usually young) dogs *can* rip it up and chew through it. It's usually repairable.

19. OK, is it dog friendly?

Absolutely, yes. Of the many 'dog gardens' we've done over the years, no more than a handful ever had any issues. Dogs love it.

They love rolling around on it and they love pooping on it. Or they pay it no attention so no big deal. Of the many dog boarding kennels we've done, there has never been a problem. We do push customers to higher-end grasses. Covered in Chapter 7.

20. What about cats?

No issues whatsoever. Nine out of ten cats prefer it. OK, I just made that up. There is no way of asking them. And really, would you trust their answers? I'd imagine plenty of nonchalant shoulder shrugs. But I'm fairly sure most cats would not be hostile to it. We have installed it in several catteries and the owners, at least, seem satisfied.

21. What about pet pee?

The uric acid in dog wee is smelly. It kills real grass but it will not stain the synthetic version. In Ireland we have found that the volume and frequency of rain is sufficient to wash it away. Have I mentioned it rains a lot here?

Certainly I've never had a whiff of it from our dog at home. We do warn our customers that in the event of several dry summer days *in a row* (cue raised eyebrows and quizzical looks) the grass could begin to smell, particularly if your canine friend likes to use the same spot close to a window or your patio. The uric acid in dog urine can cause crystals to form which are not so soluble in water. The latex backing on the grass can soak up and trap these crystals. Not to worry, however, as the odour can be controlled and eliminated by applying an anti-bacterial non-biological spray, first developed to protect American football athletes from picking up infections from AstroTurf. If your grass supplier is any good, they should have it in stock. Zoflora is one safe brand available. Diluted vinegar and or lemon juice work as eco-friendly enzyme cleaners. If you mix in baking soda or even washing powder do not let dogs ingest.

Plus there are now specific dog-friendly grasses with a non-latex (PU) backing which does not retain odour.

22. OK, but what about poo?

Way easier to deal with than on a real lawn. That's because it's much easier to spot deposits from our furry friends as the synthetic version is shorter and more even than the real thing. How many times have you trodden on the dreaded poo as it lurked unseen behind a tuft of grass. Yuck! On an artificial lawn it can be picked up and disposed of as normal. I invested in a pooper scooper so it's less hands-on and I don't have to bend down so far. That doesn't get any easier with age. Must go back to yoga.

Even if the poo is runny and congealing among the fibres, do not panic. It can simply be washed down. Use hot water. Any diluted household bleach is fine – we've tested it. Disinfectants (enzymatic cleaners) like Dettol work well.

23. Do pets really like artificial grass?

Besides the presence of children, pets are the reason most householders opt for a synthetic lawn. Feedback confirms that they love playing and scratching themselves on the grass. It's difficult to survey dogs but observation and anecdotal evidence says Yes.

24. Is it safe for children?

This was the main driver for its initial development over half a century ago, and still drives growth today. So yes.

It's specifically designed for safe play for children, and far better for them to be outside, albeit on an artificial surface, than stuck inside on the Xbox.

The longer and more dense the pile the softer the grass, although a shorter pile height is better for specific ball games like tennis or hockey. Artificial grass has a soft smooth feel that does *not* burn skin as kids slide around. This was a myth grounded in the earlier teething problems of the original nylon sports grasses. Its density acts as a cushion in the event of a fall. School principals and crèche owners report that their first aid box (for cut knees etc.) is taken out far less often post-installation. That's most gratifying.

25. Can you put fake grass over real grass?

Eh, that would be a definite no. Maybe for a few hours on a once-off basis but it's no shortcut. It's unlikely to sit evenly and will kill the grass underneath if left down for long. See Chapter 15 for why and how to do it properly.

26. Can it be laid on a slope?

Sure thing but be warned that any more than a 15 per cent gradient can be slippery *regardless* of the surface. The build-up need not be too elaborate as rainwater will flow to the bottom, but the grass must be secured well. It's a good solution for troublesome banks where it's difficult to grow stuff and get ground coverage, as gravel and bark mulch never stay in position and your weed membrane becomes exposed, a pet hate of mine.

27. Can it be laid over a mound?

Certainly the inclusion of a mound in your lawn or putting green can help it look more natural adding interest, but be aware it takes some skill to do it correctly. Imagine spreading a large tablecloth over a mound. There will be overlaps all around the base. The solution is to cut out these triangles and re-join. Take care so that the joins are invisible.

28. We've got a trampoline. How does that work?

Not a problem. If you already have one (a seemingly obligatory accoutrement of family gardens), you will know that the grass underneath has either died from lack of sunlight or is a two-foot-high jungle that's hard to get at with the lawnmower. Or else you keep having to shift it around to stop this from happening. The good news is it can sit on top of your artificial lawn in the same spot indefinitely. Don't worry, the kids will soon grow up and you can get rid of the dangerous monstrosity. Besides many tales of woe involving hospital visits due to broken limbs and missing teeth, some of my own hostility stems from a late Christmas Eve years ago spent, instead of down in the pub with friends, out in the freezing cold trying to assemble one alone, in darkness, in time for the arrival of you know who.

29. What about garden furniture?

As above, your patio furniture won't affect it. You know the way when you shift the couch in the sitting room and you can see an indent of its legs in the carpet? Well, it's the same with heavy objects like plant pots sitting on the grass. Happily, the grass will spring back. You can help this process by coaxing and brushing it up by hand or with a stiff-bristled brush. Soon you won't even see the mark.

30. Can I fix my swing/slide/trampoline, etc. into artificial grass?

Yes. Either cement it into position and lay the grass around the uprights or simply push in spikes through the grass into the build-up below just as you did into the earth previously. Punching a small hole through the grass is no big deal and it shouldn't be visible when eventually removed. The infill build-up will hold the spike or U pin just like soil would.

31. Is it a good investment?

Rather than comparing it to the price of re-carpeting indoors, a sun holiday or even a cheap second-hand car, consider what you'll reap from your investment.

Besides boosting the value of your property – I've seen this first-hand when selling my own home – think of the additional use you'll get out of the space, never mind time saved.

32. Is it really maintenance free?

Compared to a real lawn, yes. Almost. But not quite.

Much as you still have to wash your shiny new car every now and again, a certain amount of occasional aftercare *is* in fact needed. The shiny new car does not need a service for the first 20,000 to 30,000 miles but will need some TLC on at least an annual basis thereafter. You don't march back into your dealership after a month saying the wheel arches and body are all dirty, do you? It's *your* job to wash your car once in a while. So too with your new lawn that will never grow.

33. How do I maintain and clean my artificial lawn?

We recommend an occasional brush (use a yard brush with stiff bristles) or rake (plastic fan rake not a metal one) to keep debris from building up. Work against the grain. That way you'll jazz up the nap of the fibres. If your artificial lawn is ignored for months on end, debris may accumulate and look untidy, allowing weeds to take hold. I tidy up my own lawn three or four times a year max. Far better than mowing it 30 or 40 times.

I might vacuum the hairy green carpet or use a leaf blower, hooshing the debris into a corner then picking it up and disposing of it. I'd suggest doing this a few times in the autumn depending on the volume of falling leaves, though a few leaves can help it look more natural. A reputable installer should issue you an aftercare instructions regime.

If seedlings or weeds do appear and you are averse to using chemical weed killers, simply apply a half-water half-vinegar solution on a dry day, or even lots of table salt, which will do the trick. Try physically pulling up the weeds but try to get the roots up too. In the event of snow simply clear it away with a shovel or allow it to melt away as normal. Regardless of how onerous the above might seem, believe me it's a *lot* less work than having real grass.

34. Can I use a power hose (pressure washer) to clean the grass?

If the grass is sand-filled, then no because you'll disturb the infill and will have to redo again afterwards. If it's non-infill, yes, but proceed carefully. Use a wide angle nozzle tip and keep it at least a foot away from the surface at all times. Spray at an angle – not straight down – so as not to disturb the compacted base underneath, otherwise it could shift and feel uneven underfoot and this can be tricky to rectify.

35. Can I drive and park on artificial grass?

While it's not designed for such use, it's not a cardinal sin once in a while. I doubled the width of the driveway when installing my front lawn. Somehow my wife still managed to park two of the four wheels of her Audi on it, leading to the grass being crushed and flattened. You know what? So what. No big deal. It simply looks like somebody parks on it. What would it look like if it was a real lawn? Much worse.

That said I wouldn't advocate using it for an entire driveway. With pressure on space we have installed lawns that double up as parking spots, warning people that an oil leak or sharp turns can damage or disturb the surface. If you are simply driving in and backing out and can live with seeing the imprint of your tyre tracks, go right on ahead. Note, however, that it will negate your guarantee and shorten the grass's life expectancy.

36. Can weeds grow in it?

Yes, they can. Just like they grow in your gutter, on your driveway, patio and everywhere else. Synthetic grass is more resistant than many other surfaces, after all it's plastic so minimal nutrients are available. But light and moisture are sufficient for germination so don't let them take hold. Typically they appear along the perimeter or in the small drainage holes.

The good news is that they are easy to spot and deal with. If the build-up is sufficiently deep, it's very rare that they come up from below although we have had instances of it happening. Say a deep-rooted dandelion or daffodil bulb that escaped the dig-out (bamboo shoots can be a nightmare) – in this instance, there's no point in pulling it up. You won't get the roots and it'll continue to appear. Far better to kill it (see Question 33 above) and let it die before removing what's visible.

37. Does artificial grass need to be watered?

Seriously? No. The only reason you might ever spray it down is to cool it if it's very warm and you are in bare feet.

38. Can it catch fire?

It will melt rather than catch fire in the first instance. So if a lit cigarette, match or burning coal from the barbecue falls on it, it can blacken and be damaged. Sand infill acts as a retardant so we advocate it for public areas in pubs, clubs and hotels as well as in smoking areas. It's important to be aware of windows, mirrors and other highly reflective surfaces. Sunlight can bounce off them, intensify and slowly melt the grass it hits. So if you have a mirror in your garden, make sure to tilt it up away from the ground. If cutting a hedge with a petrol strimmer do *not* leave it down on the grass, as its heat could well mark the grass. Grass with a high fire rating is available and is often a requirement for indoor installation.

39. Can it be repaired?

Usually yes. The challenge is to match up the particular batch subsequently, hence our advice to keep some offcuts just in case. Tears can often be glued back into position or a small patch can be replaced. If skilfully done it can be difficult to see where it occurred.

40. Does it fade in the sun?

Happily, no. This is another misconception based on earliest versions that *were* prone to bleaching over time. It's now fully protected and stabilised and most grasses carry a 10-year VU guarantee. After 20 years my lawn looks just as good as the day it was installed.

41. Does it go mouldy?

Typically, no. Once properly installed with good drainage, it's similar to, or better than, real grass. Mould and mildew are rarely an issue unless in dark, shaded spots and in the absence of any aftercare.

42. Can it get mossy?

As per above. Moss grows at two degrees centigrade whereas it needs to be four degrees or above for real grass to grow. That's why, with a winter head start on grass, moss often takes over Irish lawns. To be frank, many people are not bothered. It's still green and there's not so much grass to cut. Greenkeepers on golf courses are not so blasé. If it does take hold, say around trees and shady spots, it can be treated and even physically removed with a good brush and elbow grease.

43. What if it gets dirty?

No big deal. As per Question 33 just clean it off. Dust, debris, leaves and all sorts can blow in. The dog might dig up an adjacent bed and spread soil over it. The kids might throw stones on it. Your brother-in-law might barf on it. Panic not. It's plastic. It's cleanable. Disinfectants won't damage it.

44. Could having an artificial lawn adversely affect the value of my property?

As it's become more accepted it's become a desirable feature for many prospective house buyers. According to US house financing experts (and they would surely never lie?) any investment in quality landscaping can add value to your home, from 100 per cent of the costs to more than doubling your investment. A bonus to having a low maintenance garden is that it's a factor in selling your home quickly. Don't underestimate curb appeal.

45. Will it reduce creepy crawlies?

Yes. It covers the soil, which prevents access for insects and denies them a food source. Small animals like rodents and rabbits can't eat it so they'll go and annoy your neighbours instead.

46. Does it feel like real grass?

Kind of a subjective question. More or less, yes. It's soft underfoot and can be walked on safely in bare feet. In my travels internationally I've stood on many varieties of grass and they all feel slightly different – it's much the same with the fake alternatives I guess.

47. Can it be laid next to real grass?

Yes. For example, it's often put into goal mouths or around the perimeter of football fields. Sometimes our customers can't afford to get their entire lawn done so they just do whatever they can afford initially. The lawnmower can simply be run over the outer edge and will do no harm to the shorter artificial grass. Best not to have the lawnmower deck at the lowest setting to be on the safe side. You can add an edging such as a brick border for the visual effect or simply let one directly meet the other.

48. Over time will the grass squash down and flatten?

This is a question avoided by most suppliers. The honest answer is yes. With good grass and periodic brushing it'll stay looking good for a long, long time. Modern grasses with texturised curled fibres and blade shape technology have more bouncebackability.

Nevertheless with heavy foot traffic it will inevitably flatten. This fact used to bother me but after 20 years in the business I now realise it's no biggie. Like my front lawn with my wife's Audi wheel tracks it looks like what it is. A bit worn. Constantly walking to the shed or clothes line might show on the grass eventually. But I can honestly say that in all my years I've never had a complaint about it. Plus after decades of continuous use it can be replaced far more cheaply as the groundwork is already done.

49. Can I put my inflatable swimming pool on it?

Sure you can. Unlike on real grass splashing and emptying it will not lead to slippery mud patches. Have fun. But when emptying it do so gradually so as not to disturb the build-up under the grass.

Salt in seawater has no detrimental effect on fake grass whatsoever.

50. Can it be installed and used indoors?

Yes, siree! This is becoming increasingly popular. We've done conservatories, bedrooms and even a hall, stairs and landing. Elsewhere we've installed it in shops for retail displays, pubs and offices, including our own.

SAQs
(should ask questions)

1. Do you guys supply and install?

Some companies won't want to know about installing and will often fob off your questions on 'how to', claiming that it's easy to do it yourself. It's not.

2. If you do offer an installation service, is it installed by your own employees or subbed out to a third-party independent contractor?

The other guys may well be great but if something goes wrong, who takes responsibility? 'Not my problem' is something you don't want to hear. Who trained them?

3. What does 'accredited' installer mean?

Accreditation can mean they have paid a fee, have been trained by the supplier or merely been recommended by them. You need to clarify exactly who does what, who guarantees what element of the job, who is to be paid, and when. The less complicated the better.

4. What is the actual lead time?

Don't be misled here. State your own deadline from the start. If they are good they will be busy, especially in the high summer season. You might just have to wait. Watch that they don't quote you a shorter lead time to stop you going elsewhere. If they say they have a six-week lead time, ascertain whether that's from the date of their visit/quote or your formal go ahead. You might be disappointed to learn that the clock only starts from the confirmed receipt of your deposit. Note that there could be weeks in the difference. Seek written confirmation that you have been scheduled sufficiently in advance of your barbecue, holy communion, birthday party or bar mitzvah. Ideally, don't leave it until the day before. Remember Murphy's Law. Even if all goes smoothly at the last minute, we advise staying off the grass for 24 hours after installation to allow the glue to cure properly.

5. Should I do it myself?

We've devoted Chapter 15 to this question but put it this way, if you read this book carefully you know way more than most, including many in the trade.

6. Should I go for the cheapest price?

In a word, no. By all means seek the best price. But as with everything you can only have two of the following three at any one time: good – fast – cheap. If it's good and fast, it won't be cheap. If it's cheap and fast, it won't be good. You get the picture. Installing grass is a relatively expensive project, and a long-term investment.

7. When do I pay?

Different companies will have varying terms and conditions.

Don't pay all up front no matter what. If asked, run a mile. A percentage deposit, anything from 10 to 50 per cent is not unreasonable to secure a date. Stage payment over the course of a long (more than a couple of weeks) project would be the norm, but not applicable to most domestic grass installations unless part of a wider hardscaping project. Payment of the balance upon successful completion is normal. Agree in advance and make no assumptions. 'Money,' as my old accountancy lecturer used to say, 'is a very emotional topic.'

8. What happens if I'm not happy?
First of all, communicate clearly, both with operatives on the ground and with the installer's office. Withhold payment of the balance or you'll have a far weaker hand to play. Refer to your guarantee. There is always the small claims court if all else fails but most conflicts are resolved amicably.

9. Should I haggle?
By all means, particularly if it's straight forward, in the depths of winter or a particularly large installation. There may be economies of scale. A reputable supplier will have fixed overheads. You certainly won't get a discount unless you ask. After the 2008 crash, when Irish property values fell by 50 per cent, many people became streetwise wheeler-dealers overnight.

10. How can I get a bargain?
Explain that you are on a budget. Do some of the prep work yourself and it'll be discounted accordingly. Arrange to keep the soil in your garden to save labour costs.

 TIP Offer to toss a coin over the last 50 or even 20 quid. You can't lose as it won't go up but you've a 50–50 chance of it going down.

Say you are prepared to wait until the off-season or until the supplier has a cancellation or postponement. You can be the first substitution, as it might be handy for the installers to have a job available to slot in, albeit at a slightly reduced rate. If you are accommodating they may reciprocate.

11. What if I pay cash?
It might help but a reputable installer will still have to record it and lodge it to their bank account incurring VAT regardless. In this day and age it's difficult to do under the table jobs and the absence of paperwork might affect your guarantee in any case. So don't.

12. Should I visit their premises or showrooms?

For sure. Even if the salesperson has been out to your place, it's no harm to establish a rapport with the office-based staff and see for yourself the full extent of what they have to offer, rather than just seeing what the rep wants you to see. They might have grass offcuts or rejects (often with a very minor fault) lying around that you could pick up cheaply.

13. What's the deal with offcuts?

These are unused, perfectly good, smaller pieces of grass that have come back from jobs. If someone has a 7m wide × 7m long garden, then two 4m rolls are required to complete it. Therefore, a one metre strip will invariably make its way back to the yard. Combine a few of these and it's possible to construct an entire lawn. OK, you'll have more joins and several pieces but if carefully done you could get a far cheaper lawn. Companies will often sell these at a discount otherwise they accumulate, clogging up space. The challenge is matching identical batches of a particular grass, and figuring out if there are sufficient quantities to cover your area, bearing in mind nap orientation (explained later in Chapter 14).

14. I've bought the grass elsewhere. Can you please install it?

Our answer would always be a big fat *no*. Not a chance. Why would we forgo that margin, work with an unknown and possibly inferior product, and bear the brunt of dissatisfaction if things didn't work out.

15. What if you see a grass supplier at a show or exhibition?

Ask what they are going to do with their display grass afterward. By definition it's now second-hand with just foot traffic from the couple of days of the show. Typically they'll just be rolling it up to take back to languish in a corner of a warehouse. Do a deal on the spot as you might not be the only one with the same idea. Ditto with a product launch, fashion show or other public event. Often it's bought for that particular purpose and it may be a pain to take up and transport away. You can offer to do it.

Alternatively do a casual walkabout *after* the show or event. It's often panic stations with a deadline to clear the area. You could swoop in and save them hassle and yourself money. Better still, look into the skips around back. It's not unusual to see perfectly good stuff chucked away. Save the environment and liberate it.

16. How can I trust you?

Don't. Look up reviews on social media. Testimonials can be made up but genuine ones tend to be easy to spot.

17. Can installed lawns be stolen?

It's rare but it has happened.

Years ago a Dutch supplier told me about a front garden lawn in the Netherlands that went missing overnight. He kindly volunteered to replace it but waited a couple of weeks first.

'Oh no,' I said. 'How terrible.'

'Not at all,' he replied, 'I was delighted.'

The theft made all the local papers and was even reported on the TV news. His delay was to maximise the free publicity.

You couldn't buy such exposure, he explained, as the media couldn't report it without explaining what it was, getting the homeowner talking about why they got it in the first place. Well worth the expense of replacing it as a once-off goodwill gesture.

It almost happened to us once, in a relatively small front garden on a busy road in Dublin suburb. The lawn thieves ultimately failed, however. They pulled up and rolled the grass but either it was too heavy for them to drag away or they were disturbed in the act. Either way we simply relayed it, secured it more firmly, brushing in sand to make it heavier and it hasn't been touched since.

18. What happens if it snows?

No biggie. Grass is entirely unaffected and snowmen tend to be cleaner.

It rarely snows in Ireland. One year just before Christmas it did and we had a one day installation for a customer not far away. It had snowed heavily the night before and she had left for work assuming we wouldn't turn up. As the main roads were just about passable and we'd forgo income by not continuing to operate, Krzystof, my hardy foreman, and crew set off. Undeterred by a locked side gate they simply hopped over, unscrewed the hinges and got to work. The first task was clearing several inches of snow. They managed to finish before dark, reinstating the side gate before they headed for home.

Next day our office called her for payment. 'Yes,' she said, 'I'll pay you when it's done, not before.'

'But, but we did it yesterday.'

'Oh, no you didn't ...'

'Oh, yes we did.'

It was pantomime season after all. It had snowed again after our crew had left and, in fairness, by the time she arrived home her new lawn, all footprints, tyre tracks and any evidence of our presence had been covered in a nice new blanket of snow. We had to wait until she found a shovel and cleared a patch to see for herself. Lo and behold there was her brand new synthetic lawn underneath. Only then did we get paid. Mind you, it was several days later before she got to see her new lawn in its entirety.

Coming up I'll help you leave no stone unturned doing your due diligence when it comes to picking a pro.

What if the lawn is in the wrong place? Or worse, the wrong garden? There's lots of information needed in advance to carry out a successful installation. Our crews need to know the proper dimensions, how much digging and infill is required, what access is like (about a quarter of our domestic installs are for terraced houses where everything goes through the house). Drawings, photos and even videos are routinely provided for the crews the night before in order to prepare and load-up. Normally this works like clockwork. They need to know about manholes, utilities, power cables, gas lines, water availability and of course the names of our customers (or their nannies) and, critically, where exactly they live.

Can you see where I'm going with all this?

In 20 years and thousands of gardens this has only happened once. To my knowledge. If no one is home, we make arrangements for a key to be left out or a side gate unlatched. So it was one day for an average-sized install in a large north Dublin housing estate.

Readers will have had frustrating experiences with their own satnavs, I'm sure. Google Earth and Google Maps have been a boon for businesses like ours. We can check people's gardens from outer space in advance, even roughly measuring them. Britain and Ireland have many housing estates that are very uniform with row upon row of identical houses and gardens. Moreover, they have confusing and illogical numbering systems. Individual roads are marked 'the Way', 'the Lawns', 'the Crescent' and so on. No prizes for originality.

So on this fine day, Dominic, our sales director, visited the crew mid-morning to check on progress. Only there was no sign of the lads. *Ring, ring.*

'Eh, where are ye?'

'We're here,' answered the foreman. "We're flying through this job.' *Nooo!*

With a sinking feeling Dominic looked around and spotted two of our vans over the far side of a large green area outside the wrong house. It had the same number and a similar address as the correct one. Moreover, it too was a corner house with a side gate halfway up the garden. It even had, as described, a mound of rubble outside. Dom waved across to the lads. But it was far too late.

That entire lawn had already been dug out with most of the hardcore in. The fact that it was a terrible lawn in bad nick raised no eyebrows with the lads. That's par for the course.

These are the phone calls from site that one dreads.

'Mark, bit of a problem here …' No way. OK. *Stop!* Half of the guys were sent to start the correct garden across the way. Meanwhile Dominic composed a short polite note. Along the lines of 'Sorry for accidentally ripping out your garden. Please call us on …'

They called alright.

The lady of the house came home at lunchtime and was livid. Couldn't blame her, I suppose. Solicitors were threatened, the works. We offered them their choice of a free artificial lawn or a replacement with new rolled-out turf. She consulted her husband who, in fairness, could see the funny side, and they opted for the latter. We got busy sorting this while garden number two was also underway. The erroneous install was reversed and for a couple of hundred euro we bought and carefully laid nice new instant lawn turf. We scrambled, working hard and fast, and by the time the husband got home from work they had a brand new much improved rolled-out lawn. So in the end no harm was done and the correct garden got finished with some overtime and reinforcements.

Plus I got a tale to tell, though I have never admitted to it before now. Keep it under your hat, would you please.

Chapter 13

Buyer's Guide: How to pick a pro and more

'When you make a choice, you change the future'
~ Deepak Chopra

As with all human pursuits there are varying degrees of competence within the landscaping industry. The same goes for artificial grass installers. When faced with a choice how do you choose the best supplier and manage them once appointed?

For a few years the choice in Ireland was easy; it could only be the pioneering specialists – us guys, unless you went to a sports grass company for whom artificial lawns were a sideline at best. Since then, there are dozens of new competitors, which keeps us on our toes and it drives standards. That's all good news for you.

Six good reasons to pick a professional to install your grass

1. Professional know-how
There's no one size fits all technique. Pros have the experience and knowledge to use the most appropriate methodology for your circumstances.

2. Necessary equipment
Purchase or hire costs for DIYer will quickly mount up so factor this in when comparing the cost of DIY versus picking a pro.

3. Time
What do *you* earn per hour? While you might fancy tackling the project yourself, don't forget the opportunity cost. Pros will be faster, having learned from their mistakes, and they know what to expect. In Sanctuary we frequently (and sheepishly) get called in once DIYer gives up, belatedly realising the magnitude of the work and volumes of materials involved.

4. Energy

Pros don't need gym memberships as it's a physically demanding job. Digging out heavy compacted sod and soil, roots, obstacles and utilities is heavy work. Pros handle all this without damaging trees and blocking drains. So save your energy for something else.

5. Avoid the stress

Many wistfully look out at the gardeners on a nice sunny day and wish they had their job and lifestyle, forgetting about the rainy days. Earlier this morning (at time of writing) it was minus 5 degrees. The guys would have swapped places with our admin staff, in their snug offices, in a heartbeat.

6. Avoid costly errors: Measure twice, cut once

Measuring and cutting must be extremely accurate as mistakes can be costly. Seaming the joins correctly is critical. Let that be the pro's problem.

Ten point checklist when considering a landscaping professional

1. Do they have membership of professional associations?

Every country will have representative bodies for their landscaping industry. Membership indicates a willingness to stay up to date with industry trends such as technological improvements and changes in materials, engineering and practices, including ecological practices. Reasonably stringent membership criteria apply, often based on one's portfolio and peer approval. In Ireland top garden designers are part of the GLDA and the best contractors are in the ALCI (SGD and BALI are the UK equivalents). We are corporate members of both. They frequently run seminars, training programmes and award schemes. We participate in and sponsor many of these on an annual basis.

A small outfit may not have the interest or resources to be involved.

I know several who, for their own reasons, eschew participation but would still be deserving of consideration. Some simply prefer to plough their own furrow.

Finally, be aware of subterfuge. There are several designations, 'guilds' and 'awards' that are either bogus or bought. Have they attempted any show gardens like RHS (Royal Horticultural Society) shows in the UK, or Bloom in Ireland? Participation here demonstrates ambition, technical ability, creativity and the ability to work to deadlines. When weighing up your options this should certainly tip the scales. I have at least two competitors who advertise their grass as 'award winning'. Sorry guys, I call malarkey on that. In 20 years I've never seen an award ceremony for artificial grass.

2. Do they have the requisite insurance?

If they are legitimate they should be happy to furnish insurance certification, specifically public liability and professional indemnity. This protects you in the event of unforeseen disasters (flooding, landslides) caused by their presence. If an accident befalls an operative on your property, let them sue their employer in the first instance and not you. What if they cut down a tree and it falls on your neighbour's jacuzzi or pet turtle (that poor guy would have no hope of getting out of the way quickly enough)?

Certification is routinely required *in writing* in the construction industry before any site work commences. A professional landscape company will have it on hand and can simply email you a copy. You have every right to ask and they should be happy to provide it as it immediately differentiates them from those outfits that cannot. Don't be fobbed off with 'my secretary is on holidays'.

3. Are their vehicles insured?

If they slap into your neighbour's Prius who pays? This happened to us recently, except it was a (badly parked) Peugeot. Our insurance paid and one of our drivers got an earful.

4. What qualifications do they have?

Contractors need a workforce with a certain level of proficiency. What training do they have? 'Hang on a sec,' I hear you say. 'These guys are just labourers.' OK, but my crews possess, at a minimum, a manual handling cert, a Safe Pass (safety training is mandatory on building sites) abrasive discs cert, first aid training, tickets for mini digger, crane hoist, skid steer and fork lift trucks as well as driving licences for trucks, Covid-19 safety certs and on the job specialist training. These are the basic requirements of a professional crew.

But remember while degrees in horticulture and other certifications can look impressive, the reality is that the person who left school early can be as good or better. They may not know the Latin names for what they are planting but they can identify everything by its common name and know their habits and preferred conditions.

5. Have they an operator's licence (if applicable)?

More pertinent in the USA

6. Do they have a track record?

Can you view their previous work, similar to what's proposed for your own garden? Much of their work will be private gardens and in deference to previous clients it's not fair to intrude. However, there could be front gardens or commercial work visible to the public.

Failing that, check their references and testimonials. In the US there are strict rules about using testimonials. On this side of the Atlantic, GDPR issues notwithstanding, not so much. Tripadvisor and Google Reviews are open to abuse, both by the service providers, the service users and competitors. I find 4.7 out of 5 stars somehow more plausible than top marks.

 TIP Ask 'Where are you working at the moment?' Then swing by and your eyes will soon be opened. Don't be shocked to find something of a mess. This is something we try to warn clients of in advance. Often a garden will appear to be in a terrible state before coming together at the end.

7. Do they have a portfolio or videos?

Do they have a nice informative brochure? Are they local? We'll shortly look at how to judge a website. Get past the home page and dig into their repertoire. How extensive is their gallery? Do they only have shiny 'ta-da' pics? Or before and after pictures, preferably shot from the same angle, showing progress chronologically? It's easy to cut and paste other people's work.

Everybody has video recorders on their phones now. Or a GoPro, or drone. We find time-lapse videos work wonders. Have they enough pride in their work to have taken the trouble to document it?

8. How long have they been in business?

Are they a sole trader, partnership or limited company? Do they have a headquarters you can visit (this makes it harder for them to disappear should you have issues later)? By all means take a chance on a newbie. You might save money as their overheads will be lower and their enthusiasm higher so possibly a win-win. Maybe buy them a copy of this book.

9. How do they behave and appear?

It's not rocket science to conclude that if someone is tardy and scruffy *before* you hire them, it's a good indicator of what they'll be like once the job is underway. The first test is if they show up on time for your initial consultation. If they can come immediately, are they not that busy? On the other hand if they can't see you right away, but set a firm date for a consultation then great. I know which outfit I'd choose.

If they call you to reschedule no problem but watch out for a pattern. It boils down to respect. A charming rogue will jolly you around but they're a rogue, nonetheless. Don't expect a suit – you aren't buying life insurance – but muddy boots are not really acceptable. Sure, they might be coming from a job but can they not have clean gear in their jeep? Don't expect polished shoes but expect them to remove their work boots at your front door.

Are they sporting a company logo? Do you get a firm handshake? A weak slippery one gives me the creeps (not applicable during pandemics).

Do they make eye contact? When was the last time their vehicle was washed? Is the dashboard littered with coffee cups and old newspapers? This might be an indication of professional pride or the absence thereof. Does their vehicle have a landline phone number? If not, why not?

As regards their telephone manner, what etiquette applies? Are calls answered promptly and politely? Bear in mind many grass companies are owner operated and the person you are calling may be on their knees and in no position to answer calls when busy, dirty and wet (from either rain or sweat). I would urge patience. Someone working in an office might be used to being answered virtually by return but that's not practical for an operator out on-site. They might want your business but already have a commitment to their current client.

TIP Never mind leaving long-winded voice messages. Text them instead but be succinct. Better still, use WhatsApp and at least you'll know that your message has been seen (unless the receiver has this function switched off). Plus they will know that you already know that they have seen your message.

10. Review the warranty

Do take the trouble to read it, assuming there is one. Longer is not necessarily better. Sometimes the smaller print the more uncomfortable you should be. There are likely to be disclaimers. Some reasonable 'does not apply if ...' provisions are OK but too many may be designed to be your supplier's get-out-of-jail-free card. 'Your grass is guaranteed for × years.' Great! But what does that mean? What specifically does it cover? Just UV fading or more?

A supplier will, in turn, be relying on their manufacturer's guarantee to them. If you want to be pedantic, ask for examples of what has gone wrong with other lawns in the past, and how the situation was remedied. From personal experience I can look people in the eye and say that my own lawn is down over 19 years and is still tickety-boo and in daily use. So, depending on traffic volumes, aftercare regime, type of use and aspect (sunlight, trees, roots, etc.) you can expect your lawn to last at least twice as long as the warranty period. The reality is that despite claims to the contrary, the fibres will gradually flatten down somewhat over time. Unless of course it's never been walked upon.

A warranty can be printed on crested parchment with a wax seal and signed in blood but still be worthless if not honoured. Think Trump University degrees. The manufacturer is most likely far, far away and with the best will in the world may not have the capacity to help. Your beef, in the first instance, will be with your installer, the issuer of your warranty. They are the guys with the logistical ability and moral obligation to sort you out.

Daniel O'Connell, the famous nineteenth century politician, was responsible for both Catholic Emancipation in Ireland and possibly coining the famous phrase 'the pen is mightier than the sword.' He was capable of kicking ass when he needed to, having once fought and won a duel, with pistols, in Bishopscourt near where I grew up. A certain Arthur Guinness (who also brought a lot of happiness to the Irish), happens to be buried at the top of the hill overlooking that very spot. Anyway Daniel, aka The Liberator, was famous, by virtue of his rhetorical skills, for being able to 'drive a coach and four' through any contract or opposing argument. So choose your supplier carefully. Either they are willing and able to fix things for you or, well, there'll be wigs on the green.

If you are using a third party, such as a landscaper buying from a wholesaler or indeed a builder who digs out and stones up, ready for the installers, clarify who takes responsibility for what. When issues occur it doesn't take long for the finger pointing to start. Of course nowadays the fear of a bad review on social media hangs like the sword of Damocles over the supplier's head. On the other hand, and this is something installers should be cognisant of, if a complaint is promptly dealt with, consequent endorsements can be very positive.

Our complaints policy

As my accountant says, it's hard enough to make a living laying an artificial lawn once. Doing it twice cannot be profitable. So we do all we can to do it right the first time. When finished we issue written aftercare advice, posting or emailing our guarantee. Hopefully this reassurance is put in a drawer and never seen again.

Should a problem occur, it's documented and popped into a 'callback' tray. The system tracks which operatives did the job as well as the nature of the complaint. The purpose being to spot trends and respond accordingly. Is the problem due to dog damage, loose joins (did it rain heavily that day?) or unsecured edging (human error)? Was the problem caused by our trade customers, their end users, non-matching batches with colour variations? We need to know if the landscaper messed up and is trying to pull a fast one. Sometimes accidents happen.

It's how it's dealt with that counts.

How to judge a synthetic grass website

Searching for knowledge but drowning in information

If you are reading this, then you have probably been wise enough to use Amazon rather than Google search for your research in the first instance.

Online savvy should be part of every school's curriculum. Society's online BS detectors are still evolving. It's the new Wild West. I'm old enough to have been impressed by digital watches. Before remote controls were invented I myself *was* the remote control[43]. I have now largely got with the programme. Besides being on our fourth generation website we have over 10,000 followers on Facebook, Twitter, LinkedIn and Instagram. I draw the line at Snapchat and TikTok.

My older brother Joe is the tech geek of the family. I grew up playing Jet Set Willy on the old Sinclair ZX Spectrum 48K. Google only started the year before I went into the landscaping business.

In the Golden Pages directory, competing businesses were lumped into the same category geographically and listed alphabetically. Now you millennials know why so many AA or AAA insurance brokers and laundromats, etc. exist.

43 I distinctly remember the excitement of being kept at home from school sick one day as a kid and watching a man taking away our old black-and-white TV and installing our first colour one. Then he turned it on and tuned in a station (there weren't many) on which there was some kind of street parade. The colours were amazing. While researching this book I discovered that it was 1977. I was watching Elvis Presley's funeral.

You had to compete on the strength of your budget which dictated the size of your listing. Twitter was not the first to impose restrictions on the number of characters allowed.

Looking for information on the internet is like drinking from a fire hose.

There are over 1.6 billion websites and counting, with over 500 million blogs and over 2 million daily posts. That's 20 times more than the combined broadcasts of all the TV, radio and newspapers in the world. Given Google's everchanging algorithms, it's a deep rabbit hole. I once saw a post from a guy complaining that he popped online to check the weather forecast in 2004 and had been stuck there ever since. With the advent of Facebook and other social media platforms it's become a dangerous echo chamber of fake news. Beware of confirmation bias.

There is frighteningly sophisticated profiling. Judging by the recent proliferation of data centres being built in Ireland thanks to our cool temperate climate (at least all that rain is good for something) the amount of data is increasing exponentially. Advertisers are the paymasters and you, dear readers, are the cannon fodder. Keyboard warriors abound and everyone is suddenly an expert. Medical doctors' heads must be wrecked. It's a field day for quacks and a nightmare for hypochondriacs.

Remarketing is Machiavellian targeting of a punter who visits a site and suddenly sees ads for the very thing they had been looking at. If you send a Gmail to a pal saying you can't wait for the skiing trip, isn't it disconcerting how you are inundated with ads for ski paraphernalia? That's online commerce. Understand where Google is coming from. It's a for-profit search engine that's now a big part of our lives. It exists to serve you with the most relevant content possible. Google's AdWords is a multibillion dollar science that makes the Yellow Pages look like the scratching on a caveman's wall.

Is the website you're looking at secured, with an SSL status? Are there spelling mistakes, language quirks or grammatical errors in the content? Evidence perhaps of being poorly translated with zero editing and therefore unreliable information. If a potential supplier's website is not well designed, how can you expect that same outfit to design your garden? Excuses like 'my brother-in-law did it for me as a favour' don't wash. Is the content current? Is there a blog section with 'Lorem ipsum' or other such gobbledygook place fillers instead of text? Is it fast-loading? Mobile friendly? Does it read just like the last bland website you have just been on? Or is it hassle-free, easily navigable with working links, a visible menu, good flow with some originality?

Judging a book by its cover

(If it's a big hairy green book, don't worry about a thing.)

Who is the author of the content anyway? I've put my name on the cover of this book. Unlike *The Art of the Deal*, there was no ghost writer. Much online content is anonymous. Not a good sign.

Several of our competitors shamelessly proclaim themselves 'Ireland's leading providers of synthetic grass'. By definition they can't all be right. Imitation, they say, is the highest form of flattery but sometimes it gets old.

A new competitor's website was once brought to my attention. They were an ex-trade customer and now suddenly another self-proclaimed leading expert. Turns out their FAQs were identical to ours. As I looked closer I began to laugh. In cutting and pasting the lot they (or their website designers) failed to spot the occasional 'we in Sanctuary Synthetics suggest ...' Needless to say I never said a thing. It probably remained there for years.

Finding a reputable outfit

Word of mouth is a good if not infallible way to start. Do you trust the recommender? Ask someone in the industry or a related industry. You may not know any landscapers personally but you may have gone to school with the general manager of the local hardware store. Ask them about local landscapers; they'll know who the messers are. Otherwise you'll find their advertisements online and in local papers. Get a second quote to keep 'em honest.

Agreeing all the details

Estimates, quotations and retention

Beware of unrealistic prices – if it sounds too good to be true, then it is too good to be true. For example, if you get three quotes and two come in at around €4,000 and the third is €2,000, alarm bells should ring.

It's perfectly legitimate for them to give you a verbal estimate at the conclusion of the site visit but do expect a prompt written confirmation via email once they have had a chance to digest your requirements. Detailed design work will naturally take longer so be patient but ask for a realistic timeframe. What deposit and stage payments are requested? Are bank transfer details included? Note that builders give estimates but landscapers typically quote fixed prices with any deviations or extras agreed along the way.

In terms of a retention amount, construction contractors are used to having anything from 2.5 percent to 5 percent of the overall payment withheld for an agreed period of time to cover any contingencies and future issues. Perhaps suggest you'll keep the last hundred euros for a month to make sure all is OK. Maybe post-date a cheque. This will act as an incentive for the contractor to return that bit quicker should there be any issues.

Are all the materials and quantities specified and costed separately? There's no industry norm or obligation on the contractor to do this and there could be commercial sensitivities involved. They might not want to. Period. Your dentist could have just charged you €500 for some work with no question of a breakdown whereas your garage itemises every last washer and widget for their repair work.

Is the preparatory work included? Do they tidy and clear your garden or is that your job? Who gets rid of that old shed in the corner? What about all that junk in it? It's not as easy to dispose of as you think. Watch out for such grey areas or suddenly you'll be hit for extra costs you had not budgeted for. Also seek physical samples rather than photos of their product(s).

Job duration and lead time

Is this clearly communicated in advance? Often your work will be scheduled forward and you just have to wait. So if you have that first holy communion coming up, make your deadline super clear. If they are available immediately for no good reason (say a postponement or cancellation), then smell a rat. The reality is that landscape projects often come straight after construction work and – newsflash – builders often overrun (and overcharge).

How long will the work take? Will they commit to finishing once started? Again, builders have a reputation for doing more than one job at a time. Does your contractor have the resources to do the same? What weather conditions could lead to delays? Will your pets have to be boarded elsewhere? Be sure to factor that often-overlooked expense into your budget.

 TIP Get your job done in winter. People tend to close the curtains and forget all about their gardens for the winter. Your lead time is sure to be shorter as it's a quieter time, plus it will be less rushed. Overtime will be limited by daylight. If it takes a bit longer, due to adverse weather, so what? It will involve less disruption to your lifestyle given that you are unlikely to be using your garden at this time of year. Being done off-season means you'll have it sorted by the time the weather *is* good. We get loads of customers saying let's do it ... but wait until the spring. Saint Patrick's Day, in the middle of March, is the traditional start of the gardening season. Then there's a mad scramble to be done in time for the oncoming summer. Knowing this, time your project for the off-season, haggle accordingly and you could get a better price and a more unhurried finish.

Access

How difficult is it to get into your garden? Bulky machinery and materials will have to be transported there somehow. What about noise levels? Should you notify the neighbours? A courtesy warning is recommended due to potential disturbance, extra traffic, tight parking and deliveries to site. It's a good excuse to knock on doors and say hi in any event. Assure them that a proper tidy up will be done on completion, then make sure your contractor delivers. It's all very well to have a beautiful garden and new lawn at the end of a project but having resentful neighbours might mean your celebratory barbecue could be boycotted.

As many as one in four of our city gardens are done through terraced houses which means a day or so of inconvenience for the householders but then it's sorted for good. It might cost a bit more though, due to the extra time and care it takes, especially with steps, level changes or tight internal corners.

Read the small print

There may be none. Read the full quotation carefully. Some contractors will be as vague as possible on details such as sizes and quantities. Any deviations from the original plan should be clearly identified and explained. There could well be legitimate reasons.

When you first meet, if you can't get a word in edgeways, be wary. A good contractor should spend more time listening and questioning than talking. Then let them propose solutions. A nice person is not necessarily the right choice. The person who provides a professional service at a fair price is.

Read their terms and conditions, assuming there are any. It's certainly better to have done so rather than relying on verbal utterances. 'Shur, I told you about that before we started ...'

The terms and conditions should be clear. Tiny print is tiny for a reason –

to discourage people from reading it. So too is obscure and industry-specific terminology. Dense legalese is specifically designed to confuse and leave wriggle room in favour of the authors.

TIP

Maybe leave this book lying around so they can see you have already done your homework.

Are payment terms included in the quotation or terms and conditions? Is there a description of the works to be done? Any drawings? Are there guarantees on the workmanship and materials? Are arrangements for preparation work and post-job site clean-up included? Note that it's not unusual for the supplier to retain title of ownership until payment has been made in full.

Starting the work – running a smooth operation

Have you discussed the use of toilet facilities/the kitchen/a kettle in advance? It's your privacy that's being invaded and you are well within your rights to dismiss the crew member who knocks on your back door asking to use the bathroom, but consider the consequences. For starters they'll feel less guilty about having a wee-wee behind your shed. They are unlikely to have brought a Portaloo (a temporary toilet in a small plastic cabin). If forced off site to seek relief, that'll cost time and money and could cause resentment.

Are the crew well organised? How and where will tools and materials be stored and secured? Give them access to power, water and a key to your shed for a few days.

TIP

Warn them not to unplug your freezer.

Lay down guidelines and expectations. Things like taking off boots upon entering your house. Is someone going to be home during installation or are you being asked to give the run of your house to strangers while you are away at work? Can you lock certain doors internally and confine them to the kitchen and downstairs toilet?

A safe and tidy site

Tell them that's what you expect.

TIP If they leave behind a mess on day one, tidy it all away neatly, then praise them profusely the next morning, announcing to all and sundry that you had been afraid they might leave it as a sloppy dangerous hazard but that you were in fact delighted to see that they took such care. So here's a pack of chocolate Hobnobs as a little reward (cost €1.29). They might look at each other with raised eyebrows knowing well it was not them … maybe they'll figure it was your partner who did it unbeknownst to you. But with luck you'll find they'll continue to keep up the standards you've secretly set for the rest of the project.

Are the crew all wearing logoed gear? It'll make them more easily identifiable thus protecting your security. I've heard of charlatans rocking up during work, boldly asking the house owner for a stage payment/cash for extra materials 'acting on the boss's instructions'. They often unquestioningly get paid and are never seen again.

Are they wearing high-visibility jackets and steel-toe-capped safety boots and not runners or sandals (you may recall my earlier hostility to sandals)? You are well within your rights to question their attire. Hard hats are not a requirement for gardening projects. Yet.

Are they blaring loud music without consulting you? Have they blocked a neighbour's driveway? What do they do with their cigarette butts?

The reality is that their boss won't always be on-site so it's in your interest to politely police things from the start.

Do they talk you through what they are doing?

It's entirely reasonable to ask them to explain as they go. This is not to say you have carte blanche to be constantly in their ear.

TIP

Stock up on tea, coffee and snacks, preferably chocolate. For the sake of a few quid it'll get them on side big time and save constant disappearing off to the shops, thereby finishing the job more quickly. Plus they are more likely to go the extra mile for you, for example chopping off that low hanging branch. When I phone the crew and they've been given a cup of tea by mid-morning I know the job will invariably go a lot smoother. That's probably due to a combination of the good nature of the customer and the consequent gratitude and dedication of the lads.

Do casually question them on things like ongoing maintenance requirements. You'll get more honest answers from the crew than from the salesperson. It's not unreasonable to expect to be able to communicate easily with at least one person contracted to work on your property.

Waste disposal

Sometimes a licence is required to transport, treat and dispose of waste. Sod, soil and spoil from your garden qualifies as waste but in Ireland landscapers have an exemption from this requirement. Before the work begins, ask where the waste is going. Preferably to an approved recycling centre rather than being dumped down some lay-by.

Why do unscrupulous operators always dump in areas of natural beauty? Obviously because these areas are often quiet and isolated, but what kind of git do you have to be to destroy such spots with rubbish?

If you take the cheapest price from a dodgy outfit, *you cannot* wash your hands of moral responsibility for despoiling the environment by claiming ignorance.

During the work – dos and don'ts

*   Make sure the grass that arrives on-site matches the sample you got. Allow for minor batch variations in colouring and the fibres being squashed down. In Sanctuary if stuck for stock we offer a free upgrade but we make damn sure to get agreement in advance. If this happens, check the supplier's range and prices online.
*   Do check if the contractor is digging as deep as they said they would.

They might have valid reasons to deviate but verify, nonetheless. Make sure the workers on-site are aware of any badly drained soggy areas in the garden. Just because you explained it all to the salesperson don't assume it has been communicated to the work crew, as in all fairness, it's often weeks or months later when work commences. Even if the supplier has top of the range project management software (like us), do allow for human error. It might have been minus five degrees, early and dark when the crew loaded up to get to you and they might not have read every detail of your job in advance.

- It might not be your job to apprise all personnel on-site as to the specific requirements but it is certainly in your interest.

- Check their methodology. Was it as described? We have seen competitors with elaborate side elevation drawings and descriptions who fail to carry out the same on the ground. If they are using cement borders, make sure it has 'gone off' (hardened) before gluing the grass down.

- Ensure the joins are done with proper seaming tape and the correct glue. This is no time to improvise. Otherwise although it might look fine initially, the joins could split open within a short period.

- If the weather is bad don't pressure the work crew to finish. Not only might they resent it but it could also compromise quality, e.g. the joins not being glued correctly. If it's very warm, offer water or ice creams. It's the simple things that make for a happy and smooth job.

- Regarding the joins, in all my years in the business I have never claimed that joins should be totally invisible. They certainly shouldn't be obvious and standing out, but it's the nature of the product and an unavoidable reality that joins are necessary. If unsure, let others, say a neutral visitor or neighbour, take a look, preferably without biasing them by mentioning your concern in advance. See if they independently spot or point out the joins.

- Make sure all fibres are facing the same way. It sounds basic but amateur installers are particularly prone to this mistake. If possible, check it from an upstairs window as it will be more obvious from a height. Don't second-guess yourself and be hoodwinked by the installers. And no, brushing it up will not match it in. Most grasses are not multidirectional. It's like my mechanic says, if you think there is something wrong there invariably is. Ask them to stop immediately because once cut and glued into position, it's a much bigger job to fix. Waiting weeks to 'see if it beds in' makes it difficult to match in the same batch. I've seen entire lawns having to be ripped out and replaced.

Having said all that, do remember these are not multimillion euro contracts. Go easy and use common sense. A landscaper I know was recently asked for his last year's set of accounts. Although tempted to retort with a request for verification of his prospect's salary, he simply walked away.

What else could possibly go wrong?

Flooding

A properly prepped subsurface and synthetic lawn should easily stand up to the heaviest of rainfall. Even after surface pooling with standard percolation rates, it should quickly escape and disperse. In the event of serious flooding a raised water table can disturb the base and upon receding can leave behind an uneven lawn at best. It may have to be taken up and either replaced or cleaned. Also be cognisant of potential sewage contamination – fixable but undesirable.

Oil spills

On more than one occasion we've been called in following an oil leak. Many gardens have an unsightly tank containing hundreds of litres of home heating oil. Pipes, however well protected and buried, can burst. If this occurs, the soil of a real lawn or the base of a synthetic lawn becomes contaminated. And smelly. Often it's a case of starting again.[44]

---

44 Yes, [sigh!] it happened to us. Once upon a time, long ago, in a far-off city – Limerick, actually – not everything went as smoothly as planned. On this occasion, in order to maximise a playing area for kids, we were asked to chop down a large, already dead, tree that was right up against the neighbour's fence. Krzystof was experienced in tree surgery and correctly and systematically chopped the upper branches first. So far, so good. When it came to the main trunk, we latched on a couple of ropes to guide the tree the right way once the precision-angled cut was deep enough.

It didn't fall the right way. Instead it wobbled tantalisingly before crashing into the garden next door. Timber! Oh, dear. The fence was smashed to pieces but luckily nothing other than an old clothesline got flattened. The neighbours were not amused but turned out to be fine about it. A new clothesline and a few new fence panels later and we were all friends again. The new fence enhanced the look of the job and both families got enough free firewood to last the entire winter.

The story does not end there, however. About five years later we got a phone call from the family who owned the tree.

'Remember us? You need to come back and replace the entire lawn.'

'Whaaat?'

This time it turned out the neighbour's oil tank had sprung a leak and slowly disgorged its contents, which had leached into both gardens. We're fairly sure it wasn't a belated act of revenge for the earlier tree incursion. The insurance company covered the cost of decontamination, we got another full installation out of it and, to the best of my knowledge, the neighbours are still firm friends.

High winds

If the lawn is properly secured high winds are never an issue. However, a section or flap could come loose if inadvertently skipped with the glue or staple gun. Usually it's quickly repaired unless torn. Even then a new section can be added back. Beware of wind when covering balconies and rooftops. Make sure your installers take extra precautions.

Non-matching batches

This is not the same as incorrectly orientated fibres but the look will still be 'off'. Often the difference can be quite subtle but enough to be annoying. Make sure it's not just a shadow before complaining. Don't pounce too quickly as the first half of your lawn may have been laid before lunch when it was bright and sunny, whereas the rest might have been put down just before dark. So they won't initially appear identical as half has been exposed to sunlight and the fibres will naturally fluff up.

TIP

Brush up a section of each against the grain to compare properly.

As we've seen, the appearance of the same type of grass can vary from one production run to the next. Two slightly different pieces could end up in your garden. It's unlikely to be done deliberately but can happen inadvertently. Even the most efficient stock rotation system can break down. If it was loaded or laid in the evening or early morning, then the light levels might not have been good enough to spot any mismatch.

Weeds

Shock, horror! Weeds can grow everywhere and anywhere. This fact hardly comes as a big shock. So why the big surprise if some appear in your artificial lawn? Even with several inches of stone build-up, weed barriers, a strong latex backing and polypropylene fibres, weeds can manage to take hold. Periodic brushing, blowing or even vacuuming will minimise the chances of this happening.

But happen it does. The good news is that they are easy to spot and physically remove and can be sprayed without damaging the grass. If the problem persists, call the contractors. Send them photos. Their concern will be whether they are being seeded from above (unavoidable and not their fault) or if somehow they are managing to come up from below. If it's the latter, a reputable installer should return and assess, treat and alleviate.

The inside track – final insights and tips

How the pro picks you
Do you wanna dance? Just like in the old days in the nightclub you may have been checking out the talent, but remember they were probably checking you out too. A busy professional will be wary of timewasters and tyre kickers. They won't want or need to work for every prospect who calls them up. Even in a bad economy they will know there's no point working for nothing. Far better to sit out the odd dance and work on lowering one's golf handicap instead.

It's a regrettable fact that landscapers are not held in the same regard as other tradespeople or even lawyers. Often the general public look down their noses at 'gardeners'. They don't have the same prestige as other common or garden (!) service providers. Why is it that when an office-based professional gets in trouble, they are put out on '*gardening* leave'?

My theory is that most people consider themselves well capable of planting a few shrubs, laying a lawn or even throwing down a few patio slabs. How hard can it be? Only they don't have the time. Or the inclination. But they'll be damned if they are paying through the nose for someone else to do it. These same folk think nothing of paying hundreds to the plumber for just showing up and confirming that they have a problem and will gladly pay the mechanic to merely check out that worrying rattle in the Audi.

I think landscapers love their work and thus can be more easily exploited. Even garden designers suffer from this. While architects demand up to 10 per cent of the value of the job in fees, the designer is sadly often under-rewarded.

The reality is that a good landscaper not only has extensive horticultural experience, training and knowledge but must also be proficient in many other trades. They will design (designer), draw up (draftsperson), plant up (horticulturist), price (quantity surveyor), install lighting (electrician), irrigation systems and water features (plumber), walls (brickie or stonemason), plastering (eh, plasterer), painting (eh, painter), decking, pergolas, gazebos (carpenter), lay patios (groundworker) and install artificial lawns (Fake Grass Man) to name just some of their abilities. Consider this: how many interior designers do you know that will not only pick your curtains and granite kitchen worktops but can hang and install them too? Unlike with the landscaper, you'll find this is *not* all part of the service.

It's a far bigger industry than you think. Take the UK, for example. BALI figures for 2017 show landscape services contribute £6.8 billion to GDP, with 200,000 jobs directly involved. This amounts to £880 million in tax contributed to the exchequer (over 6 years, nearly enough to pay the cost of their new aircraft carrier the *Queen Elizabeth*, excluding F-35 fighter jets). Not an inconsiderable sum for an increasingly important, if undervalued, and frequently overlooked industry.

Within this landscaping world artificial lawns are a growing niche (no pun intended) that's fast becoming mainstream. It's a slightly annoying fact that the dramatic increase in popularity of synthetic grass has not been fully appreciated and acknowledged by the wider industry, the media or society at large.

Someone ought to write a book about it.

Maybe it's because it's mainly confined to back gardens and largely out of the public's gaze. Its promotion and sale is mostly online, with suppliers and customers communicating via websites and email. Perhaps for fear of ridicule the early adopters kept it quiet for a while, despite being perfectly satisfied. We still encounter some reticence lest it be judged weird or objectionable by some. It's not, by the way.

The security alarm

Leave it off for the duration of the work. Please. Most are motion sensitive and often the first pickaxe in the ground or start up of a compaction plate sets off the bloody thing. At the very least give the foreman the code. A blaring alarm going off intermittently wrecks everybody's heads, including your neighbours'. Besides, unless directly hooked up with your local gardaí or monitoring company, it will be completely ignored by all and sundry regardless.

Dog poo

Very often the reason we are brought in is because the family's pet dog has wrecked the lawn in the first place. As installers it's one of our biggest pet hates (see what I did there? *Pet* hate ... never mind).

There's nothing as disgusting or gut-wrenchingly smelly as discovering dog dirt embedded on the soles of one's boots. Having to go around the garden clearing it before starting is not a pleasant task. Please have the

266

courtesy of doing it before the arrival of your installers.

Mind you, I've seen worse.

We had a big job in Dublin a few years ago, where on the first morning there were many, many used nappies of various vintages strewn about the garden, obviously thrown from an upstairs window. The client had known for weeks that we were coming. In retrospect we should have declined to continue. The client was initially as nice as pie and we did a great job, including elaborate patterns in their new patio. That was eight years ago. We never got one penny for our troubles, despite numerous reminders.

Don't stare

I've talked about keeping an eye on proceedings and what to watch out for. That said, please don't interfere too much. The crew get freaked out if shadowed or stared at all day long, even if you are working from home. By all means take a day or two off to 'supervise' proceedings if you so choose. We've had people pull up a chair and watch every move day in and day out. Please … get a life. That's just creepy.

A client attempting to micromanage is every tradesperson's nightmare. Any initial charm soon slips. The attitude can be 'I am the brains, you are the brawn.'

And don't second-guess our every move by asking Alexa or Siri. Chances are we've mixed cement more often than both you and that pair. We do it how we do it regardless of someone else's YouTube pontification. If it works it works. Yes, you are paying, but have some trust and allow the crew the dignity of progressing unencumbered by your constant attention. We don't mind small, fascinated children or dogs staring, however. That's expected. You've done your due diligence. Relax and let the crew get on with it. Thanks.

Don't panic
(in the immortal words of Douglas Adams in The Hitchhiker's Guide to the Galaxy*)*

As previously stated, your garden is going to look a whole lot worse before it starts to look good again, typically towards the very end of the project. So no need to be unduly alarmed. A pro will have forewarned you about this to save panicky phone calls as the garden is ripped asunder. As the saying goes 'You can't make an omelette without breaking eggs.'

Keep off the grass

Please observe the contractor's instructions. So, for example, expect to be asked to keep the kids and dog out of the garden for safety reasons. It's typically just for a couple of days. It won't kill them and it'll be worth the wait. Even a small dog can quickly disturb carefully prepared and levelled groundwork. This admonition includes *you*, the paymaster. If I had a euro for every time we got a panicked phone call during a job going something like, 'Hey, the joint is loose/ three of the slabs on the patio are wobbly', I'd be a rich man. 'Oh, really,' we reply, 'and how do you know that?'

'Well, I'm standing on them' or 'I've pulled up the grass to check.' OMG! You were asked to stay off the damn patio/grass. The glue/cement needs to dry for God's sake. We did tell you not to … 'Oooh,' they say, 'I see.'

Now the slabs will have to be relaid and the glue join redone. Great. Thanks a bunch.

Pay up

Please meet the agreed payment schedule. A percentage in advance will certainly relax your installers. Not only does it help them with cash flow, it also demonstrates that you are serious and less likely to cancel or postpone. Don't forget it also increases your installer's moral obligation to honour their side of the deal.

A deal is a deal

Haggle away initially but *don't* attempt to re-haggle at the end.

(This is separate from any negotiations regarding changes or additions.)

If a price has been agreed in advance, don't go looking for further discounts taking advantage of the fact that the 'goods' have already been delivered and the contractor is in a weaker position.

That's just not cool. Or fair.

If a pro does a job a lot quicker than expected, so what? It's probably because they have spent a long time honing their techniques.

They won't slow down according to your expectations. We've had disgruntled customers complaining we are done and dusted 'so soon', wanting a discount as it was 'so easy'.

Whether it's a small job or a high-spec, high-end project, an unscrupulous client can always find something however immaterial to pick up on, to leverage a further discount or concessions. Don't go there. Let them move on to their next job, and pay everyone involved. Besides, leaving a bad taste over just a few quid is unwise. One could well need their help or advice in the future. Believe me, getting stiffed is never forgotten. One could be blacklisted by the local landscaping industry and not even realise it.

I loved this story told by a local builder friend.

Sitting in the front room of an affluent couple's home in a leafy Dublin suburb, they discussed extension plans. All was going swimmingly until the woman revealed, in a throwaway remark, that her husband was a barrister. As it turns out, she was a solicitor. Mr Builder nodded slowly, closed his diary and politely declined the work.

'But, but …' they asked, as they chased him out the door. 'But why?'

'Because,' he answered, 'you'd have me strangled in legal letters and actions over the tiniest details until the cows come home.'

So no thanks and good luck. It was a sizable job. 'I didn't care,' he told me. Bitter experience had taught him the virtue of caution. He was trusting his instincts, right or wrong. There's no law, to my knowledge, to say you have to work for someone if you don't want to.

Don't cry wolf

A reputable contractor will willingly return if there is an issue. But be aware they will soon tire of you if it's for vexatious complaints. For example, we had a 'Come quick, my lawn is *destroyed* with weeds' call. One hundred and fifty kilometres and several staff hours later I'm presented with the offending 'weeds' back in my office. Both of them. Smaller than my pinky finger. If that client subsequently has another, possibly genuine issue, how quickly do you think we'll respond?

Be careful who you approach for grass

Context is everything. It can be mixed up with the illegal stuff.

In the end picking a pro boils down to trust and it's always a bit of a gamble, but take the trouble to load the dice in your favour. It's a fact that suppliers with integrity simply expect to be believed and if not they firmly believe in simply letting the passage of time prove them right.

Now let's continue with the important process of picking the right grass, properly measuring and accurately pricing.

Chapter 14

Buyer's Guide: How to choose, measure and price

Should-dos before getting started

1. Decide on your ideal garden layout

What do you like, need and want? Look online but stay away from those cat videos. Consider the practicalities. Try to look past what's actually there right now. Visualise.

2. Make a plan

Start with the end in mind. Decide where your new lawn is going. We'll examine how to measure up shortly, but do a rough sketch for now.

TIP

If you want zero waste, make sure your lawn is an even number in metres in width or depth as rolls are 4m and 2m wide. 'Shur, it'll be grand' is not a good idea. Lots of our work involves undoing bad ideas.

3. Determine your budget

Designers and landscapers will help you in this process if you are stuck. Be realistic. Remember: buy cheap, buy twice. Consider doing the job in phases.

4. Understand the order of work

There is a logical order in which hardscaping ought to be carried out. To-do lists are your friend.

5. Make sure you are allowed to do what you are proposing

Beware of boundary issues, especially if adding height. Neighbours tend to get upset if not consulted. Local authorities can be very prescriptive.

Some US cities specifically outlaw the conversion of front gardens to artificial grass.

6. Locate underground utilities

Ask your utility company if you are unsure where these are. There are gas lines (which explode), water pipes (which gush), sewage pipes (which … well, let's not even go there) and electricity lines (which can kill). It's your responsibility. We've hit all of the big four over the years – so have learned our lessons – and it's costly to rectify.

Speaking of unpleasant discoveries, the lads were just starting on a routine installation in Crumlin early one morning when all hell broke loose. The family had a large Great Dane puppy who, as we started sod cutting, was digging away, showing particular interest in one corner of the garden. He soon unearthed a bundled up old nightdress and immediately screams emanated from the bedroom window upstairs.

'Gerrit off him, gerrit offa him!'

Moments later the owner, dressed only in his jocks, emerged from the house to give chase. Thinking this was great fun the dog ran away with a bemused and bewildered Sanctuary crew watching on with bits falling from the bundle as, egged on from above, yer man dived around after him in the mud. Turns out the nightdress was wrapped around the mortal remains of their last pet, who had been lovingly buried in what turned out *not* to be his final resting place. Which is why we always ask about buried utilities and anything else we should know about in advance.

7. Establish what utilities are required

Figure out what you will need such as extra drainage channels or ducting and cabling for power for your shed/home office, water feature or lighting. Make sure it's adequately rated, protected and sufficiently deep or someday your ancestors or new occupants will curse your memory.

8. Outsource

Most homeowners will not have all the skills required. It's likely you'll need outside professional help. As per Chapter 14 watch out for the cowboys.

Consider this tale of woe which happened to my friend, whom I'll call Bob. Bob started out around the same time as myself. A hardworking chap, he's a horticultural college graduate, specialising in groundwork. Less interested in administration, he's happiest 'on the tools'. We often meet to compare notes and share gripes.

Some time ago he suddenly started getting irate phone calls asking when he was coming back to finish a job. Only he didn't have a clue who these people were. 'What job? What mess?'

It transpired that there was an identical white van doing the rounds sporting his exact logo and name 'Bob's Landscaping' minus a phone number. The doppelgängers were trading on his good name, going around taking substantial deposits then quickly disappearing, often leaving behind an unholy mess. 'Just popping out to the builder's merchants to get some materials, Boss ...' Only that was the last they were ever seen or heard of.

Bob was naturally livid and flabbergasted.

He called the gardaí but before any action was taken he managed to track the culprits down himself. Bold as brass they claimed it was just a coincidence, 'An honest mistake, Boss', and were unmoved by Bob's threats of legal action.

Threats of another kind became necessary.

The bad guys soon moved on, no doubt to pull the same stunt elsewhere, and Bob's reputation was restored. So be sure of the calibre of the person with whom you are dealing. Assumptions can be costly.

9. Prepare the site

Weeds, like Jehovah Witnesses, are by definition mostly unwanted yet they tend to keep on coming. Physical removal may not be sufficient (some of those religious folk can be heavy!). Use weedkiller or the eco-friendly alternatives carefully, according to the instructions and in the right climatic conditions, i.e. not on windy days. Allow sufficient time for it to take effect and reapply as required. Do this well in advance of commencing other works. Remember it can take 10–14 days, depending on humidity, for it to take effect. There's absolutely no point in spraying one day and digging out the next. You might as well sprinkle water around instead. Or loose change.

10. Establish if demolition or soil removal is required

Soil does not have to be removed entirely. We encourage customers to retain as much as possible, perhaps filling raised beds adjoining the lawn. Don't undertake demolition work casually. If it's too daunting, hire someone or bribe students with beer. Groundwork, despite the fact that it looks basic, ain't always straightforward!

11. Check your soil quality

Soil quality is often the luck of the draw. Is your house at the end of a row? If so, your garden could have been a construction staging point with heavy machinery compacting your ground beyond redemption with a thin layer of good stuff then sprinkled on top as the builders made for the exit. Some 'finds' are the stuff of urban legend. I heard of a landscaping crew who came across a metal bar while digging a back garden. They couldn't shift it. Digging further down they came across a seat, then a steering wheel. Eventually they excavated an entire three tonne dump truck that, having gone past its sell-by date, was simply buried by the builders.

Or it could be the opposite, with a huge amount of topsoil dumped in to bring your 'garden' up level with the house. There's a test if you suspect it is a swamp: push a crowbar, or even a brush handle, into the ground. If it goes all the way in, you know you are in trouble. I've demonstrated this to shocked customers before.

12. Construct walls, fences, paving or patios

These are jobs that should be completed in advance of installing the lawn.

TIP

Good foundations are key. the deeper and wider the better.

13. Source materials

You get what you pay for, so don't scrimp, but by all means scrounge. My wife and I built a really nice rockery by gathering up stones lying about the site. We did the builders a favour really. Look up free-cycling websites. One person's rubbish is often another person's treasure.

14. Grade and level

Use string or a spirit level. For God's sake be aware of the damp proof level of the outer walls of your house.

15. Don't murder your plants

Salvage what you can. A synthetic lawn looks more natural when laid around the trunk of a nice specimen tree. Keep some life in your garden.

How to choose your grass

'If you see a gravy train, then it's too late to climb aboard.' When I started out, the artificial grass train was still very much in the station. A UK supplier sent me a handful of different samples. I say different in that they had different name tags and prices – they all looked the same to me at first. So fear not if you've the same initial reaction. Slowly I started to spot variations. This is a product that requires close inspection. I learned that the shorter cheaper ones were typically for budget gardens, the tougher, denser, mid-range ones were more pet-friendly and the slightly longer grass was for general family use. My new supplier had to patiently educate me.

Don't let yourself be bamboozled. Is the grass for sports or leisure? What's the expected function and frequency of use – light, moderate or heavy foot traffic, or is it merely ornamental like a front lawn that never gets walked upon? Is it for children's play or for entertainment? Or is it multipurpose?

Consider the 4 S's

1. Style of blade – skinny, wide or firm?
2. Shape – what is the shape of the yarn and what bouncebackability technology does it have?
3. Sheen – does it have a matt or shiny finish? Does it absorb light or is it reflective? Many people like bright grass in a shady garden and the converse is also true.
4. Softness – softer does not always equal better. You need a balance between feel, performance and resilience.

Factors to consider when choosing your grass

- How good is the backing?

 TIP

If you can physically tear the backing, then walk away.

- What testing for harmful substances has the manufacturer done? EU standards are often very different from those of south-east Asia.
- Is there a warranty (see below)? How long is it for? What does it cover?
- Is the grass fire resistant/retardant?
- Is it brand new or used? Perhaps a factory second?

- How about the blade recovery technology? The vendor should at least know about different yarn shapes.
- What are its environmental credentials? Is it recycled? Is it recyclable?
- Does your supplier have a showroom, or is it an online business only?
- Do they provide an option of adding underlay/shockpad? Does that shockpad come with certification?
- Does the grass have an accompanying specification sheet? You cannot compare properly without this information.
- What does it smell like? Be wary if it smells too much like petroleum.
- Don't necessarily compare your sample(s) to the real grass you already have in the garden. Once it is removed, any comparison is moot.

How to measure your garden

'Measure twice, cut once'
-Tradesman's saying

If I had a euro for every time we showed up to verify measurements which turned out to be totally wrong, I'd certainly have enough for a fancy meal out. For two. Including a good wine.

People consistently fail at this relatively straightforward task. I say 'relatively' as depending on the shape of the lawn, including nooks and crannies, it *can* get a little bit awkward.

Nap orientation

First things first. Nap is the direction in which the pile fibres naturally lie. Grass rolls usually come in 4m and 2m widths (with limited 5m wide rolls available). It is important to realise that the vast majority of domestic artificial grasses are *not*, in fact, multidirectional. Instead the nap goes with the grain and stitch lines. Therefore, you *cannot* simply cut off a piece and add it back perpendicular to the other piece. *All must go the same way* which can restrict your options. Laying grass in different directions can result in different amounts of square metres required. A competent installer should automatically pick the orientation that produces least waste while facing the optimal way. The choice is laying it east to west or going north to south (i.e. side to side or up and down). You may prefer it laid one way or the other but there could be a difference in volume and cost. If in doubt simply lay down a piece, brush it up and see for yourself. Then rotate the grass and look again. You must allow for a combination of factors including pile direction, waste, cost and the number and direction of joins.

I always say there are three right ways and one wrong way to lay your grass.

In a typical back garden scenario if you lay the grass facing away from the back of the house, it will look shiny and fake as the sun's rays are reflected more easily from your viewing point. This is the wrong way.

If you flip it with the nap facing into the back of the house, it will look much better and more realistic. Or finally, depending on the position of the necessary joins and your viewing points (e.g. from the patio in the sunny corner), it could be rolled out left to right or right to left.

Don't worry if you are scratching your head.

If you are even vaguely aware of this as an issue, you are far less likely to make a muck of it. It'll become quite obvious once the grass has been opened up on-site. Laying carpet is way easier. Remember what it cost to redo the hall, stairs and landing before complaining about the price of carpeting your garden, please.

Recently, 'multidirectional' grasses have come on the market. While attractive, with a less obvious nap, they must still obey the 'all pieces must be laid facing the same direction' rule.

Now, back to that bugbear of mine pertaining to people's inability to take accurate measurements and the constant misunderestimation (as George W Bush would say) of lawn size.

Measuring no-nos

'Oh, it's quite small, only about 20m^2, I'd say.'

'Fine, that'll be approximately €1,500 including VAT for a full installation,' we'd answer. Later we discover the garden actually measures more like 40m^2, possibly including some unavoidable waste.

'So your total price is now €3,000,' we'd say.

'Oh, no,' we'd be told with a scold, 'the person in the office said it would be no more than €1,500. That's way too expensive.'

Jesus wept.

Or we'd get, 'Hang on, I'm just going to measure it now,' … long pause … 'It's 20 of my feet, hang on … by 15 and a half of my feet.' We've learned not to get into how large people's feet are.

Here's what *not* to do.

Ring the supplier and attempt to describe the shape. 'Yeah, it's four across, [four what?] then it tapers in a curve to the dog kennel, then it's about the same again to the fence with a standard-sized shed in the corner. How much do you think that would be?'

Stop! No can do.

That's just asking for trouble. Your supplier is not a clairvoyant.

I can only surmise the problem is a subconscious hope that it might cost less than it should, fooling themselves (and sometimes the poor suppliers too) that a smaller amount of grass will be sufficient for the area. This common phenomenon can lead to nasty shocks and the occasional row, sometimes between the homeowners. Nobody wants that.

Please also be aware that there can be slight variations between production runs of the same grass. Even if your supplier tries their very best subsequently to get a matching batch to beef up the shortfall from your initial order, it may well be too late or impossible. If it doesn't match perfectly, it could stick out like a sore thumb. This might lead to having to start all over – happens all the time – then more rows over money, lost time and waste.

Of course most grass companies will happily send out a representative to measure for you or to verify your measurements. But please understand they are, in the interests of efficiency and costs, likely to attempt to give you a phone quotation *and* qualify you as a prospect first. You might love the idea of getting it but have no clue as to what it might cost. We in Sanctuary are at pains to give people a reality check in the first instance.

'You realise you are probably looking at thousands, not hundreds,' we'd often say.'

'Whaaat ...?'

Hurray! From our commercial point of view that's time and money saved from the get-go. That's why we want people to get some kind of realistic handle on the likely cost of the project before going to the expense of a 'free no-obligation visit and site survey'. That's also why we painstakingly built an online calculator on our website (which helpfully converts feet to metres) so that people know in advance what the ballpark figure is likely to be. Thereafter, if they like our samples and still want to talk we'll happily show up and measure everything up precisely

TIP

To convert feet to metres, multiply the feet by 0.3048.

Ten most common scenarios

Scenario 1 – Even-metred lawn

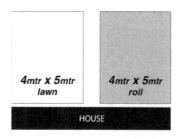

4 metre wide roll cut to length (x 5 metre) - no wastage

= wastage

4 metre wide roll of artificial grass - up to 25 metres long without a seam break

You may be lucky and have a lawn that is either an even or slightly short of an even number of metres meaning there will be virtually no waste. For example, 4m × 5m.

If you are laying out a new area and can control the size to match the above criteria, then please endeavour to do so. Failing that, know that there's an average of 5 to 8 percent waste in most synthetic lawn installations.

Scenario 2 – Not all same-sized gardens are the same

'But I know for a fact that Fred next door got his done only last year for a lot less than you are quoting me.'

Well, besides inflation, there might be legitimate reasons for the price difference between seemingly identically sized gardens. Although housing developments are often quite uniform and Fred's lawn comes in at 40m^2, yours might well require 44m^2 (or 38m^2). At a glance they are identical but even a few inches can throw out the total required.

Newsflash! Walls and fences are *not* always exactly parallel and uniform. Furthermore, right-angled corners are not always 90 degrees. If your garden is exactly 8m wide, east–west at the outer edge of your patio, you could well find it's 8.1m in the middle and 8.2m at the back. This 0.1 or 0.2 difference can become problematic. If it's not spotted, your grass could be ordered, cut, despatched, paid for and laid out in the garden only then to discover a long triangular sliver of a shortfall. There's no point in complaining to your supplier, your partner or the unfortunate installer. Don't feel too bad though. Engineers and architects frequently make similar boo-boos.

Your supplier won't have a selection of spare matching long narrow triangular slivers on hand. Assuming the batch is still in stock, the unfortunate householder may well have to buy a full 2m long piece just to get the long sliver out of it. Bummer.

We try our best to accommodate of course and there are solutions. Maybe make a feature bed, squaring off the area. Put in sleepers, stone or cobble sets. Try flipping the grass 90 degrees, possibly leaving the gap at the back end of the garden where it's less visible. Maybe place the shed strategically so that the long narrow triangle becomes at worst a short narrow triangle. Square it off and plant in some flowering wall climbers perhaps.

We usually have offcuts from other jobs on hand but there's no guarantee we'll have the right size, I'm afraid. Plus we wouldn't stay in business too long if we are chopping off random slivers from full rolls, making the rest far less saleable.

Think of it like ordering carpet. They too may have shortfalls and generate offcuts, but remember that rooms in houses tend to be a more uniform shape than the typical garden. So try to get it right the first time. Hey, the grass company can also make the odd mistake. You may well have given them precise measurements and end up second guessing yourself when you discover you are a couple of feet short. Human error is unavoidable, but a reputable company will quickly compare what was requested with what was delivered, and should replace it without fuss.

Instead of scribbling on the back of an envelope get your hands on some graph paper. Then draw out your contours, to scale. If your lawn is 10m deep, then draw a straight line through 10 boxes. By all means send that sketch to your preferred supplier and they'll get back to you with an accurate layout and total requirement.

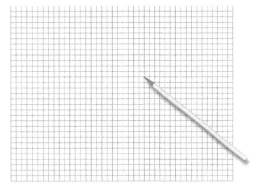

TIP We recommend ordering slightly more than you need to allow for minor size discrepancies. Plus there may be some loss in trimming the edges and prepping for doing the joins.

Whatever about the disappearance of privacy, it's now very easy for us with Google Earth to have a bird's eye look at your garden, allowing us to at least roughly verify measurements using its measurement tool. But there really is no substitute for actually being in the garden.

Scenario 3 – Ideal 4m wide lawn

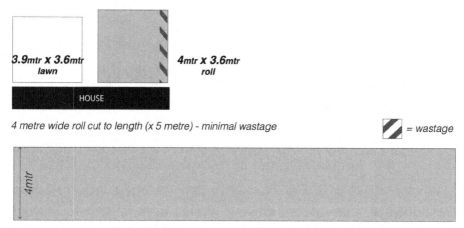

4 metre wide roll of artificial grass - up to 25 metres long without a seam break

If the lawn is 4m wide then there's no waste. Doesn't matter how long it is, once it's under 25m then there are no joins needed. If it's a bit less than 4m wide, then there's a bit of waste but no joins required. For example, a garden measuring 3.9m × 3.6m (total actual area 14.04m²) requires an order for 4m × 3.6m = 14.4m². Multiply by the cost of the grass per m². Simple!

Scenario 4 – Square or rectangle shaped lawn

If your lawn area is actually a square or rectangle, then all you need to do is multiply the length by the width to get the total area and exact square meterage. In Europe, thanks to Napoleon's adventures around the turn of the nineteenth century, we mostly use the metric system. So your total figure will be in metres squared. So as per the example in Scenario 3, the 7m wide and 5m long lawn area is 35m².

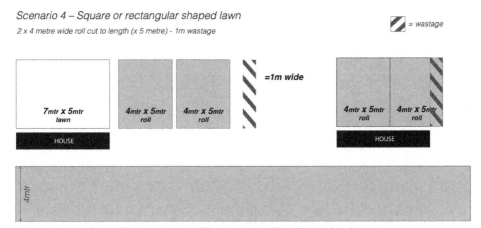

4 metre wide roll of artificial grass - up to 25 metres long without a seam break

Hooray, we now know what size it is.

Sorry, but that's not enough. Back to maths 101.

You now know that grass rolls are typically only available in 2 metre and 4 metre widths, (that's 6.56ft and 13.12ft respectively by the way) and typically 20m to 25m long. So what do you need to order to cover your 35m²?

'Anyone? Anyone?' (Remember that history teacher in the 1986 classic *Ferris Bueller's Day Off*?)

Unfortunately for you, the answer is you'll have to buy 40m². Or 42m² depending on the optimal orientation. Either you must get two 4m wide pieces to cover the 7m long side, resulting in a 1m long piece of waste, or get a 4m and 2m piece to cover the 5m length, also with a 1m strip of unavoidable waste. The waste (aka offcuts) is yours to keep. Often our fitters will make a door mat or two from them and offer to take the rest away.

TIP

Keep some of these offcuts. Throw them into the back of the shed in case of the unlikely event you might need a bit for repairs someday. Maybe that new puppy the kids have been begging for will grow up and go wild if left alone in the garden for too long and rip up a bit.

Which must you get: 40m² or 42m²? The above example shows both options. If you do it one way, the 7m length requires a join perpendicular to the rear of the house 4m in. Doing it the other way, with a 4m and 2m roll going east–west (or right to left if you prefer), means the join is parallel to the viewing point.

Ultimately, it's your call but listen to the opinion of the fitters too. They'll see the optimal way taking all factors into account.

TIP

Don't get ripped off. Although unfortunately you must buy 40m² to cover your 35m² lawn, you should only be paying for 35m² of installation costs. Study the quote to ensure that fact is reflected and accounted for. This is why you should have a handle on measurements yourself. If you are unsure, request a breakdown of costs between grass and labour.

Right, that's the easy scenarios done.

Don't be daunted – even some professional landscapers struggle.

It's just a bit of maths and geometry. I'm asked to figure out requirements for our trade customers on a daily basis. So, even if you are not confident you have figured out your actual requirement (and remain in the dark regarding the cost), at least map out your measurements. Then photograph your piece of paper/back of the envelope and send it to your supplier who should be quickly able to calculate what's needed and quote accordingly. If they cannot, then your 'chancer' alert radar should be going off.

Send photos of the garden too, along with any relevant notes, for example confirming that there is side access. If it's a sketch, make sure to indicate where the house is in relation to the garden. Also write 'shed', 'patio' or 'deck' on the sketch where relevant.

Scenario 5 – L-shaped lawn

This is common, especially for the many suburban gardens that feature the obligatory garden shed. Typically it's nestled into the back corner, thereby creating an L-shaped lawn. Applying your expertise gleaned from the above scenarios you will know to get measurements for all points around the perimeter as in the illustrated example. Good. As before there will often be more than one way to lay the grass and consequently different totals and prices:

Scenario 5 – L-Shaped Lawn

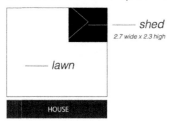

shed
2.7 wide x 2.3 high

lawn

HOUSE

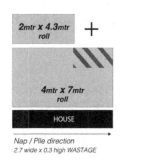

2mtr X 4.3mtr roll
+
4mtr X 7mtr roll
HOUSE

Nap / Pile direction
2.7 wide x 0.3 high WASTAGE

Option A - East-West (left to right)

0.3 x 2.7 used for here

+

4mtr X 6mtr roll
4mtr X 3.7mtr roll

HOUSE

Nap / Pile direction

1mtr wide x 3.7 high 'WASTAGE' bercause

Option B - North-South (top to bottom)

= wastage

4mtr

4 metre wide roll of artificial grass - up to 25 metres long without a seam break

Option A: east to west (left to right)

- 4m × 7m long piece = 28m²
- That leaves a 2m × 4.3m = 8.6m² piece above it from house to shed, so a total of 36.6m² is required with a 4.3m long join.
- The actual area is 6m × 7m = 42m².
- Subtract the shed's footprint, 2.7m × 2.3m = 6.21m², and the area that needs to be covered is 35.8m².
- Happy days! You only have 0.81m extra to pay for, less than 1m² of waste.

Option B: north to south (up/down)

- The actual area, minus the shed, is still 35.8m² (ish).
- So lay a 4m × 6m piece and then a 4m × 3.7m piece for starters. This time the join is parallel to the house rather than perpendicular to it. Now all you are missing is a thin strip in front of the shed. It's 2.3m × 0.3m to be precise.

Luckily you've a 1m × 3.7m long offcut (from the 4m × 3.7m piece) that's more than enough to slot in here. Doing it this way means using three pieces not two, and you also now have two joins not one.

• Your total grass requirement is 38.8m², so 3m² of waste, over three times that of Option A. It's still a modest percentage.

TIP

Consider laying paving slabs at your shed door.

So on balance, despite having a perpendicular join by going left to right, the nap of the grass will face the back of the house, waste will be minimised and only one join required. Be aware, however, if we tweaked the measurements even a little, then Option B, with the nap going sideways, might be preferable.

If the patio doors were on the right of the house, then I'd lay the grass left to right so you are looking into the nap as you emerge from the house. If there is a large viewing window on the left side, then I'd recommend reversing the grass.

Scenario 6 – Cut-off rectangular lawn

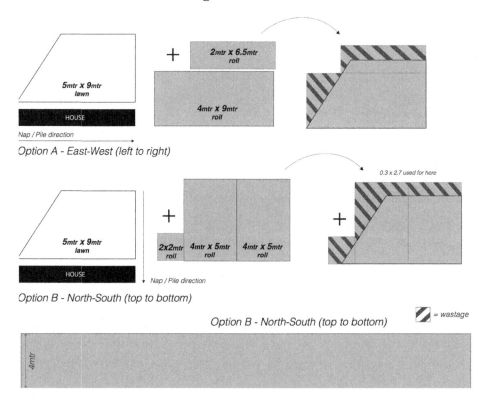

Maybe you have a corner site.

The actual size in this example is 6m × 5m = 30m^2 plus (5m × 3m) halved = 7.5m^2, so a total of 37.5m^2.

By definition, offering straight pieces of grass to such an angle will inevitably lead to unavoidable waste.

OK, let's just order a 9m × 5m piece I hear you say and forget the upper triangle.

No can do, I'm afraid.

Neither figure is an even number and, to repeat, most suppliers will only supply 2m and 4m rolls. Sure, they'll cut them down for you but you'll still be charged for the full piece. So how about a 10m × 5m = 50m^2, made up of (4m × 5m) × 2 and a 2m × 5m.

Or perhaps a 9m × 6m = 54m^2, made up of 4m × 9m and 2m × 9m.

Yikes, that's 13.5m^2 or 16.5m^2 of extra grass to pay for! Let's take a closer look, shall we. Besides no matter what, there will be joins needed within the new lawn.

Option A: left to right

So a 4m × 9m = 36m^2 piece, then a 2m × 6m = 12m^2, totalling 48m^2. More than the actual but a lot less than the above. Really, you'll need a 2m × 6.5m, as the 0.5 bit at the end is needed to cover the upper triangle. Alternatively, if you can live with a second join, just get a 2m × 3.25m piece, cut it into two 1m × 3.25m strips and add them above the larger piece. But don't forget that your larger piece going the full 9m long will have a triangular piece of waste cut off it too. Insufficient for the rest but enough for a piece of it.

At some point it becomes too messy so either the client or supplier must bite the bullet and call it.

Option B: north to south (up/down)

First use a 4m × 5m = 20m^2 piece, then another, so we're 8m along.

A 2m × 2m will be more than sufficient for the rest, so a total of 44m^2.

Better than Option A but an extra join is needed.

Both, however, are better than the initial figures above.

Scenario 7 – Triangular lawn

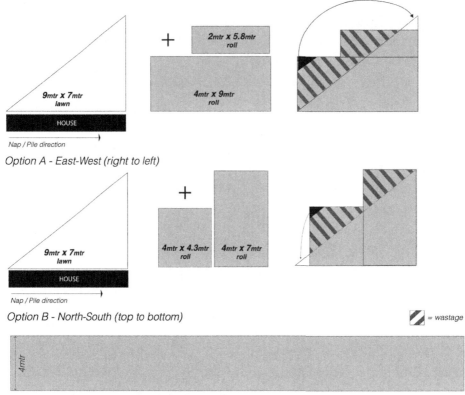

Option A - East-West (right to left)

Option B - North-South (top to bottom)

= wastage

4 metre wide roll of artificial grass - up to 25 metres long without a seam break

God bless planners and architects!

Remember Pythagoras and his theorem? Only joking. No need for it. First, square the area off as illustrated. Worst case scenario this amount is what you'll need. Here the garden is 9m × 7m = 63m².

As before an even number is needed, so treat it as 10m × 7m = 70m², or worse again 9m × 8m = 72m². Oh no! The actual area is only half the 63m² at 31.5m². This won't do at all. So let's look at our options.

Option A: east to west (left to right)
4m × 9m = 36m²

Then figure out how far along the 9m length a 2m piece on top should go. A 2m × 5.8m piece should do the trick. Now we've a total of 47.6m². Not bad by comparison.

But what about the last bit? A 4m and a 2m roll will only go up 6 of the 7 metres on the right-hand-side axis. Fear not, my eagle-eyed friend. The offcut from the end of the big 4m × 9m piece is more than enough to be transferred (taking care to match up the pile direction) to the top, the last piece of the puzzle. It's still approximately 30 per cent waste but that's the nature of the shape, I'm afraid.

Option B: north to south (up/down)
Start with a 4m × 7m = 28m² piece, then a 4m × I'm thinking about 4.3m (do it to scale and use a ruler for accuracy) = 17.2m², so a total of 45.2m².

Not far off Option A – closer to 25 per cent waste this time. Again, the last remaining little triangle is more than covered by the initial offcuts.

TIP An unscrupulous supplier would take your initial measurements and happily deliver 70m² or 72m² to your door and let you worry about the unnecessary waste and expense. So, do the maths and only get what you need.

Scenario 8 – Oval-shaped lawn
Quite common and rather attractive in the right setting. But no prizes for guessing – yes, there's plenty of waste no matter what. It's always a trade-off between what's desirable and what fits. Between aesthetics and waste.

By now you know the drill. Square it off: 11.3m long × 6.5m wide.

That makes 73.45m² needed, right? *Wrong!* If you haven't been paying attention, go stand in the corner. If you have managed to stay awake and trudge this far, you will know it's gotta be either 12m × 6.5m = 78m² or 11.3m × 8m (two 4m rolls) = 90.4m²!

Fear not. Let's break it down.

Option A: east to west
Let's do a 4m × 11.3m = 45.2m². So there's 2.5m × something left. Either above or below. Or both, if you split it. So if we did a 2m × 10.5m (21m²), we'd get the whole way along the top. Then a 2m × 2.5m (5m²) piece at the bottom and we've a total of 71.2m². Less than the worst case scenario above.

Option B: north to south

Let's centre up a 4m × 6.5m twice (52m²) and add a 2m × 6.5m (13m²) piece. This leaves 1.3m bits at either end. Being generous, let's add two 2m × 3m pieces (12m²). Great! That comes to 77m² but with five pieces and four joins.

Scenario 9 – Dreaded circular lawn

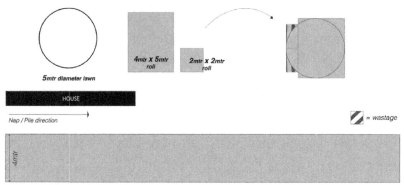

4 metre wide roll of artificial grass - up to 25 metres long without a seam break

I say dreaded due to the fact that there's lots of waste, plus securing the grass properly becomes slightly more challenging, as you'll learn in Chapter 15.

In this example all we really need to know is the diameter.

It's 5m.

For the record, to get the actual area simply apply Archimedes' constant – the formula πr^2. [Designer, for this formula, please insert the pi symbol and a lower case r followed immediately by a superscript 2, i.e. r squared.] The radius (r) is half the diameter so:

3.14159 × (2.5m × 2.5m) = 19.63m²

If squared off, the 5m becomes 25m², so that lesser amount looks about right.

We don't have the luxury of Option A or B this time as there is no up or down. I'd take a 4m × 5m (20m²) and add a small piece to one side or the other, a 2m × 2m will be plenty, and there you have it: 24m² required to cover a less than 20m² space.

Scenario 10 – Mad-shaped lawn with lots of curves, nooks and crannies

Take on board what you've learned from above and don't be daunted.

Draw it out to the best of your ability including all the measurements you can. Then redo once back inside at the kitchen table and tidy it up, making it as close to scale as possible. A ruler, pencil, rubber and that lined graph paper I mentioned would all be useful. Don't fret, if a couple of your measurements are missing, your supplier should be able to extrapolate them from the rest of the information (and hopefully photographs).

This should give you a good handle on how much grass you will have to order.

Then simply send in that sketch requesting a free estimate on the square metres required (the actual area, you will know by now, is irrelevant). It'll be quickly done as it increases their chances of getting your business by obliging you.

How to price
Now let's figure out what it will all cost.

TIP Watch out for quotes that don't make it clear if the total amount is a net figure, i.e. exclusive of VAT, or the gross, including taxes.

It is said that the bitterness of poor quality still remains long after the sweetness of a cheap price is well forgotten. Once you are happy with the overall requirement, there are still a couple of things you need to understand regarding how pricing works.

When calculating, please remember that when joining two pieces you will often lose a couple of centimetres trimming both sides to get a nice clean straight edge. This is usually necessary so that the join is invisible when finished. If in doubt, overestimate. After all, 'it's better to be looking at it than looking for it.'

TIP When comparing prices make sure you are looking at like for like. Obviously a price per square yard will be less than the price per square metre. A good supplier's website will have a metric/imperial measurement converter. In the US turf is generally priced per square foot.

There are two ways to price:

- supply only
- supply and fit

Supply only

This is where you buy the grass and arrange your own installation.

Beware of hidden costs such as delivery charges. These will vary from supplier to supplier depending on their logistics – capacity, delivery routes, stock levels, location and general hunger for business. The delivery charge could be waived (perhaps haggled away if it's a decent volume), it could be at cost, (perhaps sent by a third party) or at a set rate depending on weight, mileage and urgency.

 TIP If the bank holiday weekend is coming up and you are finally going to sort out your lawn, don't leave it until the end of the week to order your grass. I'm constantly amazed at how frequently even large amounts of grass are ordered at the very last minute. Even if still available and deliverable, you could well pay a premium that would have been avoidable with better planning. 'But I've nowhere to store it,' I hear you cry. Eh, hello, it's waterproof. Just leave it around the back until you're ready.

If ACME Grass only charges €20/m² for your 30m² order but wants €150 to deliver, that comes to a total of €750. Meanwhile, ABC Grass Inc charges €25/m² but has a flat €24 delivery fee, so their total comes to only €745.

Maybe it's a nicer grass, available more quickly. Moral of the story: the cheapest grass is not always the cheapest option.

Then take the necessary tape and glue into account. ACME Grass might only supply 10m long rolls of tape as standard and only the larger pots of glue. But ABC Grass Inc can provide the exact amount of tape you need and no more. Maybe they can give you smaller glue tubes instead of an entire tin, which might also be more efficient.

When it comes to glue, it pays to carefully calculate your exact minimum requirement in linear metres. ACME Grass might sell you the tub because that's what they happen to have in stock. ABC Grass Inc, knowing how many linear metres of joins you have, would provide sufficient tubes for your job and no more (300ml tubes usually do about 3m long). Even if they are more expensive per unit of weight, it could still work out cheaper.

TIP There's an easier-to-use alternative to the professional fibreglass and glue joining system – it's basically an industrial Sellotape which can be both single-sided (for regular installs) or double-sided (for hard-surface installs or onto shockpad).

Supply and fit

With supply and fit there is the price of the grass plus the price of installation.

The same principles apply although the installer should have given you a set price. If they happen to have offcuts from their previous job which match your batch, then great. They might pass some waste reduction saving on to you or simply say nothing and charge as per our earlier calculations. At least now you know what to watch out for and maybe you'll save a few euro.

Be aware that if ACME Grass charges you €3,100 for 40m^2 and ABC Grass Inc quoted €3,000 for 38m^2 installed, and both companies had completed a site survey, this *could* be totally legitimate and in good faith. Each supplier may envision laying it differently.

As we'll see in Chapter 15, methodologies vary. A lot. Just compare YouTube videos and you'll see exactly what I mean. Don't just follow the first one you chance upon if doing it yourself.

Typically, suppliers will send you a sample pack of grass free of charge – but it's only fair for you to have at least some homework done in advance. Thereafter, the 'no obligation' site survey is usually also free. If you are asked to pay, you should expect the cost to be deducted from the total price upon completion.

Dodgy installers typically will have considerably fewer overheads. They might not worry about trifling things like insurance or tax. This allows them to charge much less and you'll find them most interested in cash deals which avoid any messy paperwork. Be careful. No paperwork equals no guarantee.

We secretly enjoy being called in to sort out the mess left by unscrupulous fly-by-night installers. 'I knew I should have got you guys to do it in the first place'… indeed.

I recall one recent retiree, who asked us to visit and quote for their back garden. We naturally obliged, sent our quote, followed up once or twice but heard nothing. Then about three months later a rather sheepish call came into the office the morning after a storm. It transpired their new lawn was in a crumpled heap in the back corner of the garden. Upon investigation it was actually our grass, bought by a walk-in stranger. Inexplicably he requested and got two metre lengths. Maybe he figured they would be easier to carry. The garden size merited 4m wide pieces. He had scraped off the original grass, failed to dig down, sprinkled some sand on top and used 6 inch nails sporadically along his joins and the perimeter to secure it.

And it looked just fine to the client. The cowboy got paid (in cash) and off he disappeared.

Until the first high winds.

Unfortunately for his victim we had to charge full whack to start again with new grass.

Example

Let's say I'm asked to price a 45m² (*required*) garden. If the customer chooses grass priced at say €33/m² including VAT, that's €1,485. If the *actual* size of the garden is only 40m² at €45/m², then installation/labour comes in at €1,800 so it's a total of €3,285.

For private jobs we always quote VAT-inclusive figures. Sundries like tape, glue, fixings, etc. may be separate line items or incorporated into the overall price.

 TIP Don't be fooled when comparing square metre prices. Even for virtually identical grasses, with all the various possible hidden add-ons, the lower price per square metre quote may well work out as a more expensive installation in the end. Your €3,285 quote could suddenly entail an additional €150 miscellaneous extra, plus €300 for that skip, and the bottom line becomes €3,715 before you know it. This means that for your actual lawn area it's working out at €92.87/m² even though the list price quoted was €82/m².

Also consider the issue of sod and soil removal and disposal. With some companies that's your problem/responsibility. If removed by cowboys, it often gets dumped in lay-bys or off quiet country roads. Otherwise, a skip will be required. But who pays for it? Who orders it and has it collected? How long will it be sitting there blocking up your driveway? Will it turn up on time?

Perhaps you are thinking, great, here's my chance to clear out the shed or attic (be aware some of your neighbours might suddenly be thinking the same thing). You might all be disappointed in any case as it could well be filled to capacity and more before you get the chance. Skips are increasingly expensive as landfill prices and government levies increase. If overfilled, the refuse company may refuse to collect it. I've seen instances where the lorry simply has not got the power to lift an overfilled skip. (People often add old doors, radiators on their side and planks of wood around the edges of a skip to increase their capacity. I love what they call this: it's called using greedy boards.)

A good grass company should have the capacity to take the sod and soil away themselves. Sometimes a licence is required, although an exemption for landscapers is not uncommon in many jurisdictions. Don't assume it'll be taken care of. Ask the question. Where is it going? What'll happen to it? The reputable company will be delighted to explain how they properly dispose of/recycle your waste, sod and soil. The dodgy ones might be more vague.

The information in this chapter should serve to give you a better handle on what's involved in getting a new artificial lawn. It should allow you to truly compare apples with apples.

Now there's only one thing missing. What's that, I hear you cry? As you are about to find out, it's the installation process. At last it's time to examine all the ins and outs of doing it yourself, the dos and don'ts of installing properly, including some tricks of the trade and rookie mistakes to be avoided.

Chapter 15

Buyer's Guide: How to install

'Complexity is the enemy of execution'
~ Tony Robbins

Do you enjoy assembling furniture and, unlike this writer, rarely have components left over? Then read on. If you have never done much more than top up your car's windscreen wiper fluid, I refer you to the previous chapters instead.

Most artificial grass company websites provide some kind of installation guide. Some even have a handy video. Many breezily say DIY is easy. It's easy, alright. Easy to make a complete balls of it! Yet self-installing can save you money. You may have no choice. It's important to get it right. You must have sufficient time, energy and inclination. Be warned, DIY is not for the faint-hearted.

Do It Yourself is a bit of a misnomer. Unless your lawn is tiny, installing fake grass is a job for at least two people. So start recruiting. Are the kids old enough to learn the value of hard work and be pressed into service? Is your brother-in-law coming to stay and raid your fridge again? Tell him 'great news', he now has an opportunity to earn his keep. Alternatively, as previously alluded to, invite your mates over for a barbecue – the only catch being that they have to give you a dig out first.

First draw up a checklist or mind map for project 'I'm getting a new fake lawn come hell or high water'. Who'll be home when the grass is delivered? Who'll unload? A lone van driver may not be inclined to help. Ask in advance. Is it a third-party courier? Rolls of bulky expensive grass plonked in the driveway have been known to go missing. You need to get it out of sight.

Figure on a weight of about 3kg per m^2, so for a full 100m^2 roll (4m × 25m) that's 300kg, almost a third of a tonne. Think of it as a big carpet, 12 feet long with a diameter of 2–3 feet. The more expensive the grass, the heavier it will be. Will the delivery crew have a carpet trolley, which would greatly assist shifting the roll down the side of your property? You don't want to put your back out wrestling with an awkward delivery before you even get going.

Has your property got side access to the lawn? Otherwise *everything* must go through the front door. Or window. Is there a straight run through to the back? Corners and tight angles are not your friend. To minimise joins it's preferable to use the full width of the roll when installing, but sometimes there's no choice but to cut it into smaller, more manageable strips. Don't force it as there's not much bend in the rolls. It might have to fit into a lift if it's the only way onto your balcony or rooftop garden.

In terms of access, perhaps there is a back lane behind your property but can a *van* fit down it? If not, can you go through a neighbour's back garden? Or over their wall? No judgement but it's a bit sad how many people 'can't' ask their neighbours because they are sworn enemies. Perhaps the grass company has a crane or hoist on their truck?

TIP

Don't bring the rolls onto site if there's insufficient space to open them out and manoeuvre them. Instead measure and cut off-site, even out on the road if necessary, preferably in off-peak hours. This is where 'measure twice and cut once' comes into play.

Another bit of advice would be to verify the measurements, preferably when the delivery truck is still there. If not possible and you are asked to sign for it, note 'not measured' on the docket. It's no good spotting a discrepancy much later, when it's stopped raining and you're about to lay it with volunteers lined up and raring to go. It would be a shame to send them home.

Remember Murphy's Law: if things can go wrong they will go wrong.

Things you'll most likely need

- a sharp knife, preferably retractable (e.g. a Stanley knife or box cutter) and some fresh blades
- gloves (a) to handle tools and grass and (b) to protect your hands from the aforementioned knife
- a shovel
- a pickaxe
- a compaction plate (a whacker), hand roller (perhaps water filled) or a hand tamper
- a spade or, better still, a mechanised sod cutter
- a yard brush
- hammer
- nails
- U-pins
- a glue gun/applicator
- treated timbers (2in × 1in and/or 4in × in) for edging, or quick-set cement for same
- string liner for levels
- two rakes (metal for the stone and plastic for grass)
- builder's line marker or spray paint
- spirit level or a levelling app on your smartphone
- leaf blower (or elbow grease in conjunction with a yard brush)
- vacuum cleaner (optional but handy at the finish)
- a power hose (also for the clean-up)
- a staple gun and staples
- power cable reel
- transformer
- a generator if no domestic power is available
- air compressor if using one
- a nail gun
- a carpet kicker (stretcher)
- wheelbarrow(s)
- weed barrier membrane (Mypex/Terram)
- a radio (or a booster for your iTunes/Spotify)
- tea/coffee and chocolate biscuits
- an eye for detail
- patience

Hard-surface installation

Let's start with the most straightforward jobs. With no option but to self-install it was wise of you to find this book. If you live in the middle of nowhere, or the area you want covered is just too small, your supplier might either decline to quote or charge a prohibitively expensive amount. A legitimate company will have set overheads and your job simply might not meet their break-even threshold.

The good news is you don't need them.

Laying on flat concrete, tarmacadam (bitumen or asphalt in the US), timber or composite decking, wetpour or smooth paving slabs is relatively easy. Simply cut the grass into shape, roll into position, pull it taut and secure it, typically but not necessarily by gluing it. End of story.

There are a couple of things to bear in mind, however.

If the area currently holds water, it's a good idea to rectify that first. You can cut a drainage channel to the nearest point of relief or introduce some levelling compound to smooth out the worst humps and hollows. If you don't, the grass could be squelchy underfoot and lying water can be stagnant and smelly. Plus once covered, the water will be slower to evaporate.

Prepare the ground

Remove all debris, giving the area a good brush beforehand. It's your last chance. Use a power hose. Sort out any pronounced undulations, such as gaps between your old paving slabs. Re-grout them with a dry or wet sand and cement mix or one of the instant grouts now on the market.

Timber decking

A couple of decades ago Timber decks were all the rage. Not necessarily the best investment ever given our climate.

If you are covering timber decking, perhaps because it's too slippy or old and tired-looking, replace the worst and most rotten wood. Don't worry about matching the rest, just keep it level. Once covered, it won't be seen. Our advice is to clean it and give it one last treatment with preservative. Know this: all timber will eventually rot. Covering it with synthetic grass will *not* halt this process. After all, it's designed to let rainwater through. We frankly tell our customers that deterioration will, if anything, be accelerated. Basically, covering decking is a quick fix.

Nevertheless, covering a deck has the immediate advantage of making it a safer, less slippy and brighter area. It's *not* a permanent solution but at least if a piece of timber rots and falls away underfoot, the grass will prevent your foot from falling through. This has happened to me more than once. Admittedly, I am well over 18 stone.

Watch out for the gaps between the timbers which can vary. If the gap is too wide or the pile is too short, the grass can fall into these gaps and that will look odd. Consider adding a thin layer of shockpad underneath to mitigate any undulations. This work won't affect any vermin who make a home under your deck.

As the saying goes – No one ever saw a small rat or an ugly baby, lol.

Composite decking

Made partly from recycled plastics, composite boards are a fantastic invention. Typically they are at least 30 per cent more expensive than regular timbers, will last much longer and lend themselves to being easily covered in grass without you having to worry about rotting.

Securing the grass

It can either be nailed, screwed or glued down. If the area is sheltered, perhaps it's sufficient to just lay it down and walk away, but not necessarily recommended. Consider placing a couple of plant pots in the corners or brushing in some kiln-dried silica sand to act as ballast in the event of high winds.

Watch the pile height. Grass is typically between 15mm and 45mm high and this could cause a slight trip hazard when walking onto it. This can be alleviated by tacking on a border strip made from plastic, timber or metal. Next, test if you can open the door out onto the area once the grass is in position. The fibres might be too high to allow it to swing easily. What do you do if the ground level can't be lowered or the door can't be raised? Try cutting out an arc or putting in a shorter grass here instead.

If you notice the grass is wrinkled or uneven, don't panic. It's likely due to being badly rolled, stored or bent in transport rather than being flawed. It should naturally flatten out over time. Sunshine and heat help (it softens when it's warm and becomes stiffer when cold).

Allow rainwater to escape

Always just spot glue, skipping a few inches between each dollop, rather than gluing a continuous line. This will allow water to continue to go wherever it always did, depending on the gradient.

Part installation

Another way to save money is to do some site preparation yourself and get your installer to discount accordingly.

If your lawn is an overgrown jungle and covered, God forbid, in dog poo, it could well cost a bit more than a regularly cut, poo-free lawn. If the soil is already dug out sufficiently deep, your installer will allow for this as it means less labour, time and disposal. Or tell your installers there's no need to go to the trouble of taking away the soil.

We encourage people to keep good soil in their gardens. It's a shame to take it away. Mind you, it's often so bad there's no option. This is probably why the lawn is being replaced in the first place.

Post-renovation installation

Much of our work over recent years is after an extension has been built. Instead of trading up, families are staying put and extending their homes, often getting a bigger kitchen/open-plan living area. This, by definition, swallows up garden space. Having been a building site for months on end, what remains of the garden is often in tatters. Even conscientious builders destroy lawns.

So now at last you have your dream kitchen, with nice shiny work surfaces and a lovely clean white tile floor. Until the kids and dog start traipsing in and out. The smaller garden has to accommodate more traffic per square metre than ever before. Moreover, there's now more glass than walls, especially with those huge (and expensive) sliding doors. So what remains of the garden is now far more visible. I get it. Though you are still saving up for new curtains, it's at this point we usually get the phone call.

With a bit of foresight you can turn this to your advantage.

 TIP Casually mention to the builder, preferably before starting the building work, that you are considering putting in an artificial lawn afterwards. Suggest he can put down 804 (crushed stone) in the area to act as a work surface. The builder will be glad and might not even charge you. With luck they'll dig out the old lawn – which they know will just turn to mud over time anyway – and stone it up for their own sake. This means a drier flat work surface for their crew, and everyone's a winner.

Thereafter you can tell your grass supplier that the base is prepared and to reflect that in their charges. Or it's now easier for your DIY project to proceed. You are welcome!

As landscapers we are very conscious that because they have been dealing with builders for weeks and months on end, with all the inevitable disruption and 'unforeseen' problems that arise, the homeowners' patience will have been well and truly tested by the time we show up. They've put up with all the builders' shenanigans and no shows, and now *we* often bear the brunt of their frustration. We could be 10 minutes late because of traffic on day one and get it in the neck despite the last crowd swanning around at their leisure for an age. *C'est la vie.*

A full-monty installation

When it comes to replacing an existing lawn, a casual perusal of YouTube 'how to' videos and many alarmingly brief installation guides on suppliers' websites will reveal worrying inconsistencies in standards, steps and methodologies. Prevailing conditions, from weather, aspect, levels, soil type and other factors, will vary from region to region and even from one side of the fence to the other. So please always apply common sense.

TIP

If self-installing, nab the delivery person and bend their ear. If they work for the grass company, they're likely to have plenty of installation experience and will happily talk to you. Especially if you offer them tea and a toilet break.

Now that you've measured, ordered and received your grass and marshalled your assistants, it's time to install it. Here's *our* 12 step process.

Step 1. Create a staging post

I mentioned the need for lists earlier. Please see the start of Chapter 15 for my list of what you'll now most likely need.

You might want to clear somewhere like your front driveway to be your staging post. Use traffic cones (they're rather like clothes hangers if you think about it – no one ever seems to go out and buy them but they seem to have just been there all along). Here is where you will be dumping your topsoil, stone and sand/dust during the installation. Warn your neighbours as a courtesy. People are understanding, especially when you explain it's a one-off project and that disruption will be limited. But be prepared for curious/nosy visitors.

TIP

Cover the staging area with tarpaulin or a plastic sheet before you begin. This makes the clean-up far easier.

Step 2. Prepare the area

Relocate your favourite plants and remove your wheelie bins, trampoline, swing, playset, etc. Rather than risking your dog escaping, confine the animal to the house or kennels for the duration.

Next, mow your lawn down nice and short. For one last time. *Bwahaha!*

If you kill off the grass in advance (not strictly necessary unless it's particularly full of weeds), allow sufficient time for it to take effect.

Step 3. Remove the sod and soil

To be on the safe side, dig out a *minimum* of 3 to 4 inches, (7.5cm to 10cm), preferably more, to make room for the new base – hence the opening quote of this chapter. We'll touch on this again but the depth will depend on how old your lawn is, soil type, how free draining it is, whether there are mature trees nearby and several other factors. If in doubt, go deeper, but realise that for every inch you go down there could be tonnes of extra soil to get out and material to be put in to replace it.

You will have to work round any drains and utilities you find. These may need to be lowered or raised to be flush with your finished level.

If you are digging it out by hand, consider hiring a mechanical rotavator first to loosen the top layers for you. A sod cutter is an even better labour-saving device. Be warned, they are heavy by design so *do not* expect to shift one on your own. If you *can* lift it, then it's probably not going to be any good, especially if the ground is dry. Note that the depth it digs can be adjusted.

Your new subsoil base does not have to be perfectly graded. Take care to remove all organic material such as loose roots, bulbs and leaves. Decomposing matter can lead to subsidence, making your lawn humpy and bumpy. If the base is not too wet, you can compact it before moving to the next stage.

Step 4. Deal with any drainage issues

Now is the time to do any necessary additional drainage. Often poor drainage is the reason the original lawn failed and is why you are putting in a synthetic surface. You are likely to be intimately familiar with the wettest patches. Consider putting in a French drain or soak holes to alleviate same. Dig a small trench to the nearest existing drain, using perforated piping, and back fill with shingle or small pebbles. An effective soak hole is made by going down an extra couple of feet, adding back some rocks, then smaller stones, then pebbles. Simple but not easy.

Step 5. Add a membrane

This is optional but advisable, especially if you are in a new development where settlement may still be ongoing, if your garden is a swamp or if it's weed infested. A good geotextile weed membrane at the base of your newly excavated area will discourage new weeds coming up from below and it will also act as a kind of blanket to prevent any unstable subsoil shifting and to bind the ballast being added above.

Step 6. Add the base layer of crushed stone

This must be sufficiently stable, not prone to later subsidence, so possibly build up in layers. Compact the stone evenly as you go. Level it, but it doesn't necessarily have to be flat. I get annoyed when customers expect their new lawn to be billiard-table flat. One client refused to pay their bill for this reason. They sent us a picture of a spirit level on top of a cheap aluminium table plonked in the middle of their perfect new lawn. You know the bubble in the solution that should be between the two lines to show that it's level, yeah? Well, this bubble wasn't exactly in the middle, 'proving' that the lawn wasn't flat. The fact that their lightweight table's legs were sitting on 40mm of newly laid grass didn't register at all. So we got stiffed. I know where I wanted to stick that spirit level.

In fact, a correctly laid lawn ought to taper down very slightly towards its borders, like a shallow inverted saucer.

Some installers only go with one layer of fill, be that crushed stone, grit or sand. Although adequate in certain circumstances, I firmly advocate more. Certainly in Ireland and the UK the base ought to be a minimum of 3 to 4 inches of crushed stone (known as 804 or CMB-crushed miscellaneous base). This should then be compacted to be 1 inch (20/30mm max) below the finished level, like the top of your patio slabs.

Drop wheelbarrow loads from the back towards the front of the area. Use a wide, preferably metal, rake to spread and feather. Then compact it. A long spirit level or timber can be used to grade it.

Next add the final inch of plant dust/fine crushed rock/decomposed granite or sand. If using sand, regular builders' sand is fine, although we'd recommend you use mortar sand or plastering sand in preference. Why? It compacts better, holding its shape.

TIP

Do *not*, for God's sake, use shingle, pea gravel or rounded stone for the base. These materials might be perfectly suited for your cobblelock driveway but they are singularly inappropriate when it comes to fake grass. Why? They are not readily compactable and will inevitably result in an uneven lawn.

Step 7. Grade the top layer

Compact well and if it sinks below the desired level, add more. A vibrating plate compactor is best. Manual compaction is also possible but less effective. You could use a lawn roller filled with water. Failing that, get or make a hand tamper. A handle and a flat piece of wood will suffice.

TIP

When compacting, pay particular attention to the borders immediately inside your timber edges. If there is any settlement and subsidence, you do not want it at the borders.

Then lightly hose down the area. By moistening the area you aid compaction. Note that with compaction the base layer level will reduce to at least 90 per cent of its original depth, so allow for this in advance. See Chapter 14 regarding sufficient material volume.

Next, run a builder's line across the area – a piece of string and a peg at either end. Unless it's a large lawn or a commercial project, forget the laser level.

Get it flat unless undulations are a design feature. As per above a one to two degree gradient from the middle to the edges was traditional for real lawns to aid drainage and, although now technically unnecessary, somehow still looks right.

Bear in mind, however, that you will have to meet existing boundaries like border walls and fence foundations which can be far from plumb. You will often have no choice but to meet what's there, adjusting accordingly. There's nothing as bad as having a fab new lawn but seeing newly exposed unplastered sections at the base of a wall, or lumps of concrete foundations around fence posts.

Step 8. Add a weed barrier fabric
Entirely optional. I would argue that a sufficiently deep build-up will prevent weeds coming up from below. Then it's just those seeding from above that you need to worry about. Some installers advocate Mypex only to differentiate themselves. Such fabrics can, however, provide horizontal and vertical stabilisation. Like the membrane underneath they can help control erosion, contamination and mixing of base layers, and may deter burrowing rodents and insect infestations.

In my own garden? I didn't bother.

TIP Walk softly on the top layer of the base. Don't disturb your nice smooth finish with footprints or indents which may be felt once the grass is laid above.

Step 9. Roll out the grass
At last! Start with the largest piece. Make sure it's smooth and firm. Pull it into position. Watch the pile direction. Always remember to soldier the turf towards the privileged viewpoint. Roughly cut and remove the obvious excess first. Cut from the back with a sharp blade and remove any remaining 'selvage' fabric from the edges (i.e., the usually black strip of material sometimes on the outer edge of a roll of grass). It's very important to note that this selvage fabric is *not* there to be used, despite appearances, to glue on the next bit. If you try to do that, you'll never get the joins right.

TIP If there are any kinks or ripples in the grass, pour hot – not boiling – water over the uneven areas. This will soften the backing and make it more malleable.

Step 10. Secure the edges

Now that the grass is all down and in position, pull it taut to ensure that there are no wrinkles, using a carpet kicker tool if necessary. Do this in conjunction with Step 11.

 TIP If you are laying grass in cold weather, try warming up the grass before laying it. How? Some people leave it in the back of an enclosed van with the heating turned up high for an hour or two. Perhaps put it in the garage near, but not too near, a heater.

Having already rough cut the edges it's time to fine cut. Bend back the grass and offer up to the edge and carefully fine trim. Mark the backing of the grass first with chalk if it helps.

Then it's time to secure the grass. Some advocate simply banging in U pins or long nails (6 inch at least). We don't. While that can work, particularly if sand is brushed in to also help keep the lawn down, experience tells us that they are too easily dislodged and lifted. We only resort to this when working around gnarly roots of trees, where there is no alternative.

Some installers put in a concrete strip around the perimeter a few millimetres below the finished level and when it hardens they glue the grass to it and job done. Many US installers work with bendable lengths of plastic board, whereas we simply use treated timber. Either 4 × 2's, 2 × 2's for long straight runs, or 2 × 1's which have more flex for curves. If the curve is too severe, cut notches into the back of the timber to allow it to hug curves more closely, or failing that, cut it into shorter lengths and place them at close intervals along the edge. Once this timber edging is in position, stake it tight to the edge and nail or screw the top of the stake to the edge of the 2 × 1.

One possible variation, favoured by some, is to place this edging 5mm away from the edge and bolster the grass into the gap. Either way, simply nail or screw the grass into the timber.

Don't use roofing or slab nails. Regular round-headed one-inch nails are just fine. You can galvanise (protected with a zinc oxide) or not – it doesn't matter. Non-galvanised nails will rust and expand and will therefore grip into the timber more tightly.

305

But what about all that rain you keep mentioning? Won't the timbers rot?

Our experience says no, once it's pre-treated (tanalised). We find it a reliable and economic way to secure the grass. Once a good stone base is in position, rainwater does not stay at the level of the timber but instead drains away underneath. Nineteen years later my own lawn is still good and secure.

If you have a long edge to secure, consider using a manual or automatic nail or staple gun. If your lawn is say 8m wide and 10m long (so an 80m^2 install), then you will have 36 linear metres of nailing to do. If you put in one nail every 6 or 8 inches (I'd recommend that at a minimum), that's over 200 nails. Thus mechanisation comes in handy. An air-driven or battery-powered gun will do in minutes what could take you hours with a hammer. Plus, you are far less likely to whack a finger. Shouting out choice expletives can upset nearby children. But don't worry, blood wipes right off and won't stain the grass.

We favour 30mm to a maximum 60mm staples, and using a gun means you can shoot many in at close intervals. If the grass ever does have to be lifted it can, only with some difficulty, be pulled back up. Sure, some fibres and backing will be left attached to the timber but it can usually be tacked back down with little visible evidence of tampering.

Infill

Older versions of grasses required sand infilling to both provide ballast and to keep the fibres upright. The introduction of curly fibres made this less critical. While some manufacturers still suggest the addition of sand infill – 2–3kgs per metre squared – for root-zone stability, in practice it's not strictly necessary.

For private gardens we rarely do this unless requested. Although it settles at the base and the sand does not then get dragged into the house, it can allow weeds and moss to establish more quickly. We add it as standard in pub smoking areas as a fire retardant. We've also done so on rooftops and balconies to weigh it down in case of high winds. We've also learned to do it immediately around the windows of hotel rooms. Despite no smoking policies a lot of unexplained cigarette butts somehow accumulate nearby.

Step 11. Seam the grass pieces together

This is the important bit and assumes you have an area over 4 metres wide. Ideally, seam the pieces together when it's dry, although many specialist glues are damp tolerant. We will proceed in drizzle but not rain. Don't assume what's been delivered is ready to go. The factory edges may not be even.

You may well have to cut in a couple of stitch lines to tidy it up.

This next bit is critical.

If you are joining two pieces across the width of the grass, mark a straight line using a flat edge (e.g. a piece of timber) on the back and cut carefully along on both sides, then offer up together and ensure both pieces marry well. Ruffle up the fibres by hand.

If, more commonly, you are joining two pieces along the vertical, please know that in order to have as invisible a seam as possible, you must ensure that the distance between the stitch lines at the outer edges of your two pieces of grass is *the same* as the distance between all the other stitch lines visible from the backing of the grass. We recommend that you cut tight to the edge of a stitch line on one of your two grass pieces, and do the opposite on the other side, leaving the flap on the other side. You could try cutting right down the middle but it's difficult to be so precise by hand. If you cut tight to the stitch line on both sides, then it'll look bunched up. And if you leave the flap on both sides, there'll be too wide a gap. Either way it's the same result. A visible join will ruin the look of your new synthetic lawn. Yes, with use and time it could become less obvious but do you have the patience to wait? It might never fully disappear.

Another way is to cut a wave pattern, perhaps using a template. Although a bit more wasteful, the join becomes well hidden.

Securing the join

Novices lay a timber along the length of the join, butt up the two pieces and simply nail into position. This can look OK but it is not a good idea as it will be too hard underfoot. Think of little kids' knees hitting that spot.

Others butt up the two pieces and punch in U pins or long nails through the grass periodically into the fill below. I would consider this unsatisfactory and bad practice. It might be OK around tree roots but not for joining grass. High winds, a kid or dog will lift it if so inclined.

The best methodology is to use the correct tape and glue. There are two types of tape. The first is an industrial single-sided adhesive specialist tape (or double-sided for hard-surface or indoor installs) which you lay onto your compacted surface. Then peel off the backing and marry the two pieces onto it, half and half. Then compress firmly to ensure adhesion. You can walk it in or press a plank of wood down over the grass. Perhaps leave said plank overnight, preferably with blocks for extra weight.

The second way is laying down a strip of specialist fibreglass tape, typically

100mm wide, about the width of an A4 piece of paper. This is sufficiently wide to ensure good adhesion for both sides. Remember, *smooth side down, rough side up.*

The smooth side blocks moisture seeping through, which could compromise the glue, and the rough side facilitates better grip.

TIP If you run a bit short of fibreglass tape, simply split the tape in half to double the length.

Next, apply the correct glue. This comes in either cartridge form, applied via a glue gun (cheap, easy to use and readily available), or from a tin which can contain anything up to 5kg and over. Sometimes the glue is a two-part mix. Do not be phased by this. Simply open the lid, pour in the powder from the separate sachet and stir. You don't need a mechanical whisk, as a good mix with a stick by hand will suffice. Be aware that once opened, the glue will cure (go off and harden) within a couple of hours. So don't open it until you are ready and apply it immediately once you have mixed it.

If, however, it's in a tube, simply use as required. Read the instructions and find out in advance how many linear metres you should expect to get from the particular size glue container you have. My advice? Don't scrimp, but don't spread so thick that when the two grass pieces are butted together, it will squeeze up between them. By definition it's sticky and tricky to remove. If it gets on your fingers or on the grass fibres, wash immediately before it hardens.

Please allow 12–24 hours for the glue to fully harden. It'll work faster when it's warm. We know it's closer to 12 than 24 hours but we tell our customers to stay off the lawn, or at the very least away from the joins, for a full day to be on the safe side. Don't let the dogs out either. From our perspective there's nothing as annoying as getting that call, 'Oh, I was checking your work and I was able to pull apart the join.' OMG! That's because it wasn't fully set you muppet. Now it has to be redone as it won't stick properly once disturbed. Once it 'goes off' that's it. We've glued grass onto all our vans and it stays firmly on year after year, mile after mile.

Obstacles

There might well be something, for example a tree trunk or the uprights of a swing, in the way. Simply split the grass at that point, cut it in around the obstacle, then let it meet again behind it. As per the above guidance, tape and glue back together. The same goes for any other feature within the lawn.

Step 12. Sweep off any loose fibres

All that's left to do is to tidy up and sweep off any loose fibres. Don't be alarmed at their presence. This is merely a by-product of cutting the edges, and once they are removed it will not continue to be an issue. A vacuum cleaner works perfectly well for this. Use a stiff-bristle yard brush or a plastic soft rake against the grain to jazz up the fibres and get it looking its best upon completion, being careful not to disturb the joins. A leaf blower is an excellent tool for this. Now at last you can sit back, relax and admire your work, happy in the knowledge that you will never have to take out the lawnmower again.

TIP Sell or donate your now redundant lawnmower to someone who still has one of those old-fashioned real lawns. Offer it to your installer who may give you money off the job in exchange.

Seven rookie mistakes to avoid

If you want to put a play surface for children over a hard surface, then don't use the cheapest, shortest-piled grass. There are specialist grasses for play areas, with a denser pile. This gives better shock absorption and longevity. Otherwise you are defeating the purpose and might as well paint the hard surface green instead.

Beware of building up against the damp course of your house. Either introduce an eco drain along the base or put in a non-permeable barrier against it. Although rainwater will not sit on the surface of the grass, as it quickly permeates through it, it's wise for your new lawn to slope away ever so slightly from the house. If there's a footpath or patio in between, then it's less critical, but always watch your levels.

Although synthetic grass can simply meet either real grass or indeed the soil of a border, consider putting in a decorative brick or cobble edge both for aesthetics and to keep the two mediums separate. This will prevent soil, bark mulch and unwanted debris spilling onto the lawn.

To repeat an earlier critically important point, do not use pea gravel or rounded stone as a base layer. It will drain just fine but it won't compact sufficiently and will shift under foot.

In our experience loose gravel and artificial grass don't mix. It's fine if it's merely ornamental but if there are kids and dogs around, it's a no-no. It won't do the grass any harm but loose stones can easily get thrown onto the grass, disappearing into it. So what? Little knees are sure to find those stones and the howls of pain will defeat the purpose of installing the grass in the first place. Sure, you can brush the stones back off it but it'll keep happening and it can be hard to find and dislodge all the pebbles.

To labour another point, the joins are critical. Don't be complacent or under any illusion as to the difficulty of getting them right. It pains me to see so many visible joins in private gardens and many public installations. It gives the product and industry a bad name.

It's not bulletproof. It's a plastic carpet. In areas where there's guaranteed to be high traffic, for example immediately outside the back door or on the way to the garden shed, consider adding a hard path or stepping stones. Otherwise, be aware that the grass will inevitably become compacted and look less attractive.

How to install a putting green

The principles behind installing a synthetic putting green are the same as those behind installing regular synthetic grass but with a few tweaks. First, a note on size. Too small is, well, too small. Don't just put a green in for decoration or for the sake of it. The synthetic grass comes in a 4 metre wide roll. It ought to be 4m × 2m at a minimum. Also, don't overdo it with too many holes. For a green between 12m^2 and 15m^2, two to three would be plenty. For greens between 16m^2 and 28m^2, there should be a maximum of three to four, and so on.

 TIP It's best to decide on pin positions during construction before laying the surface. Once the top layer of build-up is in situ, even before compaction, simply roll a golf ball, by hand, over the sand or dust and watch the trail it leaves in its wake. It may be straight or break left or right at some point. Place your cups accordingly, compact and check the arc again. This way, you can add dust to build up a break or remove it as desired. On greens between 16m² and 24m² with, say, four holes, I'd personally have three flat shots and just one with a break or level change.

While sand over crushed stone is OK for artificial lawn build-up, I'd strongly recommend using fine plant dust — limestone, sandstone or granite — when it comes to installing synthetic putting greens. In the US this may be called decomposed granite or 'fines'. Be wary of sharp stones contained therein. Check the dust. Grab a handful and squeeze. If you bleed, then don't use it. The sharp chips could also puncture your beautiful expensive new green. The reason for not using regular sand underneath is that the finer stuff will compact better and, more importantly, hold its shape. Wet it down after compacting to aid the process. There's no point in painstakingly grading your desired contours only for them to disappear in the future.

TIP

Keep all holes at least two or three feet in from the edges.

Nothing makes me cringe more than seeing square or rectangular home putting greens. There's a word for that – lazy. I suggest three ways to achieve a curved finish. The first is to use treated 2in × 1in timbers staked into the ground at intervals. To achieve tight curves you can notch the timber to get more play. Failing that, it's a matter of lots of shorter pieces, which can become messy. The second way is to source flexible plastic edging, such as the American bender boards. The third, and cheaper, way is to improvise and use some simple plastic piping. Lay it out as desired around the perimeter. Then nail or screw it into the ground at intervals and lay the putting surface over it. Cut along the edges of the putting surface and nail or screw it onto the now invisible pipe. Job done.

Finally, before anchoring down your surface, offer it up to your hole location and cut a small hole or X from below into it. That way, when you lay the surface flat, you can see where to cut from above. When cut, pare the green back around the 4 inch hole. That's it. The putting surface simply sits over the hole. Once the entire surface is secured around the perimeter, it cannot move so there's no need for any further interference, which could disturb the path of the ball as it falls into the hole.

It's one of the nicest sounds you'll ever hear.

Conclusion

Regardless of whether you've the least intention of installing the grass yourself, it's still important to have a good understanding of standard methodology. Different installation companies will, in good faith, have different ways of doing things. Now at least you can discuss the 'how to' questions with them from an informed point of view and not have the wool pulled over your eyes. Following best practice ensures your lawn functions properly, looks the part and stands the test of time, regardless of who installs it. Now you can finally relax and enjoy the freedom from endless lawn maintenance servitude.

You can stop and smell the roses.

Chapter 16

Technical information – explanation of terms

Units of measurement

Both imperial and metric units of measurement are used, depending on the source. Like carpets, the grass is typically sold by size. The length of the piece multiplied by its breadth is the total area so a 2m long × 3m wide piece totals 6m^2. Therefore, 6m^2 at, say, €30 per square metre is €180 in total. Always ask if that includes taxes. In the UK and Ireland, for example, government VAT (value-added tax) at around 20% of the total price may not be included in the initial retail price, particularly in commercial transactions. So, using the example above, what you thought was €180 could suddenly be €180 plus 23% VAT, which is €221.40, or €41.40 more than you might have bargained for.

Hey, is delivery included in that? What about the necessary tape and glue? My advice is don't assume. Ask. Installation is typically not included, I'm afraid.

Be aware of units of pricing

Euros per square yard will always be less than euro per square metre. Why?

One square yard is 0.836m^2. In other words, it's 17% smaller. So, don't be fooled; when priced per square foot it *seems* a lot cheaper but might not be.

Primary backing

This is the woven layer at the back of the grass to provide stability. Dual backing is always better than a single layer. One can often compare the thickness and robustness of such backing by sight and handling.

Is this backing recyclable? At present, combined with the grass, typically it's not. It's currently too difficult to separate at the end of life.

TIP Much as in the Pepsi challenge, be careful. Temperature can dramatically affect how pliable the grass is. The warmer it is the softer it will be. So, if one sample has been sitting on the sideboard and the other is straight out of the courier's van, results may vary.

Secondary backing, aka the second coating

The secondary backing locks the fibres in place. Several materials, like latex, can be used and the thickness varies. The more the better.

Warning: if you can pull out the fibres from the above by hand, this backing has failed so do not buy the grass. It is not normal. The rule, however, does not apply to the edges of the sample. It's entirely normal to have a little fraying at the edges given that the sample will have been guillotined or hand cut from a larger piece.

Water permeability

This refers to the drainage rate. Artificial grass drainage systems are designed to allow water to percolate through the grass and backing, through the build-up and back into the water table. Most artificial grass is perforated by a grid pattern of 5mm needle-punched holes.

This permeability rate varies with infill and base materials used. Make sure it suits local weather conditions and rainfall patterns. An acceptable standard rate of permeability would be 60 litres per square metre per minute, or 28 inches per hour if you prefer. The punched holes also act to prevent spores and bacteria from building up in the grass.

Warranty

Is it in writing? Does it cover both the grass and the installation? Don't be alarmed if warranty periods for the grass and installation vary somewhat. A good grass should have a guarantee of 7 to 10 years whereas an industry installation warranty would typically cover a period of 1 to 3 years.

What's covered? UV stability is a must. Read the small print. If a weed or two appears, that's normal and it's not reasonable to call back the installer. Weeds can be seeded from above (by wind or bird droppings) and are easily pulled or sprayed. If they are clearly pushing up from below, then perhaps the foundation layers are not sufficiently deep and a weed membrane should have been used. Insist on having that rectified. A reputable company will have no issue sorting things for you as it wants you to be happy and to recommend it to friends and family. More on this in Chapter 20.

Pile height

Pile height is measured in millimetres in Europe. For domestic lawns, a height between 30mm and 40mm is currently optimal. Any higher and the grass flattens too easily, despite the curly fibres underneath. I personally would have reservations about buying 50mm grass, however natural and attractive it looks. Hopefully this issue can be rectified in the future. Third-generation sports grasses tend to be longer, between 50mm and 60mm, because they have sand and rubber infill ballast to keep them upright.

Turf gauge

This is the distance between each adjacent stitch line, visible from the back of the grass. Usually it's expressed in fractions of an inch, e.g. 3/8 of an inch. Typically the smaller the gap, the greater the volume and the thicker and better the grass. A tighter gauge will cost more.

Stitch rate

This is the number of tuft stitches per 100cm in line direction. Again, the more the merrier. For example ⅜ is a tighter gauge than ⅝. thus ⅜ would be more expensive.

Face weight

This is the total weight, in grams per square metre, above the backing. It depends on the pile height and density. The greater the length and density, the better it should look, and it will be proportionately more expensive. So, as can be seen from the example below, two grasses can both have a pile height of 40mm but totally different qualities and prices.

Dtex

An abbreviation of decitex. This is the unit of measurement of yarn in weight, in decigrams per 10,000m. One decitex is equal to 0.9 denier, or 0.11 tex. In other words, it's the weight or linear density of continuous yarn. Again, the higher the better. This is considered a better measure than comparing the diameter of the yarn.

Denier

US version of dtex. The Merriam-Webster definition is 'a unit of fineness for yarn'. It is equal to fineness of yarn, weighing 1 gram for each 9,000m. Don't ask.

Polyolefin

A polymer composed of both polyethylene and polypropylene, now quite common in the manufacture of synthetic grass.

Polypropylene

One of the most commonly produced plastics in the world, both popular and versatile. It's what most plastic bags and bottles are made from. Given the environmental concerns we will examine it more closely in Chapter 7.

Polyamide

A nylon, now commonly used for artificial putting greens.

Shape of yarn

As we've seen, slightly different shapes of yarn are extruded in the manufacturing process of synthetic grass to give different performances or effects. At least that's what the manufacturers claim. For example:

Oval:	common, soft and durable.
Diamond:	sturdier, more durable.
W-shaped:	more bouncy.
Flattened oval with spine:	realistic appearance and stronger core.
C-shaped:	natural look, strong, feels harder so won't flatten as quickly.
Flat blade:	the softest, therefore compelling to the touch but can flatten more easily.
S-shaped:	robust but soft. Broader and becoming more popular.

Personally I'm a bit sceptical. The development of these shapes could amount to simple differentiation, standing out from the competition. In my opinion it's much more down to the quality of the yarn — which does vary — and a combination of the other factors above.

For further technical information you could call your suppliers to test them out. Thereafter consult the Synthetic Turf Council.

![sanctuary synthetics.ie logo] **sanctuary**synthetics.ie

REAL 40mm SPEC SHEET 2022

REAL

Type	Tufted synthetic grass carpet
Material	PE Monofilament straight & PP Monofilament curled (UV Stabilized)
Yarn type	7.200 / 8 dTex PE monofilament straight & 4.800 / 8 dTex PP monofilament curled
Yarn quality	Environmental friendly, free of lead and cadmium
Primary backing	100% PP black with fleece, UV Stabilized, Weight 135 gr/m²
Secondary backing	Black Latex compound with a base of styrenebutadiene (SBR), with drainage holes. Weight 836 gr/m²
Water permeability	60 liter/min/m³
Pile height	40 mm
Face weight	1.859 gr/m² ± 10%
Total weight	2.830 gr/m² ± 10%
Tuft gauge	3/8 gauge
Stitches per 10 cm linear	15 ± 1%
Stitches per m²	15.750 ± 10%
Colour	Mix of light and dark green + brown
UV stability	Meets DIN 53387 Standard (6000 hours)
Colour fastness	Xenon Test: Blue Scale > 7, Grey-scale > 4
Colour lining	Not Applicable
Roll width	200 cm, 400 cm
Roll length	20-25m
Applications	Gardens, Landscaping
Infill advice	Silica sand, gradation 0,5 - 1,0 mm, 80% roundshaped, appr. 6 - 8 kg/m2
Comments	Before installation make sure the rolls are from the same production code (first five digits of the roll number) Project.

317

List of famous folk

Here's a list of famous folks many of whom might not have expected to be referenced in a book all about fake grass. Included are numerous writers, an emperor, a king, two queens, over a dozen presidents and prime ministers, four statesmen, assorted media personalities and actors, seven golfers, six musicians, four sportspeople, some garden designers, a few mathematicians, fictional characters, engineers, a couple of Irish billionaires, businessmen, playboys, generals, comedians, revolutionaries, a pirate, a poet, a monk and a Jedi master.

Abraham Maslow, psychologist (1908–1970)

Áine Lawlor, RTÉ presenter

Alan Titchmarsh, celebrity gardener and TV presenter

Allah, God in Arabic

Archimedes of Syracuse, Greek mathematician (*c.* 287– 212 bc)

Arnold Schwarzenegger, actor and 38th Governor of California

Benjamin Disraeli, twice UK prime minister (1804–1881)

Benjamin Franklin, polymath (1706–1790)

Bob Hope, comedian and actor (1903–2003)

Boutros Boutros-Ghali, former general secretary of the UN (1922–2016)

Brady family, as in *The Brady Bunch* TV show

Bruce Springsteen aka 'the Boss', singer/songwriter

Charles Dodgson, aka Lewis Carroll, writer (1832–1898)

CS Lewis, writer (1898–1963)

Daniel O'Connell, liberator and politician (1775–1847)

Darren Clarke, golfer

David Evans, aka 'the Edge', U2 guitarist

David Gerald Hessayon, author and botanist

David Norris, Irish senator

Diarmuid Gavin, garden designer

Donald J. Trump, 45th president of the USA :-)

Douglas Adams, author, satirist (1952–2001)

Dustin Hoffman, actor

Edsel Ford, business executive and philanthropist (1893–1943)

Enda Kenny, former Irish Taoiseach

Francis Bacon, First Viscount St Alban, philosopher and politician (1561–1626)

Francis Brennan, hotelier and TV presenter

Mark with Roz Purcell

President Michael D. Higgins and his wife, Sabina

Mark with 'wild thing'

Mark at Munster Rugby

Bob Geldof

Mark with Rosanna Davidson

Francis Scott Fitzgerald, novelist (1896–1940)

Gary Player, golfer

Gavin Duffy, investor and media expert

Gay Byrne, chat show host (1934–2019)

George Lee, RTÉ journalist

George W. Bush 43rd President of USA

George Washington, 1st President of USA (1732–1799)

Gertrude Jekyll, garden designer (1843–1932)

Goldilocks, from the fable with the three bears

Gordon D'Arcy, Irish rugby player

Graeme McDowell, golfer

Grigori Rasputin, Russian mystic (*c.* 1869–1916, several times)

Hannibal Smith, A-Team colonel

Hans Christian Andersen, Danish writer (1805–1875)

Henry Ford, industrialist (1863–1947)

Homer Simpson, immortal

Hugh Hefner, playboy (1926–2017)

Jane Austen, novelist (1775–1817)

Jerry Brown, 34th and 39th governor of California

Johann Wolfgang von Goethe, playwright, novelist (1749–1832)

Johannes Gutenberg, inventor (*c.* 1400–1468)

John Brookes, garden designer (1933–2018)

John F. Kennedy, 35th president of the USA (1917–1963)

John Milton, epic poet (1608–1674)

John Wanamaker, merchant (1838–1922)

John Wayne, aka the Duke (1907–1979)

Johnny Cooper, footballer and GAA All-Star

Johnny Depp, actor

Jonathon Swift, satirist (1667–1745)

Joseph Stiglitz, economist

JP McManus, Irish billionaire and racehorse owner

Kathy Hoffman, TV presenter

L. Frank Baum, children's author (1856–1919)

Leo Tolstoy, author (1828–1910)

Leo Varadkar, former Taoiseach of Ireland

Louis XIV, Sun King of France (1638–1715)

Louis Copeland, celebratory tailor

Mario Rosenstock, actor and impressionist

Mark Ruffalo, actor

Marty Morrissey, RTÉ sports commentator

Meghan Trainor, pop singer

Michael D. Higgins, poet and current President of Ireland

Michael Gove, Conservative UK politician

Michael Jackson, king of pop (1958–2009)

Michael O'Leary, CEO of Ryanair

Monty Don, gardener

Napoleon Bonaparte, emperor (1769–1821)

Nathan Mayer Rothschild, First Baron, financier (1840–1915)

PT Barnum, show person (1810–1891)

Pádraig Harrington, golfer

Paul Hewson aka Bono, lead singer of U2

Philip Kotler, marketing guru

Queen Elizabeth I (1533–1603)

Queen Elizabeth II (1926–2022)

Rhonda Byrne, author of *The Secret*

Richard Branson, entrepreneur and businessperson

Rory McIlroy, golfer

Scooby-Doo, animated franchise cartoon character

Sean Connery aka James Bond, actor (1930–2020)

Seána Kerslake, Irish actor

Shane Lowry, golfer

Sir Francis Drake, pirate, naval officer (*c.* 1540–1596)

Starsky and Hutch, from the eponymous 1970s TV cop show

Stephanie Preissner, Irish writer

Steven Spielberg, filmmaker

Sun Tzu, military strategist (*c.* 544–496 BC)

Terry Pratchett, fantasy author (1948–2015)

Theodore Roosevelt, 26th president of the USA (1858–1919)

Thomas Jefferson, third president of the USA (1743–1826)

Tiger Woods, golfer

Tom Selleck, Magnum in *Magnum P.I.*

William Blake, poet (1757–1827)

Winston Churchill, UK prime minister (1874–1965)

Vinnie Jones, footballer and actor

Vladimir Ilyich Ulyanov, aka Lenin, Russian revolutionary (1870–1924)

Yoda, fictional Jedi master, *Star Wars*

Yogi Berra, baseball professional (1925–2015)

Special offer

It would of course be invidious of me, after all we've been through, to use this opportunity to nakedly promote my business. So I've decided to be invidious.

Thank you for choosing to read *The Big Hairy Green Book*. I'm truly flattered. If you are so inclined, please, please give this book a favourable review on Amazon or Google. Word of mouth works too. Should you go to www.thehairygreenbook.com or the Sanctuarysynthetics.ie shop and buy three copies for family or friends (or indeed enemies), we'll send you a free hairy green doormat worth €15. When visitors wipe their feet and admire it, you can tell them where it came from. As your reward for trudging through this book to the bitter end, I'm issuing you with a *secret password*. It's only available to readers in the Republic of Ireland, I'm afraid, and it will self-destruct (expire, really) a year after publication. By simply adding the words 'I survived *The Big Hairy Green Book*' in any communication with us, you may claim a 5 per cent discount on any of our products. This excludes the installation, though. Our sample packs and site surveys are already free of charge. If you refer someone else, either to this book or directly to us, and an order materialises, let me know and we'll send you a free gift as a thank you. Sign up to our newsletter for ongoing information and offers at www.sanctuarysynthetics.ie.

Finally, if you have a property in Ireland and are interested in our grass, we would be delighted to send you free samples/brochures. Thereafter, a no-obligation site survey can be arranged.

Meanwhile, please spread the word.

I am available to clarify my assertions or to answer any readers' questions. I welcome your comments, suggestions, criticisms and corrections. Where do you see things going with artificial grass? I'll endeavour to update or correct stuff in any future editions. Please write to me at mark@sanctuarysynthetics.ie or Grassland, Military Road Industrial Park, Naas, County Kildare, Ireland.

I didn't make anything up – didn't have to. Please research and verify any statements for yourself. There are two US sources of further information you can consult: the Synthetic Turf Council and the Association of Synthetic Grass Installers (ASGI).

Acknowledgements

At the outset I had no idea that writing a book, ostensibly a solo pursuit, would be such a collaborative effort. Many have helped. Many won't get a mention. Sorry, but you know who you are. I've namechecked my family in the dedication. I would like to thank key colleagues in team Sanctuary without whom, well, you know the drill. They include the inimitable Dominic O'Donohoe, director of sales and chief of morale; Mary Purcell, office manager (think Monica from *Friends)*; Ann Harney, the real boss who runs the show; Keith 'Spanky' Willis, lover of hairy green jeeps; Tommy Mills, warehouse manager and jack of all trades; Krzystof 'No problem' Cygan, my faithful foreman for 15 years (now retired back to Poland); and Henryk, Raf and our installation crews who do the real work. 'Teamwork makes the green dream work.' A trifle trite but true.

Hey, Vicky Frazer, your relentless encouragement eventually rubbed off. The same goes for self-titled evil bald genius Jon McCulloch, Chris Cardell, Donna Kennedy, Megan Macedo, my auntie Rena Harford, beta readers and first draft editors Eilish and Paul, and superb copy editor Mary McCauley. Fair play to James O'Sullivan at WebBuddy.ie and my cousin Paula Nolan for design and artwork, and to Christine, Jeremy and Brian at Lettertec, always available with printing advice, and to Brian Flynn. Brian Cregan is responsible for some of the best photography, particularly in relation to Bloom. Also thank you to Thomas Bartlet for helping to get it out into the world.

My thanks to Jackie at Kildare Local Enterprise Office and mentor Blaise Brosnan. Thanks, too, to Gary Graham and Kerrie for setting a high bar at Bloom. Hats off to our thousands of domestic customers. Same to our trade customers. I'm very grateful for your business and friendship over the years. I take nothing for granted.

I must also acknowledge the many other sources, not always credited, from which I've borrowed in the course of my research.

Finally, dear reader, a big thanks to you too, *especially* if you aren't related to me. Your feedback, comments and even criticisms would be much appreciated.

About the author

There's more than enough about me in this book already, so here's a claim-to-fame story instead.

My first big break on the silver screen was starring alongside Sean Connery who, at the time, was better known (to me at least) as James Bond. To make a long story short – right time, right place – I was playing in the garden as a kid when a guy in a big white Jaguar drove up our avenue. 'Are they your sheep in that field?' he asked. They were. This film director urgently needed a flock delivered to Trinity College Dublin and had driven out of the city stopping at the very first farm with sheep that he spotted.

Amazingly, on his return from the mart, Dad relented to my pestering and agreed to hire them out. We soon loaded over 100 discommoded and noisy sheep, trucking them up to the old university's Parliament Square. The idea was that our errant flock would help Connery's horse-drawn-carriage's escape from custody by obstructing the pursuing men in blue (the Peelers). In the absence of any other skilled shepherds on set we were press-ganged into 19th-century rags and had to drive our sheep across the set umpteen times to get the right take.

I had an absolute ball.

It was 1978 and I was all of 10 years old.

Not only was I handsomely paid, meeting James Bond and getting his autograph – I remember him as being very charming – but I also had a big juicy hamburger for lunch.

Several months later, our entire family was invited to the Irish premiere of *The First Great Train Robbery*, most of it having been shot in Ireland. It was a good film but I couldn't really concentrate as I was busy looking out for myself. Where the hell were we? The movie was clearly drawing to a conclusion with Sean's conviction and escape – those dastardly sheep – but still nothing. Then a flash of two shepherds, for only half a second – my dad and little brother. Damn!

The End

Freeze frame.

Roll credits.

Hang on a sec ...

In the middle of the giant screen was a (rather dashing) young shepherd boy frozen in mid-leap, arms apart, shouting at the sheep.

Me.

Not only was I instrumental, albeit unknowingly, in assisting the hero's

324

escape, but my giant image remained on screen, slowly dissolving to sepia, for at least five minutes as the music crescendoed and the never-ending credits rolled up the screen.

My sincere compliments to the camera operator and editorial crew.

From that moment I knew I was destined for greatness.

Admittedly, the next 30 or 40 years, apart from one or two school plays, were a bit quiet.

An Afterword

Who we are today is a product of both our inherited DNA and how we have reacted to the various people and events we have encountered during our life's journey – some call this the relationship between nature and nurture. We cannot do anything about our DNA other than to thank our parents for it. But we do have some jurisdiction over how we react to and learn from events in our lives.

As we travel through life, we are influenced by various people and events and, in turn, we become influencers of others.

As Mark travelled on his journey to date, he often had the wind blowing into his face. Sometimes it blew sideways and sometimes, at critical eureka moments, it blew into his back. In the earlier stages, he followed the strategy 'When you don't have a plan, try many things.' This really is the R&D stage of the journey. This is where we are most influenced. Having successfully come through these 'hairy' stages, Mark, now as the Fake Grass Man, is an influencer of others.

In this book, Mark has generously shared the downs and ups of his journey, which make him a great role model for others to follow on their respective journeys.

I had the privilege of facilitating Mark on part of his journey, and I would admit that I probably learned more from him than he from me. Both our lives have been mutually enriched.

The standout trait or skill I observe in Mark is his ability to beat the odds, but in a creative way. How he has optimised this creativity in making a commodity sexy is a real eye-opener for all of us who aspire to be more successful.

Thank you, Mark, for sharing your journey with us in this book. It will become a vehicle to allow you to influence an even bigger audience, to their advantage.

Boldness underpinned by creativity and style is the sauce.

Blaise Brosnan, author and business consultant

Printed in Great Britain
by Amazon

15338258R00188